THE BACCHANTS

OF

EURIPIDES

AND OTHER ESSAYS

CAMBRIDGE UNIVERSITY PRESS
London: FETTER LANE, E.C.
C. F. CLAY, Manager

Edinburgh: 100, PRINCES STREET
Berlin: A. ASHER AND CO.
Leipzig: F. A. BROCKHAUS
New York: G. P. PUTNAM'S SONS
Bombay and Calcutta: MACMILLAN AND CO., Ltd.

THE BACCHANTS

OF

EURIPIDES

AND OTHER ESSAYS

BY

A. W. VERRALL, Litt.D.

FELLOW OF TRINITY COLLEGE, CAMBRIDGE

Cambridge :
at the University Press
1910

Cambridge:

PRINTED BY JOHN CLAY, M.A.

AT THE UNIVERSITY PRESS.

TO MY FRIEND

GILBERT MURRAY

REGIUS PROFESSOR OF GREEK IN THE UNIVERSITY OF OXFORD

PREFACE

O F the Essays contained in this volume, four
have been published previously—"The First
Homer" in *The Quarterly Review*, "The Lady of
Cos" and "The Death of Cyrsilus" in *The Classical
Review*, and "Christ before Herod" in *The Journal
of Theological Studies.* They are here reprinted
with the consent of the editors and proprietors of
the respective journals, which I acknowledge with
thanks. The other Essays now appear for the first
time.

In preparing the book for publication, I have
received valuable assistance from my colleague
Mr C. E. Stuart, of Trinity College, Cambridge,
and from Mr M. A. Bayfield, as well as from the
staff of the University Press.

A. W. V.

August, 1910.

CONTENTS

THE *BACCHANTS* OF EURIPIDES.

The Bacchae is a most glorious play....It is often very obscure; and I am not sure that I understand its general scope. But, as a piece of language, it is hardly equalled in the world. And, whether it was intended to encourage or to discourage fanaticism, the picture of fanatical excitement which it exhibits has never been rivalled. *Macaulay.*

In a perplexed and difficult question, we should start, if possible, from some proposition which is universally accepted. And concerning the *Bacchants* of Euripides, this, if anything, seems to be so accepted, that the play, in some way and for some reason, is conspicuously different from the average work of the poet. Whether this difference marks a change in his opinions, and if so, what change,—that is a question variously answered; but it would not be debated, if the difference itself were not conspicuous and indisputable. We will begin then by asking, where the difference lies. In detail, more than one distinction might be taken; but it is not upon details that such a general impression depends. The main distinction, the broad and general difference, seems to be this: in the *Bacchants*, and nowhere else among the tragedies of Euripides, we have a drama consisting, from first to last, of incidents which, upon the face of them and according to the prevalent belief of the persons represented, are miraculous and supernatural.

The story (which we may conveniently recapitulate) is one of the legends of Delphi, presenting the events which led to the recognition at Delphi of the Man-God Dionysus (Bromius, Bacchus, Iacchus) and particularly the celebration of his peculiar rites, in every alternate year, upon the sacred mountain of Parnassus. The names Dionysus and Bacchus were widely spread in Hellas, and were attached to many observances very slightly connected, if connected at all, with the religion which is the subject of our play. But this religion, in its true and proper character, differed profoundly both in theology and in practice from ordinary Greek types. In theology, it asserted the affinity and possible union of the divine and the human nature ; Dionysus was of both natures ; he proceeded from the supreme Deity (Zeus) not by a single but by a double generation ; he was born first as man from the body of a woman, and secondly as god from the body of the Deity himself. The practice and ritual consisted, so far as it was essential and peculiar, totally in the cultivation and stimulation of the divine element in man by the voluntary production of ecstasy; the prescribed means—according to this play, the only means prescribed or generally used— was "dancing," exercises performed in common by companies assembled for the purpose in remote places, and more often at night. The point, all-important to the religious conception, that by these performances the celebrants were raised, for the time at least, into participation of the divine nature, was indicated by the fact that they bore, as such and for the purpose of the performance, the name of the god, becoming *bacchoi* or *bacchai* according to sex. Doctrine and practice are plainly and closely connected. Both (let us again remark) were alien from the Hellenic spirit, which was not disposed either to merge the distinction of god and man, or, speaking generally, to regard excitement as a thing desirable and deserving stimulation. It may be convenient or necessary to have a comprehensive name for religion of this type, and the name *orgiastic*, though it does not by etymology[1] indicate the essential features, is in modern use appropriate, and may serve the purpose.

According to the legend, which to this extent may safely be accepted as historical, this orgiastic religion was introduced into Greece and specially into Delphi, at a time comparatively recent, from the north (or, according to Euripides, from Asia, where it was native, by way of the north) through Thrace and Macedonia, and was not received without a sanguinary contest. Rites violently exciting, performed by preference in the dark, and specially attractive to women, were open, whatever their purity, to revolting interpretations, the more so if, as was

---

[1] The word *orgion*, if native Greek, which is not certain, may signify merely an *act* or *performance*.

certainly the case in the historical celebrations at
Delphi, there was no separation of the sexes[1].
The attempts to prohibit and suppress the performances, and their ultimate triumph, were condensed
into the story, quite possibly true in the main, of
Pentheus, King of Thebes, who, in trying to capture
or disperse by armed force a company of women-
bacchants performing on Mount Cithaeron, was
shamefully routed and was torn in pieces by the
enraged fanatics. In the original story, so far as
we can judge in the almost entire loss of all versions
earlier than that of Euripides, the new religion was
founded at Thebes by the Man-God (Dionysus) in
his own avowed person, and it was under his direction, as general of his Bacchants, that the unarmed
women won their victory over Pentheus and his
army. Such is not the account of Euripides, who
eliminates the battle, and otherwise shapes the story
accordingly in ways that will presently demand
attention. But the battle, and the part of the god
in it, are given by an allusion in the *Eumenides* of
Aeschylus[2], and were doubtless adopted in his *Pentheus*[3], the loss of which is one of our chief embarrassments in interpreting the play of Euripides.

The Theban legend further alleged, that according to the Bacchic theology as then preached

---

[1] Eur. *Ion*, 550 ff.

[2] Aesch. *Eum.* 25, Βάκχαις ἐστρατήγησεν θεός.

[3] ἡ μυθοποιία κεῖται παρ᾽ Αἰσχύλῳ ἐν Πενθεῖ (*Argum. Bacch.*).
This does not of course mean that the plots were identical. In a
surviving fragment of the *Pentheus*, μηδ᾽ αἵματος πέμφιγα πρὸς πέδῳ
βάλῃς, someone seems to be warning the king against bloodshed.

and accepted, the human mother of the Man-God
was a woman of Thebes, Semele, who, pregnant by
Zeus, died thunder-struck in the moment of her
delivery, while the babe was taken away to be
deified. According to the Theban Pindar[1] the
mother too, though she died, rose again to eternal
life. Through the influence of Delphi, the mother-
hood of Semele, and this localization of the doctrinal
myth, was widely accredited in Greece, and has
become, through the Greek and Latin poets, familiar
to modern literature. To those who, like Euripides,
had some notions of history, and realized that the
worship of a man-god, before it entered Hellas,
was diffused over vast Oriental regions, where the
very names of Thebes and Semele, Cadmus and
Pentheus, were unknown, it must have been obvious
that the identity and personal story of the mother
was no essential part of the doctrine. We may
doubt whether, in the fifth century B.C., the Theban
elements of the legend were established even in
Macedonia, which is for Euripides above all other
countries the proper seat of the religion. For the
purpose of preaching, the birth of the Man-God
could be, and was, located with infinite variety ; while
to the believer the mystic fact, not the circumstances,
was of sole importance. The "Mother" was properly
anonymous, and Euripides, as we shall see, actually
suggests this. But, for Theban recipients, the
personality of Semele was part of the creed. The
legend there made her a Theban princess, daughter

----

[1] *Ol.* 2. 25.

of Cadmus the founder of the city and the royal house, and thus nearly related to the opponent and persecutor of the new religion, King Pentheus, grandson of Cadmus through another daughter, Agave.

According to Euripides—but here we pass from legend to rationalism—when the preachers of Dionysus come to Thebes, the royal family, and particularly Agave with the other surviving daughters of Cadmus, indignantly reject the affiliation of the man-god to their dead kinswoman, who, as they have hitherto maintained, was slain with her offspring, as a punishment for imputing to Zeus (upon the suggestion of her father) the fruit of some illicit connexion! Cadmus himself, who still lives though he has ceased to reign, is at heart an unbeliever; but, under the influence of the prophet Teiresias, a representative of pre-established cults in general and especially of Delphic religion, he agrees to perform the new rites. His submission however, and his persuasions, only exasperate the resistance of his grandson, King Pentheus, who, returning from a temporary absence, learns with disgust that an "impostor" from Asia (the god in disguise), supported by a train of itinerant women, has almost conquered the country. The women of Thebes especially have been seized by a frenzy of enthusiasm, which has gained even the infidel Agave and her sisters. Led by these, the Theban women in a mass have fled to Mount Cithaeron, there to practise the Bacchic dances in solitude; and though the men as yet have not followed the example, a great excitement prevails. Against all this Pentheus declares implacable war.

Such is the connexion of the invading religion with Semele and her family, as represented in the prologue of Euripides. How much of this representation has any base in fact, or in ancient tradition, we cannot say, nor perhaps is this question material to the intended effect of the drama. We cannot even determine precisely (though this is material) how much of it agrees with Aeschylus. The whole picture has a strong Euripidean colour. In particular, the persistent disguise of the god, the fact that ostensibly he takes no part in the main action of the piece, but is represented there by a personage who, for all the other actors, is merely an adept and preacher of the new religion,—this, as we have seen, is not Aeschylean. It is probably an innovation of the author, for, as we shall see, he lays great stress on it. From Euripides also comes, we should suspect, the peculiar turn given to the incredulity of the family, and their rational, though scandalous, theory respecting the misfortune of their deceased relative.

So however, for Euripides, matters stand at the opening of the action, and are shown in a prologue spoken by the god in person, who thenceforth is seen no more until all is over.

The interim, the action, exhibits the contest between Pentheus and the preacher, and the tremendous and ghastly triumph of the disguised deity. This personage, if we are to believe what is

said by himself and his more or less resolute supporters, proves his command of supernatural power
by a series of miracles such as imagination could
hardly surpass. The King, who denounces the adept
as a charlatan, and the rites as a mere excuse for
debauchery, arrests some of the fugitive women, and
commits them to prison ; but all of them promptly
escape, and this, according to the report, with such
aid as "bolts which, untouched, fly open of themselves." The King thereupon arrests the adept
himself, and takes him for better custody into his
own domicile ; but the captive cannot even be
chained, since Pentheus, in attempting it, is deprived
of his senses. The house is seen first to take fire,
and then to be ruined by an earthquake, while from
the midst of this devastation the missionary walks
forth untouched. All this however produces upon
the infidel prince not the least impression. Some
of the miracles he denies ; others, and the most
appalling, he ignores.

Meanwhile things hardly less stupendous are
being done by or on behalf of the Theban bacchants
assembled on Mount Cithaeron. The King's herdsmen, after witnessing a performance of the rites,
accompanied by prodigious and sympathetic disturb-
ances of nature, endeavour to seize the royal
mother, Agave. They are instantly routed, the
herds are torn in pieces, and the victorious women
raid the neighbouring villages, where they domineer
unchecked, display their power by many marvels,
and withdraw, when they please, to their solitudes.

All this is reported to the King, but serves only to increase his rage. He determines to extinguish the sect in the blood of its votaries, and orders his troops to assemble for the purpose. Here however a sudden turn is given to his plans, not by any fresh miracle, but by a proposal from the adept, that the King, under his guidance, should visit the bacchants, and satisfy himself as to the true character of their practices, of which the reporting herdsman has given a very favourable account. Pentheus, who throughout has rested his hostility upon the alleged infamy of the practices, at first leaps eagerly at this proposal, but is discouraged by hearing that, since the rites of the women may not be witnessed by man, it will be necessary to go disguised as a female worshipper. Between inclination and disinclination he hangs uncertain, and finally retires into the house for further deliberation with the adept.

When they reappear, the preacher is master, and the prince, in mind and body, his broken and obedient slave. His eyes delude him, his carriage is that of a drunkard. He has not only donned the feminine vestments, but is childishly vain of his appearance in them. He cannot reason, or think, or see, but surrenders himself, in besotted and fatuous triumph, to the guidance of his enemy.

The end may now be foreseen. The King is delivered helpless to the frantic enthusiasts, and is torn in pieces by their hands, his guide, the adept or god, having disappeared at the fatal moment. His mad mother, Agave, takes the lead in the massacre supposing the victim to be a lion, and presents herself at the palace, bearing, in hideous exultation, the head of the quarry in her hands. The sight is too much even for the Asiatic votaries, whose rejoicing dies in horror and compassion. Meanwhile the mangled remains have been collected and are brought home by the miserable Cadmus, who presently succeeds in calming his daughter, and discovers to her the truth.

In the midst of her lamentations, Dionysus appears as a god (probably in the air, and with the usual apparatus of a theatrical epiphany[1]) to claim his victory and sentence his foes. His sketch of their future destinies is compiled, in the common fashion of the Euripidean *deus ex machina*, from the data of legend, but contains no consolation, even for Cadmus[2], whose claim to favourable distinction may indeed appear very doubtful. Satisfied and self-approved, the god is alone in his glory. Agave, having grovelled before him in vain, turns from him with bitter denunciation of his character and rejection of his worship, to which no voice replies. " That which was expected came not to pass, but for the unexpected God found a way. And such is the end of this story."

Such then as it is, wherein does the play differ (as by all judgements it does) from that critical treatment of vulgar belief which was habitual to Euri-

---

[1] The text at this point is defective, but nothing material to the effect seems to be lost.

[2] See *vv.* 1352–1361.

pides? Not of course in concluding with an epiphany, the appearance in power and splendour of an accepted deity, a god of the popular mythology. That is the regular way. Certainly not in any special advantage which the god here takes by his appearance, or an exceptional display of sympathy with the divine triumph. On the contrary, nowhere perhaps is the absence of sympathy so marked, or the effect of the apparition so repulsive. As a rule, the worst that can be said of such personages in the Euripidean *finale* is that they are unconvincing, and their remarks, for a reflecting reader or spectator, irrelevant. As a rule, deities whose real or alleged influence upon the events of the drama is such as humanity would disapprove, and who, if they appeared, would be attacked,—such as the Aphrodite of the *Hippolytus* or the Apollo of the *Ion*—are not entrusted with the winding-up. But the cruelty of Dionysus is censured with fury, and, what is more, he has no defender. In view of this last point, it is needless to consider here the difference between modern feelings and those of Greeks in the fifth century before Christ, respecting divine punishment or divine compassion. If the author of the *Bacchants* had thought, or meant to allow, that Dionysus, as against Agave, could appear defensible, he would have given this sentiment some efficient voice on the stage. But there is none. Cadmus, the Cadmus of this play, however pitiable, commands no respect, and has indeed nothing to say but that, if his daughters had not offended the god, they would not

have suffered. The Chorus of Bacchants are allowed
to be silent. The god, in his glory, stands absolutely
alone.

We are not without the means of comparing this
treatment with what was thought proper, in the same
age, when a divine vengeance was to be justified.
The Ajax of Sophocles is punished, for contumacy
against Athena, so severely that he takes refuge in
death. His tone, and the general tone of the play,
does not respond exactly to what modern men would
expect. We miss the note of contrition. But what
should we think, or what could Athenians have
thought, if the surviving friends of Ajax, his wife
and his brother, were made to complain of his
punishment as monstrous, and if Athena herself, by
way of conclusion, were compelled to hear their
unrefuted invectives? That is how Dionysus is
handled by Euripides in his *finale*; and if in this
play he seems unusually indulgent to popular beliefs,
that is certainly not because, in sum, he favours
the character of the presiding deity.

Nor can much be made, for this purpose, of
sympathy extended to the worshippers and the
worship. It is true that into the choral odes, especially the noble hymn to Holiness[1], Euripides has
put more elevation and religious feeling than perhaps
anywhere else he associates with a popular cult. It
is also true, and very important to the scheme of the
drama, that upon the bacchic discipline and the
bacchic morality he here intimates a judgement much

[1] *vv.* 370 ff.

more favourable than in the *Ion*, the only extant play which offers material for a comparison. It is there implied that on Parnassus at all events, under the patronage of Delphi, the bacchic rites were grossly ill-conducted[1]; and nothing is said to show that the disorders of Parnassus were exceptional or alien from the character of the religion. Here on the contrary we have uncontradicted testimony that the performances are sober, virtuous, even severe; and, whatever we may think of the Chorus, the Asiatic women who accompany the preacher, we cannot think that they are either corrupt themselves or knowingly engaged in spreading corruption. Whether the opinion of the *Ion* is thus retracted, or whether Euripides does not rather suggest a distinction, a distinction of place and time, we will consider elsewhere. For the present it will be enough to say, first, that against the virtues and sublimities of the bacchants must be set their fanatical fury, and further that, while their crimes are clearly imputable to their religion and their patron, he has small apparent claim to their merits. It is most remarkable, that neither as god nor as man does he show any interest in those moral pieties which half redeem the violence of his devotees. The sole concern of the deity is to dominate; and the adept, in this at least, is his human double. And indeed, the better his adherents, the worse for him, since they can hardly bear to look upon the horrors which he does not scruple to inflict.

[1] *Ion*, 550 ff.

What then is it, we have still to ask, which sets the *Bacchants* among the tragedies of Euripides in a class by itself, broadly different from his usual manner, and opposed to it? It is the treatment of the supernatural, the strange and startling departure which, in the use of the supernatural as matter of dramatic story and theatrical exhibition, the author here seems to make, not only from his own practice, but from the general rules of the Attic stage. The novelty is this, that, though the scene is laid in human life, apparently not the least regard is paid to the ordinary limitations of human experience.

Manifestly this is so, if we are to accept the facts or allegations of the story at their face-value. Thebes, the place of action, is, for the time, and by the presence there of a person infinite in power, exempted altogether from the known conditions of the world. Anything may happen. There is scarcely a scene, in which we do not see or hear of something not normally possible; and all is attributed to Dionysus.

Now for us modern readers, the inference is, at first sight, inevitable, that Euripides, by composing such a play, was willing, and even desirous, to confirm belief in Dionysus. We reach this conclusion by a process brief, instinctive, and irresistible. First, we take it for granted that the marvels of the play, the alleged miracles of Dionysus, are to be accepted according to the allegations. They are facts, truths, for the purpose of the story, just as the foresight of witches is a truth for the purpose of *Macbeth*, the magic of Prospero a fact for *The Tempest*, the omniscience of the Delphic Apollo true for *A Winter's Tale*. But at the same time, in the same instant, we perceive, if we have any acquaintance with the state of religion in the age of Euripides, that to treat Dionysus and his miracles as matters of mere artistic hypothesis, without bearing on belief, was then impossible. The bacchic festival of Parnassus, of which the establishment and vogue are predicted by the prophet Teiresias as a result of the events which the play exhibits[1], was, when Euripides wrote, an actual holiday, famous and popular. Those who attended it were encouraged to expect sensations, raptures, mystic experiences, similar in kind, if less in degree, to those which are reported in the play as accompanying the rite of the bacchants on Cithaeron. The God, so believers believed, took part in it. How then should the allegations of the play be without bearing on belief, mere artistic assumptions of no religious import? Such a pretence, on the part of an author, would then have been idle and dishonest. The true Shakespearian parallel is not that of *A Winter's Tale*, where an oracle of the Delphic Apollo was commended, as a fictitious assumption, to an audience for whom Delphi and Apollo were mere names, but that of *Macbeth*, where the spells and predictions of witches were exhibited to spectators, for many of whom witchcraft was an article of faith, disputed indeed, but therefore the more warmly maintained.

[1] *vv.* 306 ff.

Or rather we must seek a stronger case, a still nearer relation to the religion of the day. In the age of Euripides, a playwright, exhibiting miracles of Dionysus and prophecies of Teiresias, was like the authors of *King Henry the Eighth*, exhibiting the baptism of Elizabeth by Cranmer, and his forecast of her felicitous influence in Church and State. As surely as those authors knew, that their scene would be taken as a recommendation of the Anglican settlement, so surely must Euripides have known, that the *Bacchants*, if it propounds the existence and power of Dionysus as assumptions of fact, would be taken as a recommendation to practise obediently the rites of Parnassus. And since such a recommendation is contradictory to what we know, from our own observation confirmed by contemporary testimony, to have been the general tendency and effect of Euripides' work, we class the *Bacchants* apart, and suppose it, rightly upon the premises, to bear, in some sort, the character of a retractation.

But are we sure of the premises? Is it certain that the marvels of the play, the miraculous allegations, were intended by the author to be accepted, *everywhere and by everybody*, at their face-value, as assumptions of fact? This is a question which, at all events since the publication of Professor Norwood's book, *The Riddle of the Bacchae*, is not to be lightly dismissed. The purpose of this essay is to review the question, adopting, controlling, or supplementing, as the evidence seems to point, the conclusions of Professor Norwood and others.

But before entering on this discussion, let us be clear on a point which, in my experience, I find specially liable to misapprehension. I do not contend, I should think it absurd to contend, that what I have called the "face-value" of the story is not, according to the intention of the author, *a possible interpretation.* He must have known that, for many or most of a holiday mob assembled in a theatre, the face-value of the spectacle is the sole value; that the idea of criticising their impressions, and distinguishing between an obvious and a less obvious view of the story, could not enter their minds, and, even if it did, could not, in the conditions of the theatre, be applied or pursued. And there was more than one good reason of practical necessity (perhaps even of art) why a legend of Dionysus, exhibited in the theatre of Dionysus, should be so exhibited, that it might be taken for truth by those who were unable or unwilling to dispute it. It is legitimate therefore and necessary that, as an alternative, as one side of the author's intention, we should view the play as it would have been taken by the pious, the indifferent, and the ignorant. Moreover it may be thought (though this is a question of individual taste and interest) that, in our days, when, since no one believes in Dionysus or his legend, criticism upon them has no practical purpose, the view of the pious and the face-value of the story are the preferable and the more important. And further still, if, by an interpretation of the play, we mean a transference of it into thoughts and terms of our own, a translation,—then some *one* view, one only, we must adopt and pursue. A work of irony and ambiguous suggestion, though such works are many and have been very important in the history of literature, is delicate and difficult enough in the freedom of a single mind and a native idiom. To transfer it, uncoloured, to an alien and distant medium, would be a chimerical attempt. And therefore I do not reject, but heartily admire and approve, such a presentation of the *Bacchants* as is given to English readers in the translation of Professor Murray, where the face-value and the pious view are altogether dominant. It is not an uncoloured representation, as we shall presently see, and as the translator is doubtless aware. But in a translation, if we are to preserve life, some colouring is inevitable, and the chosen hue is one of those which the chameleon was intended to bear.

But the only hue it is not, and cannot be. The play was not designed only to satisfy the demands of popular belief and poetic piety. No extant work of Euripides is so designed. In several of the most important, as I have endeavoured to show else-where[1], double interpretations are imperative, and the critical or sceptical reading by far the more true and vital. And of all his extant works, the *Bacchants* is that which requires such an interpretation not the least but the most, precisely because the face-value

---

[1] See *Euripides the Rationalist*, and *Four Plays of Euripides*, especially the essay, in the former volume, on the *Alcestis*, and in the latter, on the *Heracles*.

is so extravagantly inconsistent with the dramatic
principles and practice of the author.   It is not too
much to say that, if the facts of the piece were really
as miraculous as at first they may look, if no other
way of explaining them were open, then the play,
produced as it was posthumously and without the
direct guarantee of Euripides, could not have been
accepted then, and should not be accepted now, as
his genuine and unadulterated work.

It is not quite easy for us moderns to place ourselves, in this regard, at the standpoint of Athens
in the fifth century.   Respecting the admission and
treatment, in grave drama, of the abnormal, miraculous, supernatural, our approved standards, so far as
we recognize any, disagree fundamentally not only
with Euripides, but with all Attic tragedy so far as we
know.   The current notion, I suppose, now is, that
the question is merely one of keeping.   Anything,
any incident, is admissible, if the general tone of the
work is in harmony.   Shakespeare certainly suggests
no other limitation.   In his most famous tragedies,
supernatural experiences often make an essential part
of the story, are exhibited without scruple upon the
stage, and—a most important point—are so exhibited as to emphasize, not minimize, the strangeness
of the sensation, the departure from normal experience.   The ghost-scenes in *Hamlet* and *Macbeth*
will illustrate all these qualities.   Goethe's *Faust*,
the most celebrated tragedy of later times, is wildly
fantastic in imagination.   The classical tragedy of
France, otherwise severe, becomes looser just when,

as in the *Iphigénie* of Racine, it suggests an analogy
to the Greek.   If we descend to work of less authority, or pass to book-drama, such as Byron's *Manfred*
or Shelley's *Prometheus*, the balance is still on the
side of freedom.   Even opera, since Wagner at
least, has some effect in the same direction.

But Athenian tragedy, even in Aeschylus and in
Sophocles, shows in these things an economy and
caution astonishing when we consider its legendary material.   Aristophanes makes Euripides claim
realism, conformity to normal experience, as his
speciality and distinction ; and truly, as compared
with him, his predecessors are fantastic.   But they
might pass rather for realists, if compared with
Shakespeare or with Goethe.   Even Aeschylus, so
soon as he comes within the range of humanity (the
Prometheus lies altogether outside), shows a strong
disposition to make the abnormal, if we may so say,
as normal as possible.   The ghost of Darius in the
Persians is a ghost very different from those which
appear to Hamlet and Macbeth.   Except in the
bare supposition, that a dead man may return from
the dead, the scene is hardly abnormal.   Similarly
in the *Eumenides*, where gods mix with men, the
effect is not so much to expand the human range of
action, as to restrict the divine.   Athena, Apollo,
and the Erinyes, appearing in Athens, conduct a
criminal trial in the forms of Athenian law.   Sophocles, as we know him, is more severe, eliminating
supernatural persons and incidents from the main
action presented on the stage, or (as in the Athena

of the *Ajax*, heard but remote) reducing the contact to a minimum.

The principle or tendency, suggested by our extant collection of Athenian tragedy, is confirmed by the theoretical exposition, which, a century later, was formulated on the basis of such examples by Aristotle. Aristotle is indeed no mere realist; he is an adversary of the notion that art lies simply in exact reproduction of nature. But he assumes everywhere in the *Poetic*, that, in tragedy, in a theatrical work which is to be taken seriously, the business of the artist is to keep as near to the normal and the probable as he can. Departures from it may be variously justified or excused. But they need excuse. The dramatist may, for example, accept things abnormal or improbable as data of a story already fixed, and, by judicious handling, may pass them upon the audience. But he will not seek them. There is no room, within the survey of Aristotle, for such a production as *The Tempest*. We have every reason to suppose that even in the earlier tragedy of the classic century, even in Aeschylus or Phrynichus, and *a fortiori* in Sophocles, nothing similar could have been found.

But the temperaments of Aeschylus, or the refinements of Sophocles, we need not further consider, because Euripides, as every one knows, rejected such methods in favour of a thorough-going pursuit of reality. As Aristophanes, after his death, makes him declare, in words which cannot be too often recalled and remembered, he made it his business to exhibit natural experiences, "the things which we handle and among which we live[1]." The supernatural world, the world of the gods and mythology, is in Euripides, for the most part, not even postulated as an extraneous condition of the story, at all events not as necessary. There is hardly one extant tragedy of his which hangs essentially upon supernatural or transcendent assumptions, as the plays of Aeschylus and Sophocles do. And in the field of drama proper, in the action, he admits, as a rule, nothing, either as matter of exhibition or of accepted report, which exceeds the common experience of mankind. Our extant collection (apart from the *Bacchants*) confirms completely the principle stated by Aristophanes, the exceptions being so rare, and subject to such obvious reserves and remarks, that in summary they would properly be ignored. And in particular, the rule, which excludes things not normally possible from actual exhibition within the main body of the drama, is absolute[2].

Moreover the realism of Euripides was progressive. It grows on him, or, as we may say more respectfully and more fairly, he perfects it. In the *Orestes* of 408 B.C., one of the last tragedies exhibited at Athens by himself, we may see the type to which his method tends, a play which, under legen-

---

[1] Ar. *Frogs* 959 οἰκεῖα πράγματ᾽ εἰσάγων, οἷς χρώμεθ᾽, οἷς ξύνεσμεν.

[2] The *Rhesus* (see *vv.* 595 ff.) is of course excluded for this purpose. Whether composed by Euripides or not, it is not in his manner. As to the *Heracles* (*vv.* 822 ff.), see *Four Plays of Euripides*, pp. 165 ff.

dary names, exhibits a world not merely possible but familiar, clothed in the circumstances, political, religious, and social, of contemporary life. And the *Iphigenia at Aulis*, which, like the *Bacchants*, was produced by his representatives after his death in Macedonia, shows, so far as we can judge from its imperfect and interpolated condition, no change of method, but rather, in the pitch of the characters and language, an advance beyond the *Orestes* towards the pure imitation of reality.

But in the *Bacchants*, upon the view which for the moment we are assuming, Euripides discarded both his own realism and the temperate supernaturalism of his most approved predecessors, and suddenly produced a tragedy, the like of which, for audacity in miracle, Athens, so far as we know, had never seen. Such a vagary is conceivable. But presumption is strong against it. How should Aristophanes accept such a work as bequeathed by the realist of the *Frogs*? A personage who, bearing the human form and passing for a man among men, commands at his pleasure the protection of an earthquake,—this is not exactly one of " the things among which we live." A change so whimsical, so abrupt a reversal of established habit, could not and cannot legitimately be supposed, unless the natural assumption, that Euripides thought and wrote like himself, be first exhaustively disproved.

And this cogent presumption, that the play, in its true intent, is realist and rationalist, is confirmed by many conspicuous features, some of which we will note briefly before proceeding to a general interpretation.

First, it is surely significant, that as usual, the main action of the play presents no supernatural person, none that is recognized as such. The god, as god, is relegated, like the gods of Euripides generally, to the prologue and epilogue, and himself insists, in the prologue, upon the point that he acts in disguise[1]. Why should this Euripidean form be maintained, if not to open to our choice, as it plainly does, the belief that the truth lies the other way, that the man of the play is the reality, and his divine pretensions false?

Again, it is remarkable, if Euripides here meant to abandon his realism, and to present miracles as matter of fact, that he should present them, according to his former habit[2], as ill-attested. Some witness, some one witness, should surely be provided, whose competence and good faith are beyond doubt. Either Cadmus or Teiresias, though perhaps not unimpeachable, would have been a witness comparatively impressive. But neither of them attests anything. The miraculous allegations come all from persons who may reasonably be charged, as they are charged, with imposture or delusion,—the adept, his women, a string of superstitious and ignorant slaves. Herdsmen and guards report incredible things. Pentheus does not believe them. But why should he? In the first report from Cithaeron, it is

---

[1] *vv.* 4, 53 f.
[2] *Andr.* 1147, *Heraclidae* 847, *Iph. Taur.* 268 ff. etc.

expressly indicated that not every one, who saw the alleged marvels, shared the impression which they made upon rustics[1]. To this sort of thing the admirers of Euripides were accustomed, and they knew what it had meant. How should they interpret it otherwise in the *Bacchants*?

And again we observe that, though Euripides has changed (*ex hypothesi*) the habitual pitch of his facts, he has not changed, as *ex hypothesi* he should have done, the habitual pitch of his characters and style. The whispered incredulity of Cadmus[2], the misplaced rationalism of Teiresias[3], the undignified aspect of both[4],—these things, and others, are out of keeping with the purpose supposed. They would not have been tolerated by Aeschylus or Sophocles. They ought to signify, and would naturally be taken to signify, that the world of this play is no fantastic and ideal world, but the accustomed world of Euripidean realism.

But above all it is strange—a thing which, in fairness to the author, we ought not to assume without reluctance and severe scrutiny—that, if the miracles are real miracles, real effects of supernatural power, designed to prove and expose the hardness and obstinacy of a recalcitrant mind, they should be so ill-planned and mismanaged as, for this purpose, they are. Admirers of the ideal, who like a liberal use of the imagination and dislike the habitual plainness of Euripides, are wont to make,

---

[1] *vv.* 717 ff.   [2] *vv.* 333 ff.
[3] *vv.* 286 ff.   [4] *vv.* 170 ff., 248 ff.

in his supposed interest, the best they can of the
Bacchants, and therefore to praise, among other
things, the vigorous picture of rebellion against
deity, which they find in the person of Pentheus.
But the author deserves no such eulogy.   Pentheus,
ex hypothesi, is depicted not strongly, but absurdly.
He is simply impossible.

The type of a hardened mind is the Pharaoh of
Exodus, and in the plagues of Egypt we see the
elementary principles of such a story.   The essence
of the effect lies in the gradation of the prodigious
punishments, and in the fact that the rebel, though
his heart is hardened against them, nevertheless
does feel their force like a man and in a natural
proportion, so that he repeatedly wavers, and the
crowning stroke, the destruction of the first-born,
produces for the time a complete submission, from
which he only so far recovers as to provoke his final
fate.   This is defiance, this is bravery, presumptuous
indeed, criminal, even monstrous, but conceivably
human, and therefore interesting to us as men.

But the prodigies of Dionysus (supposing them
real) are such that to defy them, to brave them, would
be impossible to man; nor can it properly be said that
they are defied by Pentheus.   The imprisoned god
evokes first such a blaze of fire that the palace
appears to be burning, and, on the top of this, a
shock of earthquake, which " dashes the building
on the ground[1]."   These tremendous phenomena,
be it observed, are no delusions,—that is to say, if

[1] *v.* 633.

delusion there be, it is not in the mind of Pentheus. Both the fire and the ruin of the palace are seen, in their exterior effects, by the bacchants waiting without. Now if Pentheus defied these warnings, if, that is to say, he were represented as feeling their force, but resisting nevertheless, the scene would be intelligible, though it would still be chargeable with gross exaggeration. To brave an earthquake is too much for mortality; it should be kept, as in the *Prometheus* of Aeschylus[1], for a god. Suppose that in *Exodus* the palace of Pharaoh were treated by Moses as Dionysus is supposed to treat that of Pentheus: the story of the plagues would surely be ruined. The King of Egypt must cease to resist, or cease to convince and to interest our imagination. And Pentheus does more than brave the earthquake; he utterly ignores it. We see him instantly afterwards[2], fresh from the shock; but in nothing that he says or does do we see any trace of such an experience. It has impressed him no more, so far as we are allowed to perceive, than if a fly had settled upon his hand. This is not the behaviour of a hardened man, or of a man at all; it is the behaviour of a stone.

Satan, in *Paradise Lost*, defies the horrors of the fall from Heaven to Hell and the nine days wallowing in the fiery lake. And his defiance moves us, because

> Nor did they not perceive the evil plight
> In which they were, or the fierce pains not feel.

[1] *P. V.* 1080.　　　　[2] *vv.* 642 ff.

If he were indifferent, so should we be. Macbeth braves the prodigies of his last hour, the marching forest and the foe not born of woman, knowing and confessing their full significance. But if he ignored them, what would they matter to us ?

And let it not be said, that the insensibility of Pentheus is itself miraculous, a part of his punishment. Even if this were so, it would not save the situation, since a blow not felt is no warning. But the case is not so. He is not dazed, but alert, in all his faculties unaltered and unimpaired. Only he does not notice the earthquake ; he is occupied with other things. Now that is absurd.

This objection—which, in my judgement, would alone suffice to raise a presumption, that the miraculous allegations of the *Bacchants* are propounded not for our acceptance but for our criticism—must not be confused with another, to which we shall come in due course :—that the ignorance of Pentheus and others would naturally make the audience incredulous of the earthquake as a given fact. We are here assuming the contrary, that, upon the statements of Dionysus and his devotees, aided or not aided by some scenic suggestion, the audience do accept the earthquake, without question, as a fact. And we say that, on this hypothesis, the behaviour of Pentheus, being inconceivable, is unimpressive, and the scene is frigid.

Also it would be, on this hypothesis, a grave and strange error, that these stupendous effects are

placed where they are, almost[1] at the beginning of
the series, so that this topic, the miraculous demonstrations and the obstinacy of the infidel, is prematurely exhausted, and the sequel must be an anti-
climax. The report of the herdsman from Cithaeron,
which follows the scene of the earthquake, is in one
respect[2] well fitted to impress the king, even if, in
the main, he disbelieves it. It does impress him.
It leads to a pause and debate, which we are intended
to watch with interest[3]. But after the preceding
exhibition such a scene is out of place, and such an
interest can hardly arise. Doubt, irresolution, is
not natural in a man so obdurate that he disregards
an earthquake, and hardly worth attention, since we
must suppose that his perversity will prevail.

Such are some, a few only, of the traits in the
play which confirm the presumption, arising from
the known practice of Euripides, that the facts of
the story, according to the intent of the author,
are natural, not supernatural, and which compel us
to consider, how it would have been interpreted by
spectators or readers alive to this presumption, that
is to say, by all contemporary Athenians who were
interested in literature or speculation. To interpret
it perfectly is more than we can expect. Our knowledge, always defective, has here two special defects.
The Bacchic religion of the play is expressly said,
as we noted before, to be properly and peculiarly
that of the north and of Macedonia[4]. Doubtless

[1] *vv.* 447 ff.   [2] *vv.* 683–688.
[3] *vv.* 778–846.   [4] *vv.* 409–415.

therefore Euripides made use of his recent observations in that region; and, though the country and its practices were then little known at Athens, he must have counted on something different from our almost total ignorance. And again, in the *Bacchants* as in the *Heracles*, we feel our loss of the once important rationalistic literature of the fifth century. We do not know, and we need to know, how the legends of Bacchus had been handled by such a writer as Herodorus. These legends, like those of Heracles, were specially inviting to rationalistic explanation, because even the fabulists allowed that Heracles and Bacchus had been men. In the *Heracles* the effect of such speculation is obvious[1], and it is not likely to be absent from the *Bacchants*. But we cannot verify it by reference, and our conjectural observation is a poor substitute for the direct knowledge of the original readers. However we must do as we can.

Of the Prologue there is little to say which we have not already anticipated. A principal point in it, emphasized by repetition[2], is to inform the audience that, though Dionysus prologizes, no such personage will appear in the action, but only a human preacher of the rites. Moreover those familiar with Euripidean ways will not fail to remark, that, although the prologist declares his identity

---

[1] E.g. *Heracles*, 153 f. See further my essay on the play in *Four Plays of Euripides*.

[2] *vv.* 4, 53, 54. The tautology of 53, 54 has given offence (see commentaries), but the insistence is intentional.

with the preacher, he is on this point hardly consistent with himself. For the preacher is acting,
and is to act, in Thebes, supported by a company of
women (the Chorus), whom he has brought with
him from Asia; and as a fact, when the time comes
for him to play his part, it is in Thebes, as we should
expect, that he is found[1]. But the last words of the
prologist[2] are that he is now going "to the glens of
Cithaeron," to join the performances of the Theban
women there assembled. We may no doubt make
suppositions which will fill the gap; but the discrepancy would not have been created, if the prologue
had been conceived by the author as continuous
with the play,—a part of the action. The contrary
is apparent. The theatrical deity, having done his
service, discharges himself, after the manner of
Euripides[3], from further appearance, and, from this
point till the *finale*, we have nothing to do with him.

Not that it would make any difference to the
interpretation, if we took the prologue as drama,
a part of the action presented. In that case, the
prologist is certainly the preacher, a man; but
whether he is anything more, whether, as he says,
he is truly a god and his human form is a disguise,
or whether, on the contrary, his divinity is a mas-
querade, a pretension which he assumes when it
suits his purpose,—these are questions not to be

---

[1] *v.* 352 (ἀνὰ πόλιν στείχοντες) with *v.* 434 ff.   [2] 62 ff.

[3] See the prologue of the *Ion*, *vv.* 76 f., *Hecuba*, 52 ff., *Troades*,
92 ff., *Hipp.* 51 ff. The only supernatural prologist, who might
seem to promise an appearance in the action, is Death in the
Alcestis (*v.* 74); and the promise is not kept.

answered upon his mere authority.   We shall see in
the sequel.

But one thing is clear.   The history, which he
gives, of himself and his religion is on the face of it
improbable, and—which is odd—the improbability
is pressed upon our notice.   He is young.   His
human grandfather is still living.   Since he was
born, some twenty years may have elapsed ; and in
this interval, before ever visiting Thebes, his birth-
place, or any part of Hellas, he has diffused and
established his religion, beginning from Lydia, all
over the Oriental world :—

From the rich golden vale of Lydia I went forth, and from
Phrygia, and visited the sun-beaten regions of Persia, the fortresses
of Bactria, wintry Media, Arabia the fertile, and all Asia[1], which lies
along the salt sea, her fair walled towns thickly-peopled with
Greek and foreigner mixed together, *and came not to this town of
Greeks until first even in those parts I had done my dances and
established my rites, that my deity might be world-approved*[2].

[1] Asia Minor, especially the western coast.

[2] *vv.* 13–22

> λιπὼν δὲ Λυδῶν τοὺς πολυχρύσους γύας
> Φρυγῶν τε, Περσῶν θ' ἡλιοβλήτους πλάκας
> Βάκτριά τε τείχη τήν τε δύσχιμον χθόνα
> Μήδων ἐπελθὼν Ἀραβίαν τ' εὐδαίμονα
> Ἀσίαν τε πᾶσαν, ἣ παρ' ἁλμυρὰν ἅλα
> κεῖται, μιγάσιν Ἕλλησι βαρβάροις θ' ὁμοῦ
> πλήρεις ἔχουσα καλλιπυργώτους πόλεις,
> 20   ἐς τήνδε πρῶτον ἦλθον Ἑλλήνων πόλιν,
> κἀκεῖ χορεύσας καὶ καταστήσας ἐμὰς
> τελετάς, ἵν' εἴην ἐμφανὴς δαίμων βροτοῖς.

The last two verses repeat with emphasis (note καὶ ἐκεῖ) the effect
of *vv.* 13–19.   In *v.* 20 πρῶτον relates to the aorists preceding
and following, and means "*not until* I had done all this."

It is seen in the English, and more clearly in the Greek, that this sentence returns upon itself, insisting on the point that, though the god was Greek-born, his religion was first Asiatic. Modern readers have been displeased by this insistence[1], which seems purposeless, and have tried to get rid of it. But there it is ; and our aim should be rather to find out why. And surely this much is apparent, that the point would not have been pressed by any one, who meant the statement of the god to carry conviction. His story is a crude combination of incompatibles. He accepts the old Greek legend, framed in days when little was known in Greece of the Bacchic religion and nothing of its origins, which made Bacchus simply the son of Zeus and a Theban woman. He also accepts, with the nascent science and history of the fifth century, the truth that vast regions in the East had known religion of the orgiastic type before ever it came to Hellas. Like Herodotus after visiting Egypt, the god is aware that the traditions of Greek ignorance were a frame too narrow for recorded facts. And his device is, to force in the facts—and to signalize the compression. Such a treatment cannot be *bona fide*. It is possible that, by the age of Euripides, the legend of Bacchus, as told at Delphi and such places, had assumed the shape in which Euripides presents it ; and the god (we may note) agrees with Apollo's prophet Teiresias, a representative of Delphi, in

[1] See the apparatus criticus to the texts of Sandys and Murray.

this, that he ignores the vital doctrine of the second birth, which Teiresias expressly disowns[1]. But at Delphi (we may be sure), if they told the story so, they told it simply, and not, as Euripides does, so as to invite rejection.

What Euripides seems to suspect, as matter of historical truth, or at least what would naturally occur to a reader of his prologue, is that the precinct of Semele (a real Theban relic and haunt of fancy[2]), with its ruined house and its legend of a woman pregnant by Zeus and slain by the jealousy of Hera, had originally no connexion with the religion of the Man-God, which was incongruously annexed to the place at the time of its importation, perhaps because of the accidental circumstance that the ground was overgrown with the Bacchic leafage of the vine[3]. Whether such a speculation was current, as in the fifth century it well may have been, and whether it was well-founded, as is also possible, we need not enquire. But it is material to observe that, in Euripides, Bacchus, like the Twin Gods of the *Electra*[4], becomes a critic : his legend, in its Hellenic form, is not satisfactory even to himself.

His manner, so far, in the prologue, is animated

---

[1] *vv.* 286 ff.

[2] See *vv.* 6–9 with Sandys' notes. *V.* 6 does not show that the monument is represented on the scene, but only that it is supposed to be visible *from* the scene. And so also *vv.* 596 ff. In the absence of notice elsewhere actual representation is not likely.

[3] See *vv.* 6–12, and especially the last two verses.

[4] *El.* 1245 f.

and not undignified. But it is neither sublime, nor mystical, nor, in any sense of the word, religious. It is a plain style of narrative, having about as little elevation as is compatible with the form of poetry. It could not satisfy, and was not (one would suppose) designed to satisfy, as the style for a god, those who had seen gods presented by Aeschylus and Sophocles. And we observe that it does not satisfy Professor Murray. Mr Murray's prologue is not only more highly coloured, more poetical, but it has, what Euripides will not give, the note of sublimity and mystery:

> *Behold, God's Son is come unto this land*
> Of Thebes, even I, Dionysus, whom the brand
> Of heaven's hot splendour *lit to life*, when she
> Who bore me, Cadmus' daughter Semelê,
> Died here.

This is a fine opening, and religious. This, or something like it, is what would have been put in the mouth of the Man-God by an Aeschylus or a Pindar. But let it be compared with the original[1]. Can we suppose that the Διὸς παῖς of Euripides, or the ἥκω (a common form of his theatrical prologists)[2], had ever for any ear the arresting sound, as of some awful Revelation, which the translator

---

[1] *vv.* 1–3

Ἥκω Διὸς παῖς τήνδε Θηβαίων χθόνα
Διόνυσος, ὃν τίκτει ποθ᾽ ἡ Κάδμου κόρη
Σεμέλη λοχευθεῖσ᾽ ἀστραπηφόρῳ πυρί.

[2] Cf. Hermes in *Ion* 5, ἥκω δὲ Δελφῶν τήνδε γῆν, the Ghost of Polydorus in *Hec.* 1, ἥκω..., Poseidon in *Tro.* 1, ἥκω....

strikes in *Behold, God's Son is come*? And if Euripides wished to suggest that the speaker is a superhuman, incomprehensible Being, in whom earth and heaven are united, could he not find, as our English poet can, language fit for the purpose, and say that, by the stroke of lightning, He, the Babe of Semele, was "lit to life"? What Euripides says is simply that the lightning "delivered" the mother. And as the two compositions begin, so each proceeds to the end. The prologist of Euripides concludes his narrative by saying twice, in plain terms, that his outward appearance, for the present, is merely human : *For this cause I have taken mortal form, and changed my shape into the nature of man*[1]. From the English alembic this emerges thus :

> For this I *veil my godhead* with the *wan*
> Form of the things that die, and walk as Man.

This is, or might be, the language of godhead veiled. But in Euripides there is neither veil to see through nor deity to see.

The prologue, though it says little or nothing of the Bacchic religion on its spiritual side, lays some stress on the Bacchic costume, the dress of fawn-skin and the ivy-wreathed wand (*thyrsus*) in the hand[2]. We may take therefore this opportunity of noting that the play does not anywhere appear to

---

[1] *vv.* 53–54

  ὧν οὕνεκ' εἶδος θνητὸν ἀλλάξας ἔχω,
  μορφήν τ' ἐμὴν μετέβαλον εἰς ἀνδρὸς φύσιν.

[2] *vv.* 23–25.

treat these properties as symbolic, to connect them with doctrine, or otherwise to account for them. The costume seems to be, for Euripides, nothing but a ritual prescription, though in this sense peremptory. The peculiar dress, like the retirement into a lonely place, seems merely to mark that the worshipper is for the time withdrawn from ordinary life and given up to the worship. If Euripides had any theory respecting the garb imposed upon bacchants, it would seem to be possibly this, that its very strangeness might be a test of obedience[1]. And we may bear in mind, in this connexion and generally, that the Bacchic religion, *as described in this play*, had in the fifth century B.C. but a slight hold upon Hellas, and that in most places and ordinary times bacchic performances, of the kind here represented, were not to be seen.

With the departure of the god, and the entrance of the Lydian women who travel with him in his character of adept and preacher, the action opens, and we pass into a different atmosphere. Neither poetry, nor depth, nor height, nor mystery is deficient in the astonishing dance-hymn with which they come on. The rhythm of it, a three-time movement, slow apparently at first, but passing at the end into a precipitate race which whirls us away, cannot be precisely reproduced in English or without the aid of music. But for spirit and feeling one

[1] See the language of Teiresias (175 ff.) and Cadmus (180) and the scene there following.

would desire nothing better than such passages as these :

> Oh, blessed he in all wise
>   Who hath drunk the Living Fountain,
>   Whose life no folly staineth,
>   And his soul is near to God :
> Whose sins are lifted, pall-wise,
>   As he worships on the Mountain,
>   And where Cybele ordaineth,
>   Our Mother, he has trod.......

> Hither, O fragrant of Tmolus the Golden,
>   Come with the voice of timbrel and drum;
> Let the cry of your joyance uplift and embolden
>   The God of the joy-cry; O Bacchanals, come!
> With pealing of pipes and with Phrygian clamour,
>   On, where the vision of holiness thrills,
> And the music climbs and the maddening glamour,
>   With the wild White Maids, to the hills, to the hills!
> Oh, then, like a colt as he runs by a river,
>   A colt by his dam, when the heart of him sings,
> With the keen limbs drawn and the fleet foot a-quiver,
>   Away the Bacchanal springs[1]!

There is no reason to doubt that, with due allowance for the colouring of poetry, Euripides here describes realities, things and practices which he had seen ; though, likely enough, he had not seen them in any high degree of purity until he went out of Hellas. Indeed they are, in their inward meaning, less foreign to us than they were to him. The idea of a religion universal in application and claims capable of transference from place to place, prosely-

---

[1] *vv.* 72 ff., 152 ff. (Murray).

tizing, was strange to the primitive paganism of
Hellas, whose native cults stood rather upon privilege and exclusion, particularities of race, family,
person, and sex; but it is familiar to us, and even
fundamental in our conception of religion as such.
Again, the happiness of the congregation, the
stimulus of religious acts performed in company, is
the very root of many living cults. So it is of the
Bacchic worship as here painted. The rapture of
the initiated lies essentially in this, that "his soul is
congregationalized" ($\theta\iota\alpha\sigma\epsilon\acute{\upsilon}\epsilon\tau\alpha\iota$ $\psi\upsilon\chi\grave{\alpha}\nu$[1]),—if we may
venture an ugly phrase for the sake of its truth to
sense. The retreat, the camp of "revivals" in
solitary places, is foreign to countries like our own,
but chiefly because we lack room for it. It is perfectly congenial to the spirit of modern congrega-
tionalism, and reappears promptly where circumstances admit. The violent music and the violent
motions we have disciplined and policed away, but
even in our orderly streets we may see how gladly they
would return. And indeed Euripides himself makes
clear, when he comes to describe the actual behaviour
of the worshippers, that, however ecstatic in feeling,
they were in act not disorderly but disciplined[2], and
that the language of the Chorus, at their entrance
and elsewhere, so far as it implies the contrary,
should be taken, as the language of religion often
must be, as metaphorical. The freedom sought and

---

[1] *v.* 75. The *thiasos* is the company joined together for
religious purposes.

[2] *v.* 693 $\theta\alpha\hat{\upsilon}\mu$' $\iota\delta\epsilon\hat{\iota}\nu$ $\epsilon\hat{\upsilon}\kappa\sigma\mu\acute{\iota}\alpha\varsigma$.

extolled is that of the spirit, not of the body.   And
the same applies to the other expressions, by which
they set forth the inward exaltation of the worshipper.   When one of them exclaims :

> O glad, glad on the mountains
>   To swoon in the race outworn,
> When the holy fawn-skin clings,
>   And all else sweeps away,
> To the joy of the red quick fountains,
>   The blood of the hill-goat torn,
> The glory of wild-beast ravenings,
>   Where the hill-tops catch the day....

and when another adds :

> Then streams the earth with milk, yea, streams
> With wine and nectar of the bee,
> And through the air dim perfume steams
> Of Syrian frankincense[1]....

we are surely not bound, nor at liberty, to assume
that literal draughts of blood were part of the practices, or real springs of honey familiar to the sight
or belief of the devotees.   With such interpretation,
what would a historian make of our own prayer-
books and hymn-books ?   The spiritualists of the
fifth century B.C. were much nearer than we to the
savage base, and more easily reverted to it.   But we
must not for that reason impute to them in practice
every suggestion of their metaphorical language.

It is nevertheless true of course that, in an age
when the very rudiments of scientific observation
and reasoning were hardly anywhere popularly

[1] *vv.* 135 ff. (Murray).

diffused, the barrier between the imagination and the experience of miracles would be weak, and such visionaries as the bacchants of this hymn would be an easy prey to imposture. This also Euripides had observed as a fact, and will presently show us at large.

In theology, the Chorus have but one dogma, the double birth of the Man-God, upon which they insist[1] with a fervour specially noticeable after the neglect of this doctrine in the prologue. Nor do they agree with the prologist as to the connexion of their theology with the place of their preaching, the town of Thebes. The deity of the prologue begins with the assertion that he is the son of Zeus and of Cadmus' daughter. But the Chorus are so far from taking the Theban birth for a fundamental dogma, that, in this opening hymn, they hardly notice it. They expound their doctrine without mention either of Semele or of Thebes[2]; to the "Mother"[3] they give no name, and if any be supplied by reference[4], it is that of *Cybele*, which for Asiatics would be suitable. (*Rhea* is mentioned both in the prologue[5] and in this hymn[6] as indirectly connected with the bacchic ritual by the timbrel-music, derived from her cult; but the identity of Rhea and Cybele is not asserted, and must not be assumed.) In inviting Thebes to embrace the new religion, they address the city as "nurse of Semele," and that is here their sole reference to the local legend[7]. All this is

---

[1] *vv.* 88 ff., see 521 ff.   [2] Stroph. and Ant. 2.   [3] *v.* 91.
[4] *vv.* 78 f.   [5] *v.* 59.   [6] *v.* 128 ff.
[7] *v.* 105. See also *vv.* 519 ff.

natural and intelligible. A mystic event, such as
the double birth, may be localized with infinite
variety, and even repeated, since it was virtually
repeated in the case of every initiate who became
a *bacchos*[1]. Locality is nothing. Every place may
have its own adaptation, and the Theban story may
be accepted for Thebes. But it is not essential.

Negatively the hymn is remarkable in ignoring
the conception of Bacchus as god and giver of wine[2].
The vine is not even mentioned. What exactly the
genuine bacchants are represented as holding in
this regard, we shall have to consider later[3]. But it
appears in this opening hymn (and the whole play
confirms it) that the rapture of Bacchus, as they
conceive it, is not to be confounded or even connected with vinous excitement. This point, and the
misconception of Pentheus and others with regard to
it, are extremely important to the plot.

The mystic assimilation of the worshipper to the
god, of the *bacchos* to the *Bacchos*, is asserted expressly only of the leader of the company[4], but is
doubtless to be understood of all in due degree.

---

[1] See hereafter on *v.* 243.

[2] The ῥεῖ δ' οἴνῳ of *v.* 143, taken with the context, rather
excludes than suggests any particular attribution.

[3] See *vv.* 375 ff., 416 ff.

[4] *v.* 141 ὁ δ' ἔξαρχος Βρόμιος, and perhaps in *v.* 115, where the
false reading of the two MSS. (Βρόμιος ὃς ἄγῃ θιάσους) is corrected in
one of them to Βρόμιος ὅστις ἄγει θιάσους "Whosoever leads the
companies is a Bromios." This, or rather ὅστις ἄγῃ, as Prof. Murray
suggests in his edition of the text, may well be right. See also
v. 243 ἐκεῖνος ἐν μηρῷ ποτ' ἐρράφη Διός.

That the knowledge of certain mysteries is one of the rewards of the worshipper, and a part of his happiness, we are told both here and elsewhere[1]. But the play lays comparatively little stress on this side of the religion, and conveys (I think) no hint of what the revelations might be. It is conjecturable that they pointed to a future life. But here it is the present rapture of the religious performances, rather than any promises, upon which the preachers dwell; and in truth many firm believers in a Heaven above love more, if not better, the "little Heaven below."

Such, in outline, is the religion which has already carried away to the wilderness, in a frenzy of enthusiasm, the women of Thebes. Among the men no conversions, so far, have been made[2]; but two converts of importance now present themselves in the persons of Teiresias, the blind prophet of Apollo, and Cadmus, the ex-king. These aged men have agreed to practise the prescribed rites and to repair to Cithaeron for that purpose; and they now appear, dressed in the bacchic garb. That their appearance, in a costume certainly more becoming to the agile, may provoke some contempt, Teiresias, the leader in the action, admits[3]; but we cannot infer from this that they are not meant to command our perfect sympathy. To brave ridicule in a good cause may be more than respectable, and we may suppose the author partly to mean this. Only, to make such a

---

[1] *v. 72 τελετὰς θεῶν εἰδώς.* See also *vv.* 471 ff.

[2] *vv.* 195 f.   [3] *vv.* 214 f.

situation satisfactory, from a religious point of view,
it should be clear that the devotees are in fact up-
held and exalted above themselves by a mightier
Power. We expect to read something like this:

> *Cadmus.*　Where then shall I stand, where tread
> The dance and toss this bowed and hoary head?
> O friend, in thee is wisdom; guide my grey
> And eld-worn steps, eld-worn Teiresias.—Nay;
> I am not weak.

> [*At the first movement of worship his manner begins to change;
> a mysterious strength and exaltation enter into him.*]

> 　　　　　　　　　Surely this arm could smite
> The wild earth with its thyrsus, day and night,
> And faint not! Sweetly and forgetfully
> The dim years fall from off me![1]

Now it may be that, in the Athenian theatre, a
convinced initiate (probably not the priest of
Dionysus), or any pious and simple person, may have
interpreted Euripides to himself in this sense. And,
for reasons already given, I think it defensible as
an alternative to put such colour, firmly and definitely, upon an English version. But on the other
hand no reader of Greek, and certainly not the
translator, will deny that colour is put on, and that
the pious and simple person gets help from our
native tragedian for which he will look vainly in

---

[1] *vv.* 184–189 (Murray)

> ποῖ δεῖ χορεύειν, ποῖ καθιστάναι πόδα
> καὶ κρᾶτα σεῖσαι πολιόν; ἐξηγοῦ σύ μοι
> γέρων γέροντι, Τειρεσία· σὺ γὰρ σοφός.
> ὡς οὐ κάμοιμ᾽ ἂν οὔτε νύκτ᾽ οὔθ᾽ ἡμέραν
> θύρσῳ κροτῶν γῆν· ἐπιλελήσμεθ᾽ ἡδέως
> γέροντες ὄντες.

Euripides. To pass minor touches—such as "smite the *wild* earth," where the lifting epithet is an addition—the vital sentences

> Nay; I am not weak....
> Sweetly and forgetfully
> The dim years fall from off me!

are free composition, where everything which supports the stage-direction by suggesting mystery comes from the translation—the dreamy melodious rhythm, the bold figure, everything. The Cadmus of Euripides says just this: "We have pleasantly forgotten that we are old." Justice Shallow might have said as much to Falstaff. And moreover, instead of English notably musical, we get, by accident or design, Greek most uncommonly and rather comically ugly[1]. The excitement of Cadmus, so far as appears, may be that which is natural to an old man making an unwonted exertion, and pleased to find that it is not beyond him,—just that, and no more. Nor does Teiresias, in Euripides, prove more. In the translation he may seem to do so.

> *Teir.* As with thee,
> With me 'tis likewise. Light am I and young,
> And will essay the dancing and the song.
> *Cadmus.* Quick, then, our chariots to the mountain road.
> *Teir.* Nay; to take steeds were *to mistrust the God.*

This means, with the context, that in the strength of the God, in the strength of which Cadmus has felt the mysterious access, they may walk. If the prophet

---

[1] γέροντες ὄντες. Note the uncouth assonance.

did indeed say this, he would assent to the mystic
sensation, which, in the translation, is attributed to
the king; and such a note might redeem the oddity,
otherwise apparent, of the king's proposal to ride.
But the note is not in Euripides, whose sense is
given more exactly by Mr Way:

Nay, so were the God's honour minishéd[1].

Even this, in the poetical form and pronunciation
of the word *minishéd*, exceeds the original line,
which may fairly be described as prose in metre.
But it gives the sense, which is simply that pilgrims
must not make themselves too comfortable, and
does not suggest any miraculous exaltation.   Nor,
so far as I see, does any part of the scene.

   The case is this.   If this scene were the prelude
to a series of gigantic miracles, performed by the
Power to whom these old men are offering themselves as a sort of aged martyrs,—and that is what
Professor Murray has in prospect,—then, by every
rule of keeping and sense, the Power should be
perceptible here.   The action must rise, rise high,
and the language with it.   The translator accordingly raises the level of the whole, and, just at the
right place, goes deftly and dexterously up to the
proper pitch.   But why did Euripides stay below?
He can soar when he pleases; he has soared in the
hymn.   Here he is firmly pedestrian.   Is it unreasonable to suggest that he meant to be taken at
his word?

---

[1] *v.* 192 ἀλλ᾽ οὐχ ὁμοίως ἂν ὁ θεὸς τιμὴν ἔχοι.

The figures and characters of Cadmus and Teiresias, since neither, without forcing the language of Euripides, can be made into a witness of the supernatural, do not concern the special subject of our investigation; and we may deal with them summarily. Cadmus is transparent enough. He is decrepit, weak, and, as he flatters himself, cunning. He is attached to his family and zealous for its honour[1]. It was he who, at the time of Semele's misfortune, ingeniously attributed it to Zeus—but did not convince his other daughters[2]. What he sees in the bacchic mission—if we may so term it— is an excellent opportunity for establishing this view, and immensely improving it by the addition that the offspring of Semele has been raised to immortality. He puts this to his grandson Pentheus with a frankness which rejects all gloss. Dionysus, he says, may be a god or he may not; but surely it is not for the family of Semele to dispute it[3]. With such a disposition, the concurrence of Teiresias, an authority in matters of religion[4], is decisive, and he puts himself cheerfully in the prophet's hands. His part so far, before the catastrophe, is ridiculous; after the catastrophe, his very weakness, his extreme misery, and the irony of his suicidal success, add a poignant touch to the bacchic triumph. He helps materially to launch the movement, but finds, as with

---

[1] *vv.* 181 ff., 333 ff., and *passim.*

[2] *vv.* 26–31. Note Κάδμου σοφίσματα.   [3] *vv.* 333 ff.

[4] *vv.* 185 f., where ἐξηγοῦ suggests the professional ἐξηγητής or *director.*

more wisdom he might have foreseen, that his conversion is reckoned at its true value.   To the lesson of the play, as the picture of a religious revolution, he contributes this much : that great movements, good or bad, may, at a critical turn, depend much on the action of little men in high places.   That is true ; and it covers perhaps all that need be said about the Cadmus of the *Bacchants*.

Teiresias is far nobler and more important, and deserves a fuller study than we here can spare to him.   He fills a place which the author was bound to fill.   He represents the authority of Delphi—a function in which he was a figure familiar to the tragic stage[1],—and his views serve to show what the poet thought of the Bacchic religion as accepted by Delphi, and of its actual position in Hellas at his own day.   No one, Euripides least of all, could exhibit the conversion of Thebes without saying his word about this.   And what Euripides says, as I understand, by his portrait of Teiresias, is that the Bacchic religion, the religion of the Man-God, as truly represented by the Chorus, had been so transformed by Hellas and Delphi in the process of acceptance, had been so accommodated, clipped, and adapted to the prepossessions, the habits of thought and practice, rooted in an alien soil, that its effect, as a change, was more nominal than real; and further, that what was most real in the effect was not the most laudable part of it.   The motives of Teiresias, in supporting the invaders, are stated as frankly as

---

[1] See the *Oedipus Tyrannus, Antigone, Phoenissae.*

those of Cadmus. He sees that the new religion is
a great power, and well may see, when it has swept
all the women into the wilderness. He foresees
that it must and will be admitted upon some terms.
He holds, as I apprehend, honestly and plausibly,
that, because strong, it is divine. But he is confident,
and shows in this the sort of insight which the heads
of established religions have shown again and again,
that it will not destroy native growths, "the traditions
of our fathers." These, he says, "no doctrine, however subtle, can destroy[1]." Here he goes beyond
the truth, as Delphi was one day to learn. But it is
true that such destruction is most difficult, and that
what more often happens is what had happened, up
to the time of Euripides, in the relations of pagan
Hellas to the religion of the Man-God: the new is
absorbed, and digested. The current, judiciously
led, runs into the old channels of religiosity, quick-
ening the flow but not disrupting the conduits.

How this was to be, Teiresias sets forth in his
reply to the denunciation of Pentheus[2]. It comes
to this, that Dionysus, *suitably treated*, might take
his place, without disturbance, beside Zeus, Hera,
Ares, Phoebus, and, in short, the Olympians at large.
To him, as well as to Ares, will belong the battle-
panic[3]. He, as well as Phoebus, may inspire divina-

---

[1] *vv.* 201–203

    πατρίους παραδοχάς, ἅς θ᾽ ὁμήλικας χρόνῳ
    κεκτήμεθ᾽, οὐδεὶς αὐτὰ καταβαλεῖ λόγος,
    οὐδ᾽ εἰ δι᾽ ἄκρων τὸ σοφὸν ηὕρηται φρενῶν.

[2] *vv.* 266 ff.   [3] *vv.* 302 ff.

tion (as at Delphi in fact he shared the temple with
Apollo)[1]. As god of wine—or rather of drink—
he will pair off with Demeter *alias* Earth, who
feeds mankind with solids[2]. As identified himself
with wine, he will be poured in libation, and make
peace between gods and men[3] (a hint at the sacra-
mental conception, which is traceable in the religion
of Eleusis, but noticeably absent from the religion
preached by the bacchants in this play). As for the
novel theology, the mystery of the Twice-born, this,
the prophet concedes, as stated by the new preachers,
is objectionable; but it can be explained away by
a simple trick of words,—resolved into a common
Greek fairy-tale, like those of Hesiod, meaningless indeed, but certainly harmless[4]! The new
rites, the ecstatic dances, these too will some day be
performed on Parnassus[5]. To women there may be
some moral danger in them—so far the Delphian
patron agrees with the persecutor—but the virtuous
will resist, and the vicious must not blame the
religion for their own vice[6].

Such, set off by a sober pulpit-eloquence not
unimpressive, is this interesting discourse, and such
(according to Euripides) was the patronage which
the Bacchic religion had found in Hellas. Manifestly
between Teiresias and the bacchants there is, at
bottom, no agreement and hardly any affinity what-

---

[1] *vv.* 298 ff. [2] *vv.* 274 ff.

[3] *vv.* 284 f., suspected of interpolation, but, I think, without
reason.

[4] *vv.* 286 ff. This passage is further discussed below.

[5] *vv.* 306 ff. [6] *vv.* 314 ff.

ever. The prophet is concerned for a mass of beliefs and cults of which they have never a word to say, and denies—or, to save dispute, let us say "ignores"—the momentous doctrine by which alone their theory of the Man-God is distinguished from miscellaneous polytheistic paganism. The single innovation which Teiresias really concedes, is a rare celebration of the rites, once, as a fact, in two years; and from this, as is only too evident, he does not expect any good. How should he? Without the peculiar Bacchic theology, with its promise of divine union for men, the bacchic cult of rapture would be a mere snare, and would naturally become the scandal which, as Euripides implies in the *Ion*, the Delphian celebrations actually were. And the Teiresias of this play goes near to admit the imputation; his remarks on the moral danger of the rites are the least creditable point in his discourse.

Whether Euripides' picture of Bacchus in Hellas is exact, or what correction it needs, we have not the means to decide. General truth a modern must, in fairness and respect, attribute to it; and I am not aware of any material evidence to the contrary. The silences of the play, the total absence of allusion to the many famous practices, feasts, institutions, habits, which connected themselves *nominally* with Dionysus, Bacchus, or other associated names, imply (what is surely true) that such things in general—the Dionysia of Athens, for instance, and the mysteries of Iacchus at Eleusis—were not "bacchic" at all in any proper and distinct

sense. The *trieterica* of Delphi, held in alternate
years, were bacchic in form; and this is the only
positive example which Teiresias alleges for the
"greatness" which the new god was to acquire in
Hellas[1]. These performances, and such, Euripides
counted to his disgrace; nor was that opinion
confined to sceptics, if we may judge by Aeschylus,
whose recognition of the Delphian "Bromios," in the
prologue to the *Eumenides*, could hardly be less
warm than it is[2]. But Euripides seems also to have
thought, at all events after seeing the religion of
Macedonia, that the true Bacchus might disclaim
what was offensive in the Delphian festival, and
that there was a Bacchic religion different from that
of Delphi, stranger perhaps, but loftier and more
moral.

The passage in which Teiresias explains away
the doctrine of the Twice-born, and also the sneer
of Pentheus to which it replies[3], are by some dis-
allowed as interpolations. But no one has explained,
when, by whom, and with what motive, the insertions
can have been made and established in the text.
And without them the discourse of the prophet
would be oddly incomplete. In the sense indeed and
substance of his exposition, there would be no difference. He maintains that the importation of Bacchus
and the bacchanal worship will harmonize with
traditional Greek polytheism as received from
Homer and Hesiod. Manifestly this is impossible, if

[1] *vv.* 306 ff.   [2] *Eum.* 24 ff., discussed in my edition.
[3] *vv.* 242–247, 286–297.

the importation is to include the bacchanal theology, which signifies a view of the relation between God and man, a conception of all that religion means, radically incompatible with the Homeric. Believers in the Twice-born, real believers, would assuredly not be supporters of Ares, Athena, Apollo and the rest. One might almost as well imagine such an effect in Christianity. Whether then Teiresias disowns the doctrine, or merely passes it in significant silence, does not affect his position. But for dramatic purposes silence would be much less proper and less natural. The bacchants, in their hymn, have made apparent the unique importance of this point in their creed and cult[1]. And although Teiresias has not heard this particular statement, theatrical effect requires that his exposition of the new preaching, or rather his reply to it, should start from the base propounded to the audience. The sneer of Pentheus is a natural way of furnishing the formal cue; and the insertion of the two passages (whether by Euripides or another) was an improvement. As for the method of Teiresias' solution—a supposed ambiguity and juggle of words,—that should not surprise any one who has studied in Aeschylus, or indeed in this very play[2], the favourite devices of "mantic" interpretation. We need not necessarily suppose that the precise juggle here employed was a genuine product of Delphi. It has perhaps a touch of parody. In any case, the disputed passages, perfectly Euripidean in manner, must be extremely

[1] *vv.* 89 ff.   [2] *v.* 367.

ancient, hardly less so than the production of the play at Athens. And more than this we cannot, after all, say of any given passage or verse[1].

[1] In *vv.* 242–247 there are some noticeable details :

ἐκεῖνος εἶναί φησι Διόνυσον θεόν,—
ἐκεῖνος ἐν μηρῷ ποτ᾽ ἐρράφη Διός,—
ὃς ἐκπυροῦται λαμπάσιν κεραυνίαις
σὺν μητρί, Δίους ὅτι γάμους ἐψεύσατο.
ταῦτ᾽ οὐχὶ δεινῆς ἀγχόνης ἐστ᾽ ἄξια,
ὕβρεις ὑβρίζειν, ὅστις ἔστιν ὁ ξένος;

In *v.* 243 modern texts adopt ἐρράφθαι (Reiske) for ἐρράφη. But is this necessary? " He forsooth affirms the divinity of Dionysus! —he forsooth has been 'sown into the thigh of Zeus'!—Dionysus, who was consumed by the thunder-fire...." This is not nonsense; it implies that the worshippers of Bacchus, as they identified themselves with their God, were accustomed to attribute to themselves, mystically of course and by a religious figure, the process by which He was taken into the divine nature. Modern and familiar parallels to such religious language will occur to every reader :—"except *ye* be born again...," "*crucify* your affections...," etc. The composition, the way in which the relative ὅς reverts to Dionysus, thus becomes very abrupt, but this is not unsuitable to extreme rage. Apart from this, the only serious objection is to δεινῆς in *v.* 246. This epithet seems absurd, if we assume, with some, that "worthy of the halter" means "worthy of *execution* by hanging." But surely they are right who take the *halter* to be here, as usually in Athenian language, a symbol of suicide. "Worthy of the halter" means "enough to make one hang oneself"—a colloquial form of indignation. In such a form, which of course is not to be understood seriously and literally, the insertion of the epithet, "worthy of a *monstrous* halter," though loose, seems to me by no means unnatural or inconceivable. There is no valid objection to the metre ἐστ᾽ ἄξια.—In the second passage *vv.* 293–294 are certainly very obscure, perhaps not intelligible. The latest suggestion (Murray) that a verse is lost between them, making up the sense "he delivered the cloud-baby

Teiresias, as a type and a man, is admirably drawn. Whether such a person is to be liked and praised, is a point of moral taste, upon which people may and do differ indefinitely. The world is full of such persons still, and they play a vast part in history. The creator of this Teiresias did not love him much, —or he would not be made to say what he does about religion and vice[1]. But he is honest, grave, and in his way wise. To the play as a historical picture or symbol, he contributes perhaps the most important truth which it contains, namely that, as in other things so specially and above all in religion, revolutions, noisy and even tempestuous on the surface, may, after all, leave the foundations almost unmoved. And in the drama, tragedy, story, his importance is great. Through him chiefly—we may almost say solely—is exhibited the case against Pentheus. The futile Cadmus is a mere irritant to his stronger-minded grandson; and only prejudice will find anything conciliatory in the behaviour of the bacchants or the adept. They are sectaries of

as a pledge, [and, by giving the real Dionysus to the nymphs to nurse, saved] him from the jealousy of Hera" may well represent the intention. But the text may nevertheless be as complete as it ever was. I would distinguish, in these passages, between the two questions, whether they are *insertions*, and whether they are *genuine*, answering both in the affirmative. In a work like the *Bacchants*, on which the author was probably engaged to the last, the occurrence of such additions, perhaps imperfectly recorded and not yet worked in, is to be expected. This would account also for some roughness of composition.

[1] *vv.* 314 ff.

the most exasperating kind.　The servants and peasants have no weight.　But for all that, Pentheus is in the wrong, and, as tragedy demands, he provokes, without deserving, his fate.　And he has his chance, his fair chance, of suspecting that he is not in the right, when it appears that his attitude, his notion of the way to deal with a spiritual agitation, excites mere pity and dismay in a personage like Teiresias[1].

To Pentheus we now turn.　His character, mind, language, acts are, with those of his adversary the bacchic adept, the chief material for our present question :—whether the alleged miracles of the play are to be taken as facts.　That the miracles are ill-proved, the witnesses slight or suspect, is obvious; the silence of some who might be witnesses, and especially the silence of Teiresias, is significant; but Pentheus, and Pentheus only, expresses and maintains disbelief.　Now, as the reader will have just observed, I hold no brief for Pentheus.　He is prejudiced, rash, violent, deaf to advice.　All this is patent, and not at all affected by the equally patent

---

[1] *vv.* 358 ff.　As will be seen, I find no need to explain the acts of Teiresias, with Prof. Norwood, by a supposed private league with the adept, of which there is no account in the play. Prof. Norwood appeals to my own view of the *Andromache*, a play which I do hold to be inexplicable without the assumption of facts which it does not intelligibly state.　But he omits to notice, that what I there deduce is the connexion of the *Andromache* with some *other document*, presumably a play, which we do not possess.　Prof. Norwood's view of Teiresias would require a like hypothesis for the *Bacchae*; but I can see no need for it.

perfidy and cruelty of his opponent. His main and fatal error is that which is exhibited to us, for this reason, immediately upon his entrance :

Scarce had I crossed our borders, when mine ear
Was caught by this strange rumour, that our own
Wives, our own sisters, from their hearths are flown
To wild and secret rites ; and cluster there
High on the shadowy hills, with dance and prayer
To adore this new-made God, this Dionyse,
Whate'er he be ! *And in their companies*
Deep wine-jars stand, and ever and anon
Away into the loneliness now one
Steals forth, and now a second, maid or dame,
Where love lies waiting, not of God ! The flame,
They say, of Bacchios wraps them. Bacchios ! Nay,
'Tis more to Aphrodite that they pray[1].

Upon this ground, that the rites are vicious, he is resolved, and has already taken steps, to extirpate them. And the ground is hearsay—" I have heard[2]"; he cannot have made, and does not pretend to have made, any investigation whatever. Yet upon this hearsay he threatens death[3], and actually proceeds to every violence short of it. Upon this and no more, when his nearest friends and counsellors declare against him, he drives them away with insult and invective[4]. Upon this he arrests, imprisons, exerts, or is ready to exert, the whole terror of the state. All this for rumour, circulating amid conditions of excitement which impose the utmost caution ! In a young man prematurely called

[1] *vv.* 215 ff. (Murray).   [2] κλύω, *v.* 216.
[3] *vv.* 239 ff., 355 ff.   [4] *vv.* 255 ff., 343 ff.

to power[1], and vain of his position[2], such conduct is possible ; but it is monstrous, and it may well prove suicidal.

This error and crime of Pentheus, we should note, lies not at all in the fact that his opinion, in the particular case, is false. Not until late in the play[3] does either Pentheus or the reader learn that it is false ; and then, as we shall see, Pentheus is by no means deaf to the testimony. Such religious performances are mostly dangerous to virtue, and suspicion is only natural. Some anger too, at the violence of the enthusiasts, is, on any supposition, pardonable, not to say just. His whole sin, and it is enough, lies in *punishing upon a presumption*— the most intolerable abuse of authority.

But all this has no bearing on the question, whether, according to the dramatist, the bacchic preaching and rites are in this play accompanied by miracles. We cannot argue that, because improbable allegations are rejected by a man who in another way believes and acts unreasonably, therefore they are true. Certainly the disbelief of Pentheus does not disprove them. Considering his prejudice, it may be discounted and go for nothing, just as, for like reasons, the word of the adept on the other side is, in itself, worthless. The question is simply this. Are miracles so exhibited or so reported in the play, that the audience should naturally take them, for the purpose of the story, as true ?

[1] *vv.* 43 f.   [2] *vv.* 319 f.
[3] *vv.* 686 ff.

It will hardly be thought that the effects of the
preaching, as assumed in the prologue and at the
opening of the action—the flight of the women, their
"madness," and the general disturbance—are miraculous in the sense which concerns us here. They
do not exceed the known range of experience. It
is certain, only too certain, that religious enthusiasm,
suitably stimulated, is equal to such effects.

Nor is our question raised at all in the course of
the first scene, which displays the relations of Pentheus, Cadmus, and Teiresias, or in the entrance-
song which precedes this scene, or in the hymn (*To
Holiness*) which follows it. A single allusion occurs
in the entrance-speech of Pentheus, where, in
declaring his intention to put to death the Lydian
adept (on the charge of corrupting women), he
describes him as a "juggler and charmer[1]," which
suggests both supernatural pretensions and, in the
belief of the speaker, fraud. But the point is barely
touched and drops unnoticed. Teiresias in his
solemn exhortations and warning to the young
prince, and Cadmus in his affectionate but futile
pleading, say nothing of danger to be apprehended,
or conviction to be found, in the personal powers
of the foreign preacher, or in signs by which his
preaching has been accompanied. They do not so
much as mention him. Nor do the bacchants in
their hymns. These negations, though of course
nothing absolute can be inferred from them, are
worth notice and remembrance to this extent : it is

[1] γόης ἐπῳδός v. 234.

no datum of the play, we are nowhere authorized or asked to suppose, that, before the action begins, there have been undoubted miracles. The prologue does not say so, nor the expository scene. We come therefore, without any direction or prepossession, to the marvels propounded within the action of the play.

The first report of such an occurrence comes from the leader of the servants or guards, who execute the King's order for the arrest of the adept, and, at the opening of the second scene, bring him bound before their master :

> Pentheus, we come, who have run down this prey
> For which thou sentest us, nor sped in vain.
> This wild-beast found we tame : he darted not
> In flight away, but yielded, nothing loth,
> His hands, nor paled, nor changed his cheeks' rose-hue,
> But smiling bade us bind and lead him thence,
> And tarried, making easy this my task.
> Then shamed I said, "Not, stranger, of my will,
> But by commands of Pentheus, lead I thee."
> *The captured Bacchanals thou didst put in ward,*
> *And in the common prison bind with chains,*
> *Fled to the meadows are they, loosed from bonds,*
> *And dance and call on Bromius the God.*
> *The fetters from their feet self-sundered fell ;*
> *Doors, without mortal hand, unbarred themselves.*
> *Yea, fraught with many marvels this man came*
> *To Thebes !*　To thee the rest doth appertain.
> *Pentheus.*　Ye are mad ! Once in the toils of these mine hands,
> He is not so fleet as to escape from me[1].

For the last couplet, the comment of the King,

---

[1] *vv.* 434 ff. (Way).

Mr Way gives an alternative, representing an uncertainty in the text:

> *Let loose his hands.* Once taken in the toils,
> He is not so fleet as to escape from me.

Professor Murray translates both readings:

> *Ye are mad !—Unhand him.* How so swift he be,
> My toils are round him and he shall not fly.

I think, for reasons given below[1], that this must be nearer to the original, though not complete, and that

[1]
 μαίνεσθε· χειρῶν τοῦδ' ἐν ἄρκυσιν γὰρ ὢν
 οὐκ ἔστιν οὕτως ὠκὺς ὥστε μ' ἐκφυγεῖν MSS.

μέθεσθε χειρῶν τοῦδ' Burges, and many texts. Neither the tradition nor the correction is satisfactory. To drop μαίνεσθε makes Pentheus pass in silence the escape of the bacchanals and the man's miraculous explanation. Drama, if not reality, requires that he should take some notice of it. On the other hand, to construe the MSS., we must suppose, according to an ancient gloss accepted by Prof. Tyrrell, that τοῦδε means τοῦδε τἀνδρός, i.e. ἐμοῦ, *me*, which, if possible, is surely not natural. Moreover a direction to release the prisoner (μέθεσθε) is necessary, for released he is (see *vv.* 503 ff.), and the servants would not do it without an order. We want both μαίνεσθε and μέθεσθε, as Murray, by his version, implies. The true inference seems to be that something has been omitted, and that the original was such as to facilitate this accident, e.g.—

> μαίνεσθε· <χειρῶν τοὔργον· ἀλλὰ νῦν ὅμως
> μέθεσθε> χειρῶν τοῦδ'· ἐν ἄρκυσιν γὰρ ὢν
> οὐκ ἔστιν οὕτως ὠκὺς ὥστ' ἔμ' ἐκφυγεῖν.

Here χειρῶν τοὔργον, "it is the work of hands," completes the comment upon the alleged miracle, and replies to the ἄνευ θνητῆς χερός, "without mortal hand," of *v.* 448, while at the same time it gives a lead for the antithetical χειρῶν τοῦδε, "the hands *of the prisoner*," and the order for release. And the repetition of syllables (εσθε χειρων του) might easily deceive a copyist.

the King's words were something like this : "You are mad ! The thing was done by hands. But nevertheless you may now release the hands of the prisoner, for, once in the toils, he is not swift enough to escape from *me*." However the doubt is not important. Any way the King, expressly or tacitly, treats as absurd, not worth discussion, the suggestion of the reporter that the escape of the women was miraculous. And the question is :—with which of the two, the servant or the master, does the dramatist expect his audience to agree ?

Now let it be assumed—I do assume—that, as an alternative, we may agree with the soldier. But is it, can it be, the intention of the author, that we may not agree with the King ? If so, why does Euripides invest the miraculous account with every circumstance which, according to the habits of rational mankind, would naturally invite disbelief? Is it first-hand ? The reporter neither says so, nor makes any reference to his authority. Is he a person likely, from his standing and his state of mind, to be critical or careful ? We are shown the contrary. The man's own words, his account of his feelings in arresting the adept[1], show that he is awed and alarmed. In the state of the country, after the conversion and flight of the women, such agitation must naturally prevail. And this man and his companions, slaves and as such superstitious, have heard the declaration of Teiresias in favour of the new

---

[1] *vv.* 434–442.

god[1]. Of course they are ready to believe anything, the stranger the more likely. The imprisoned bacchanals have escaped—miraculously, says rumour. But why? By whom were they guarded? By whom but by other servants of the King, in the same state of mind as those whom we see, the reporter and his party? They, it is plain, would not, could not, have arrested the preacher, if he had not so chosen, would gladly have permitted his escape, and would certainly have reported it as a miracle. Yet, because his converts have escaped, chains must have parted and doors must have opened "without mortal hand"! In the circumstances shown, any one may have done the thing, the prisoners them-selves, their guards, the adept,—any one, or every one together. "You are mad," says Pentheus; and surely, so far as relates to the alleged miracle, that is the sum of the situation.

The effect of this incident, taken according to its natural sense, is to show us that, however Pentheus may storm and threaten, his position is weak. Served as he is, mistrustfully and reluctantly, by men who believe, or half believe, that he is fighting against superhuman power, he can be sure of nothing which he does not do with his own hands. And in particular we are reminded, that he cannot secure the safe custody of a prisoner. At the end of his interview with the adept—over which we may pass for the moment, since it throws no light on our question—he remits the captive to the same

---

[1] *vv.* 266 ff.   For the presence of the servants see *vv.* 352 ff.

servants or soldiers, by whom he has been arrested, and orders them to shut him up in the stables of the palace. At this moment our attention is again called to the fact that, as against a professor of the new religion, these men are not trustworthy. When the King commands them to replace the prisoner's bonds, he himself loftily bids them abstain. And it is evident that they hesitate, for Pentheus has to repeat his order before it is obeyed[1]. When therefore, within no long time after being led off, the man emerges again at liberty, this result, in itself, is not of a nature to impress a spectator, any more than it impresses the King, with the conviction of a supernatural agency.

But at this point, during the confinement and escape of the adept, occur, or are alleged to occur, the terrific demonstrations which culminate in the ruin of the palace by an earthquake. If these are genuine, if the audience have reason to accept them for fact, there is an end of our question : the adept and his adventures are supernatural. And to the contrary effect likewise : if these demonstrations are visibly not genuine, but a combination of falsehood, imposture, and delusion, then also our question is determined, so far at least as this, that the miraculous allegations of the play are propounded not for acceptance but for criticism.

Respecting the earthquake, and the blaze which, breaking out on the tomb of Semele, seems to set

---

[1] *vv.* 503 ff. See the correct stage-directions in Murray's translation.

the palace on fire, I have little or nothing to add to what is said by Professor Norwood in his chapter on "The Palace Miracle[1]." A voice (purporting to be that of Dionysus) is heard within the palace commanding these phenomena, and, upon this suggestion, the troop of women without, or some of them, see corresponding effects[2]. But that no such effects are shown, or are to be supposed, is proved by the universal ignorance of them, and in particular by the ignorance and silence of Pentheus —*to which the dramatist expressly directs our attention.* Immediately after the supposed shock, and while the women still grovel on the ground, the adept comes forth, and, in a rapid narrative[3], describes first certain delusions which (he says) his God imposed upon Pentheus, to prevent the King from putting him in chains, and then the production of the earthquake and fire with their alleged consequences. As he is finishing, footsteps, which he truly conjectures to be those of Pentheus, are heard approaching the door from within:

He will be here directly. *What, what will he say after all this?* However high his tone, I shall endure him easily; for a wise man should practise a prudent calm of temper[4].

---

[1] *The Riddle of the Bacchae*, pp. 37 ff.
[2] *vv.* 576 ff.   [3] *vv.* 604 ff.
[4] *vv.* 638–641

    ὡς δέ μοι δοκεῖ—ψοφεῖ γοῦν ἀρβύλη δόμων ἔσω—
    ἐς προνώπι' αὐτίχ' ἥξει. τί ποτ' ἄρ' ἐκ τούτων ἐρεῖ;
    ῥᾳδίως γὰρ αὐτὸν οἴσω, κἂν πνέων ἔλθῃ μέγα·
    πρὸς σοφοῦ γὰρ ἀνδρὸς ἀσκεῖν σώφρον' εὐοργησίαν.

"What will he say after this?" We hardly need this dramatic reminder to perceive that, when a man has seen his house strewn in ruins by an earthquake—to say nothing of minor experiences—and he comes before us fresh from the event, he will probably remark upon it. Thereupon Pentheus enters, and the scene proceeds thus:

Pentheus. It is too much! This Eastern knave hath slipped
 His prison, whom I held but now, hard gripped
 In bondage.—Ha! 'Tis he!—What, sirrah, how
 Show'st thou before my portals?
[*The Adept.*] Softly thou!
 And set a quiet carriage to thy rage.
Pentheus. How comest thou here? How didst thou break thy
 cage?
 Speak!......[1]

And not a word more do we hear, from the King or from any one, about what has passed. The prisoner has escaped. Except this bare fact, the whole appalling train of events narrated by the preacher, and seen, in part, by his devotees, remains here and ever after absolutely unnoticed.

Thus the scene, the words and action of it, is so arranged as to produce, and to put in the strongest

---

[1] *vv.* 642–648 (Murray)

Πε. πέπονθα δεινά· διαπέφευγέ μ' ὁ ξένος,
 ὃς ἄρτι δεσμοῖς ἦν κατηναγκασμένος.
 ἔα ἔα·
 ὅδ' ἐστὶν ἀνήρ· τί τάδε; πῶς προνώπιος
 φαίνῃ πρὸς οἴκοις τοῖς ἐμοῖς, ἔξω βεβώς;
Δι. στῆσον πόδ', ὀργῇ δ' ὑπόθες ἥσυχον πόδα.
Πε. πόθεν σὺ δεσμὰ διαφυγὼν ἔξω περᾷς;

possible light, a contrast and contradiction between
the story told by the prisoner and the facts which
accompany it. To suppose that the author presents
the story for unquestioning acceptance is to charge
him not merely with negligence but with perversity. Short of saying that the man is a liar and the
women dupes, he could do no more than he has done
to force this...possibility upon our consideration. We
have here no casual discrepancy, no separable pictures,
seen to disagree only if we bring them together.
Such things may be found in most compositions,
and in the theatre are of little or no importance.
They may even be admitted wilfully, if any convenience is thereby gained. We might conceivably
so explain, in this instance, the neglect of the earthquake and its effects, though visible (according to
the women) in the palace-front[1], by those who come
to the palace afterwards from without. Since one
of these persons arrives almost immediately afterwards, and before any pause in the action[2], the
explanation, even there, would be hard. We might
however apply it, and say that the escape of the
prisoner, with all its incidents, is then no longer in
view, but done with and dismissed. But it is not
done with, it is not dismissed, when Pentheus comes
out. On the contrary, we are still expecting, and
are expressly told to expect, the most important part
of it, that is to say, the effect of it all upon the King.
And this effect, the full effect of all that has really
happened, we see: the escape of his prisoner is

[1] *vv.* 591 ff.   [2] *v.* 657.

the whole subject of his discourse. Only the alleged circumstances of it, such trifling accompaniments as a fire and an earthquake, are unnoticed, forgotten, ignored. And the audience, in spite of this, are to imagine that he has seen and felt them!

And scarcely less damaging to the story of the adept are the tone and form of the story itself. This is a point not suitable for argument; but it may be seen from the commentaries, that readers are not very well satisfied with the story, as a description of such things by one who has passed through them. The style, though animated and vigorous, is too light for the themes, and lightest just where solemnity should seem indispensable. This is how the earthquake is treated[1]:

And in the midst of this came Bacchus and shook the place, and lit a fire upon his mother's grave; which when Pentheus saw, he fancied the house to be burning, and rushed this way and that, bidding his servants bring water, so that all the slaves were busy with the vain labour. Then he dropped these efforts, and, supposing that I had got away, snatched his black weapon and plunged into the interior of the house[2]. Whereupon Bromius, as I think and suppose, made an apparition in the court, upon which Pentheus rushed at full speed, and stabbed at the bright

---

[1] *vv.* 622 ff.

[2] Or perhaps "snatched his sword, and plunged into the *darkened* house," reading ἵεται ξίφος κελαινῶν ἁρπάσας δόμων ἔσω. The ξίφος κελαινὸν of the MSS. is a strange variation for ξίφος μέλαν. If the house were on fire, as Pentheus is said to imagine, the interior, to his eyes, might well appear *black* (with smoke); and this leads naturally to the phantom "light," which the god is said to raise in the court. See *v.* 630, where φῶς (MSS.) may thus be kept, as against the conjecture φάσμα.

nothing[1], in the belief that he was slaying me. *And besides this our Deity did him the further damage of dashing the house to the ground, so that it is all broken stone from stone* (?)[2], *and he has seen cause to rue bitterly the imprisoning of me.* So, wearied out, he dropped his sword-play and lay helpless, this man who dared fight against a God....

Surely it is not thus that a man would paint his rescue by an earthquake from a dungeon and the prospect of death. Nor—if we choose to suppose that the speaker is more than man and forgets the part he is playing—is the tone fit for a shaker of the earth. It is neither awed nor awful, it is not even grave. No speaker of any quality, such as the mind of man may conceive, could treat the throwing of a house upon the inhabitants—What became of them, by the way, and how is it that we neither hear nor see anything of their horror?—as a hurt or mischief added to the rest, a thing thrown in, as it were, to fill up a reckoning of cost[3]. Our translators see this. Mr Way improves the passage a little both by omission and addition:

Then did Bacchus bring *a new abasement of his pride* to pass;
For he hurled to earth the building. *There it lies*, a ruin-mass,—
Sight to make my bonds full bitter to him!

----

[1] φαεινὸν <οὐδέν>. Cf. Shakespeare's "airy nothing." This supplement is perhaps preferable to αἰθέρα (Canter and modern texts generally) because we can thus explain the omission, the sense of οὐδέν having been missed.

[2] συντεθράνωται δ' ἅπαν. But see hereafter, pp. 70, 79.

[3] vv. 632 f.
πρὸς δὲ τοῖσδ' αὐτῷ τάδ' ἄλλα Βάκχιος λυμαίνεται·
δώματ' ἔρρηξεν χαμᾶζε.

And Professor Murray makes a new thing of it :

Then *'mid his dreams God smote him yet again*! He overthrew
All that high house. And *there in wreck for evermore it lies*,
That the day of this my bondage may be sore in Pentheus'
    eyes !

Here is solemnity, not enough perhaps for such a
thing as a penal earthquake, but some solemnity,
enough, as people say, to swear by. Euripides has
none. No competent modern composer, if told to
put these translations into Greek, would offer as
equivalent what is supposed to have satisfied
Euripides.

And more : in order to get these versions, or my
own prose, or anything compatible with the supposition that the earthquake is real, we must force a
word. "It lies a ruin," "it lies a wreck," "it is all
broken in pieces,"—such we assume to be the sense
of συντεθράνωται δ᾽ ἅπαν. But there is no evidence
for this, and it seems to be a mere figment, invented
to meet the supposed necessity of this passage. An
old Greek lexicographer[1] interprets συντεθράνωται,
evidently for this place, by συμπέπτωκε, *it has collapsed*.
We moderns follow, but, having more science, with
misgiving[2]. For the noun *thrānos*, the only known
form from which we can derive *thrānoō*, the
only recorded sense here applicable is the *beam-end*
in building[3]. But this does not help to show how
synthrānōsis could mean the destruction of a building,

[1] Hesychius.
[2] See Liddell and Scott s.v. συνθρανόω and Tyrrell's note here.
[3] Pollux, cited by Liddell and Scott s.v. θρᾶνος.

the breaking of it to pieces; neither noun nor pre-position points this way, but the opposite[1]. A member or limb in a body is *arthron*, and the *synarthrōsis* of a body is not the dismemberment of it, but a joint. So also *synthrānōsis* should be the putting together of beam-ends or beams. We have no right to assume any other meaning, till this is proved inapplicable; and, as we shall see presently, we have no need.

The earthquake is a pretence, a delusion, which the bacchic adept, by suggestion, passes off upon the excited imagination of his confederates, the attendant women or some of them. He is, as Pentheus calls him, a conjurer and master of spells, a fanatic, but also upon occasion an impostor. And some of his tricks are what would now be called, or lately would have been called, "mesmeric." His escape from prison, though it needs no explanation, gives him an excellent opportunity for providing a miraculous one, thus confirming the zeal of his aids. He predicts a divine interposition in his favour[2]; and the women expect and invoke it accordingly with rapturous faith[3]. In this mood they are hailed from within by the voice of Dionysus, and see "of course" (as the adept very candidly puts it)[4] what-

---

[1] A verb like θραύω or ῥήγνυμι, meaning *break*, can of course take the preposition συν- as an intensive (συνθραύω, συρρήγνυμι) with much the same sense. But for a verb θρανόω meaning *break* there seems to be no evidence at all. It is not proved by θρανύσσω, even if we take such a writer as Lycophron for evidence that this word existed, and was classical.

[2] *vv.* 497–518.   [3] *vv.* 550–575.

[4] *v.* 605 ἤσθησθ’, ὡς ἔοικε, Βακχίου | διατινάξαντος κ.τ.λ.

ever that voice suggests.   Half a century ago this
might have seemed surprising ; now there are few
or none who have not witnessed such performances.
The scene of Euripides proves merely that they were
known, and were sometimes used for ill purposes,
in the fifth century before Christ.   From modern
experience we should indeed hardly suppose that
actual hallucination could be produced simultane-
ously in so many "subjects" as the tragic Chorus of
fifteen.   But neither does the scene so suggest.   On
the contrary, from the form of the exclamations, we
should gather that one woman only, or at most two,
are directly so impressed: *Did you see the architraves
flying asunder ?...The fire !   Dost thou not see it, dost
thou not ? On Semele's holy grave !...*[1]   It is as if she,
or they, who do promptly see done what the voice
within has bidden, are surprised to find others less
quick.   But all believe, and all lie trembling, face
to the ground, when the master, in his own person,
comes forth to interpret his effects[2].   In a halluci-

----

[1] *v.* 591 f.

εἴδετε λάινα κίοσιν ἔμβολα
διάδρομα τάδε ;

vv. 596–8

ἆ ἆ,
πῦρ οὐ λεύσσεις, οὐδ' αὐγάζῃ,
Σεμέλας ἱερὸν ἀμφὶ τάφον ;

[2] For the distribution of the parts in this scene, see Murray's
text.   In *v.* 585 <σεῖε> πέδον χθονὸς Ἐννοσι πότνια, where " Dionysus" commands the earthquake, it is perhaps not necessary to
complete the sense (with Wilamowitz).   The intended verb (σεῖε
or the like) may be drowned in the shriek (ἆ ἆ) of the terrified
Chorus.

nant working by suggestion, and having at his
disposal a company of female devotees, prepared
for impression by frantic enthusiasm and the habit
of acting under his command, such effects are perfectly natural; and the scene shows us, in part at
least, by what means, in a place where such things
were new, excitement and faith might be stimulated.

In the story of the adept, the fire and the earthquake, which have been "seen," are supplemented
by other incidents not visible outside,—a narrative of
certain delusions which he, or Dionysus for him,
put upon the King:

My derision there I made him, that he deemed he fettered me,
Yet nor touched me, neither grasped me, fed on empty phantasy.
Nay, a bull beside the stalls he found where he would pen me
    fast:
Round the knees and round the hoofs of this he 'gan his cords
        to cast,...
            ...and I beside him watching him
Calmly at mine ease was sitting[1]....

with more, which I have already cited, of the same
kind. These parts of the story Professor Norwood,
whose conception of the fire and the earthquake I
follow, takes to be true; he would suppose that the
adept really did so hallucinate Pentheus[2]. But I
do not find it natural, or even possible, to make
this distinction in favour of the reporter's veracity.
What he tells of his operations upon the mind of
Pentheus stands *prima facie* on a par with the rest,
is equally wild, impossible, destitute of confirmation,

---

[1] *vv.* 616 ff. (Way).   [2] *The Riddle of the Bacchae*, p. 105.

inconsistent with visible facts. The adept is able
by suitable suggestion to excite, in those who
passionately believe and habitually obey him, imaginative beliefs and even imaginary sensations, for
which they themselves are prepared by confident
expectancy. This agrees with nature, as we know
it now and may presume it to have been known
in the days of Euripides. But it does not follow
that, by his mere will and pleasure, he could mislead
and hallucinate a mind incredulous and hostile.
Because the bacchants, at his suggestion, attribute
his voice to Dionysus, and because one of them
even sees a fire, it does not follow that Pentheus,
without any preparation, would take a bull for a man ;
and the dramatist, by showing us the natural performance, gives us no reason to accept a report
of the unnatural. And the facts, the words and
behaviour of Pentheus, refute this as well as the
rest. The hallucinations indeed, as such, Pentheus
might be supposed to have forgotten ; but his
labours, his frantic efforts to extinguish the fire,
his pursuit and assault of the phantom-prisoner[1],—
these, whether remembered or not, are *ex hypothesi* real, and their effect should be visible. The
story leaves Pentheus "lying," as well he may, "exhausted[2]." The words are scarcely said, when
Pentheus himself comes out, vigorous as ever, so far
as appears from the dialogue, both in body and
mind ! Even for the starting-point of the story, the

---

[1] *vv.* 624–631.
[2] *v.* 634 κόπου δ᾽ ὕπο...παρεῖται.

assumption that the King himself takes charge of the
captive and personally conducts him to prison[1], we get
no warrant either before or after.   In the previous
scene the captive is remitted for confinement to the
slaves[2]; in this scene nothing is said by Pentheus,
or by any one (except the story-teller), to suggest that
this procedure was changed.   On the other hand,
it is but natural that the impostor should improve
the occasion, and should supplement the marvels,
which his associates have seen, by a few more
which they will faithfully accept.   The deluding of
Pentheus then is a lie, like the rest ; and we have
so far no reason to think that the powers of a conjurer in the way of hallucination extended, according
to Euripides, beyond such limits as may now be
observed.   The point, though of small moment here,
becomes important, highly important, in the sequel.

In the man's whole story of his escape there is
not one allegation, which is either confirmed by or
consistent with the rest of the action, except that he
has escaped.   And this, his escape, we had every
reason to expect, from the known disposition and
desires of those upon whom his safe-keeping depends.
He is let out, or never efficiently confined[3], and
that is the whole affair.

---

[1] *v.* 616.   [2] *v.* 509.

[3] The circumstances, the behaviour of the guards, would
sufficiently suggest this without other hint.   But there is another,
or at least there was.   "How were you set free?" asks a
bacchant, and adds, according to the punctuation of the MSS.,
"...having met with an irreligious man": ἀλλὰ πῶς ἠλευθερώθης
ἀνδρὸς ἀνοσίου τυχών; (*v.* 613).   The latter words, so far as I see,

Reading the story as a pretence, we shall find natural what otherwise ought to surprise us—the literary form in which it is cast, and the strange, extravagant, unseemly performance by which it is introduced. By an exception unique, so far as I have observed, in extant tragedy, we have here a *narrative* in the trochaic metre, which, originally normal for tragic dialogue, was replaced for ordinary purposes by the iambic, but retained, as an occasional variety, for moments of heightened agitation or rapid movement :

βάρβαροι γυναῖκες, οὕτως ἐκπεπληγμέναι φόβῳ...

That the scene should so commence, and that the escaped prisoner should enter as in haste, is natural enough. But elsewhere, when such an entrance is followed by a narrative, the metre, for this purpose, passes into the normal[1]; and here, where the subject

are pointless and hardly intelligible. I believe that they make a separate clause and question: ἀλλὰ πῶς ἠλευθερώθης; ἀνδρὸς ἂν ὁσίου τυχών; In the second clause the verb (ἠλευθερώθης) is supplied from the first, with the sense, "Did you find a religious man to do it?" The use of ἂν ἠλευθερώθης (as distinct from ἠλευθερώθης) signifies the suggestion of the fact as what *may or must be supposed* to have happened. Cp. Aristoph. *Frogs* 1023, etc. The woman's conjecture is natural, for the fire and the earthquake, even if they occurred, would not of themselves explain the release; and the ἀνὴρ ὅσιος, the possible person friendly to the captive or overawed by him, is provided in the leader of the guards (*vv.* 434-442). And in the question, so read, we find, what otherwise is wanting, a proper lead for the form of the reply, " *I myself* accomplished my own rescue " (αὐτὸς ἐξέσωσ' ἐμαυτόν, 614), where αὐτός rejects the suggestion of aid.

[1] Aesch. *Persae* 159-176, Eur. *Phoen.* 1335-1356.

of the story, if we are to take it seriously, is so grave, such a transition would seem specially imperative or desirable. The circumstances, às alleged, present no difficulty, since the man does not propose to fly, and indeed, if he is to be believed[1], there is no immediate likelihood of pursuit. He might therefore perfectly well have described the miracles by which he has been delivered, the fire and the earthquake, in the accustomed strain of dignity; and, if the reader will compare the practice of Euripides elsewhere, he will not easily doubt, that such would have been the form chosen, if the author had intended these phenomena to be accepted as facts and seriously conceived. But if they are a fiction the form is right. For in that case, since Pentheus, master of himself, may be expected at any moment to hear of the escape and to pursue (as in fact he promptly does), the story must be reeled off as quickly as possible. Moreover there is in the situation, so conceived, a strong element of comedy: the imposture, if it did not provoke anger, might easily provoke a smile. And for such situations the less dignified metre is employed by Euripides elsewhere[2].

Equally appropriate to the imposture, and equally inappropriate, if we were meant to suppose a real interposition of divine power, would seem, I think, to an Athenian dramatist and spectators, the *tableau* presented at the entrance of the narrator.

---

[1] *vv.* 634–637.
[2] *Orestes* 1506 ff., *Ion* 510 ff.

He finds the women prostrated upon the ground, and notes with sympathy, and of course without disapproval, this "Oriental" fashion of expressing their fear of the present Deity[1]. Nor is it strange to us. We ourselves kneel both to God and to kings. And the Asiatic prostration, though we do not use it, occurs repeatedly, as a sign of awe, in our sacred Book. But to Greeks such gestures were foreign and distasteful. For Greeks, they were associated not with religion either in practice or in story, but with servility. They belonged to subjects of the detested Monarchy, such as the "barbarous" Lydians who use them here. Even to English eyes, the spectacle of the women, grovelling and quaking, and of their director standing above them, could hardly appear dignified. To Athenian eyes it would, I believe, be offensive and grotesque,—an impression fatal to reverence, but eminently suitable to indignation and disgust.

We have discussed this situation so far without touching the question of scenery:—whether, that is to say, the resources of the stage, in the time of Euripides, were equal to the exhibition of such effects as we now should require in connexion with the words of the bacchants, supposing that the blaze of fire, and the "parting architraves" of the palace-front, are to be taken as realities. This question, as I conceive, is immaterial. The evidence, in my belief, is against the practicability, or at all events

[1] *vv.* 600–607. Note especially the invocation: βάρβαροι γυναῖκες, οὕτως ἐκπεπληγμέναι φόβῳ | πρὸς πέδῳ πεπτώκατε; κ.τ.λ.

the likelihood, of such machinery. But suppose the
contrary, suppose the effects practicable ; we have
still no right to introduce them here, since by doing
so we do not explain the dialogue (our only testimony for the scenery), but on the contrary make
inexplicable the language of Pentheus, and other
indications that the alleged phenomena are not truly
facts. And indeed many, perhaps most, of the
modern expositors who take these phenomena for
facts, have been content nevertheless to assume that
no sign of them was shown in the scenery: the
spectator was to imagine what the bacchants see and
Dionysus by his story confirms. This the spectator
might do,—*if he chose*. The exhibition, in this as
in all respects, *could* be so taken by a spectator
sufficiently prejudiced, or so explained by the exhibitors, if compelled to maintain their legal piety. But
those who adopted this explanation as the meaning
of the author, did so in spite of the scenery, and of
the dialogue, and of the action. They were not
following the dramatist, but defying him.

And if they had supposed, as modern readers
have done, that the effects of the earthquake, as seen
by the bacchants and described by the adept, were
permanent, they would have been defying the
author's express words. Modern expositors (Hesychius is a modern for this purpose, not superior in
authority and far inferior in science to those who
have interpreted the poet since the revival of learning) make the adept say, as we saw, that " Bacchus
dashed the building to the ground, *and it is all*

broken to pieces[1]." But this version is obtained by
forcing the sense of a word. What he does say is
that "Bacchus dashed the building to the ground,—
though it is all put together," or more exactly still,
"—though its beams have been all put together[2]."
There is no reason at all for wresting this remark
from its apparent sense. The story of the adept,
rightly understood, demands that, when he has used
his earthquake, and the sensation of it which, upon
his suggestion, the bacchants have experienced, he
should *get rid of it again*, and eliminate the supposition of permanent effects, because *there are none*,
either within or without, and the bacchants, on
returning to calmness, must become aware that
there are none, at all events without. Accordingly
he chooses to say—what of course is in miracle
conceivable, because in miracle all things are conceivable—that the demonstration of power has been
transitory. The building has been wrecked...and
restored! By the form in which he puts this, by
the reference to "beam-ends[3]," he points directly,
as we may suppose him to mark by gesture, to the
particular injury which was seen by one of his dupes
in the façade, "the marble imposts upon the pillars

---

[1] *v.* 633. See above, p. 70.

[2] πρὸς δὲ τοῖσδ᾽ αὐτῷ τάδ᾽ ἄλλα Βάκχιος λυμαίνεται·
　　δώματ᾽ ἔρρηξεν χαμᾶζε (συντεθράνωται δ᾽ ἅπαν)
　　πικροτάτους ἰδόντι δεσμοὺς τοὺς ἐμούς.

In the parenthesis, the δέ is adversative (*but*, not *and*) and
answers to our English use of *though*, introducing a reservation
or correction.

[3] θρᾶνοι.

starting asunder," the parting, that is to say, of the architraves[1]. For these imposts and their junctures are just what, in a stone building, would be termed *thrānoi.* He indicates that here, as throughout, there is *synthrānōsis,* and the effect of the shock has disappeared! The touch, extravagant as it is, is necessary to rectify and safeguard his previous invention. That is the way and the peril of such impostures. The women, being for the time not sane, believe him, of course ; and so must the reader, if he will have a supernatural interpretation of the scene. But the path of the disbeliever is more plain.

The expedient of the Greek lexicographer, to say that συντεθράνωται means συμπέπτωκε, *has collapsed,* would not have been admissible while the language of Euripides was truly alive. It is purely arbitrary, like many devices of antique scholarship, and rests upon the presumption formulated by the Latinist of the Renaissance in Browning,—that "those ancients could say anything." Modern scholars have perceived this, though they have not hitherto acted upon the perception (as I think) in the right way.

This however is a detail of little moment. The broad effect of the scene is to show the adept as a most dangerous mixture of enthusiasm and fraud. Pentheus—though he dismisses the suggestion of a divine deliverance with a sneer[2]—is much disturbed,

---

[1] *v.* 591 λάινα κίοσιν ἔμβολα διάδρομα.

[2] *v.* 652. The stress is on ὠνείδισας. If Dionysus did it, the more shame to him. The distribution here is uncertain and the text perhaps slightly defective. See commentaries. But I believe

as he has reason to be, by the escape itself, and astounded[1] at the audacity with which the late prisoner awaits and confronts him. He is giving orders to secure the gates of the city[2], when the situation is changed by the arrival of a herdsman with news for the King, his master, from Cithaeron.

This fellow, whatever we are to think of him as a witness of miracles, is palpably honest—as Pentheus remarks, contrasting him pointedly with the adept[3]; and those parts of his story, for which his good faith is sufficient warrant, are enough to startle the King and others, as, we shall see, they do. In the first place, his account of the rites, the first, so far as we know, which Pentheus has had from an eye-witness, contradicts altogether the adverse rumours upon which he has been acting. The women are sober and chaste, their rites "a marvel of discipline." But their fury is terrible. The herdsmen, trying to capture the King's mother, Agave, had to fly for their lives, while their herds were torn to pieces. The bacchants then took the offensive, raided the neighbouring villages, sported at their pleasure with the property of the inhabitants, routed and wounded the men who took arms against them, and have returned in triumph to the mountain. Let the King, concludes the reporter,

it to be complete. Both 652 and 653 are spoken by Pentheus, with a pause (of vexation and perplexity) between.

[1] *v.* 644.   [2] *v.* 653.
[3] *vv.* 673 ff.

submit to this irresistible Deity, especially if, "as they say and I am told, He gave man the wine that stills his pains ; if wine be lost, there is no love, nor other delight for poor creatures any more[1]."

Frank indeed, and not less simple! The boor does not perceive that these last words must revive the suspicion which he would refute, and must suggest that, whatever he has seen, the new religion does rely for aid upon the attractions of drink and of sex. It is not from such a witness as this that the author, after what he has told and shown us before, can intend us to accept without question whatever the man says and believes. What things, and how much, has he truly seen?

Now, regarded from this point of view, the story falls into two parts, widely different in colour and credibility. In the latter part, that which describes the strength and violence of the enthusiasts, there is nothing which, with due allowance for exaggeration, will not pass as perfectly natural :

> Thereat, for fear they tear us, *all we fled*
> *Amazed*; and on, with hand unweaponéd
> They swept toward our herds that browsed the green
> Hill grass. Great uddered kine then hadst thou seen
> Bellowing in sword-like hands that cleave and tear,
> A live steer riven asunder, and the air
> Tossed with rent ribs or limbs of cloven tread,
> And flesh upon the branches, and a red
> Rain from the deep green pines. Yea, bulls of pride,
> Horns swift to rage, were fronted and aside
> Flung stumbling, by those multitudinous hands

[1] *vv.* 677–774.

6—2

> Dragged pitilessly. And swifter were the bands
> Of garbèd flesh and bone unbound withal
> Than on thy royal eyes the lids may fall[1].

Though the character, situation, and mood of these fugitives are not such as to commend the accuracy of the description, we may presume that it rests upon fact. It is quite likely that the frantic congregation would revenge upon the herd the attempt of the herdsmen to interfere with them ; and the massacre of a single beast would be enough, in the temper of the country, to produce the whole picture. The raid upon the villages is the same in style and makes the same impression. We see that the bacchants showed, or may have shown, some remarkable powers, dexterity in the balancing of burdens and apparent insensibility to fire[2]. The pupils of the adept, as Pentheus remarks[3], were likely to have some "tricks." We may believe, and without the surprise of the narrator, that even spears and swords, in the hands of a few dazed and leaderless men, did not arrest their wildness,—and this without supposing that they were invulnerable or even were unwounded[4]. Everywhere, in all this part of the story, we see facts, things natural in the circumstances, and in substance presumably true, though not observed or reported precisely, and doubtless coloured by a scared imagination.

But the earlier parts of the story, the descriptions of the bacchanal life and worship, have another

---

[1] *vv.* 734 ff. (Murray).   [2] *vv.* 754 ff.
[3] *vv.* 674–676.   [4] *vv.* 758 ff.

character, and are miraculous in a different sense.
Here is something more than exaggeration:

> Then they pressed
> Wreathed ivy round their brows, and oaken sprays
> And flowering bryony.   And one would raise
> Her wand and smite the rock, and straight a jet
> Of quick bright water came.   *Another set*
> *Her thyrsus in the bosomed earth, and there*
> *Was red wine that the God sent up to her,*
> *A darkling fountain.   And if any lips*
> *Sought whiter draughts, with dipping finger-tips*
> *They pressed the sod, and gushing from the ground*
> *Came springs of milk.   And reed-wands ivy-crowned*
> *Ran with sweet honey, drop by drop.*—O King,
> Hadst thou been there, as I, and seen this thing,
> With prayer and most high wonder hadst thou gone
> To adore this God whom now thou rail'st upon![1]

Such are the preparations; and when we come to
the actual celebration of the ritual dance, the tale
takes a still higher flight:

> And there
> Through the appointed hour they made their prayer
> And worship of the Wand, with one accord
> Of heart and cry—"Iacchos, Bromios, Lord,
> God of God born!"—*And all the mountain felt,*
> *And worshipped with them; and the wild things knelt*
> *And ramped and gloried, and the wilderness*
> *Was filled with moving voices and dim stress*[2].

[1] *vv.* 702 ff. (Murray).

[2] *vv.* 723–727 (Murray)

> αἱ δὲ τὴν τεταγμένην
> ὥραν ἐκίνουν θύρσον ἐς βακχεύματα,
> Ἴακχον ἀθρόῳ στόματι τὸν Διὸς γόνον
> Βρόμιον καλοῦσαι· πᾶν δὲ συνεβάκχευ' ὄρος
> καὶ θῆρες, οὐδὲν δ' ἦν ἀκίνητον δρόμῳ.

The translation is somewhat expanded, and the mystical tone is

"All the mountain joined in their worship, and the beasts ; and nothing there was but it moved with their speed." This is no version, exact or exaggerated, of anything which could happen in the ordinary course of the world. If the man *saw* these things, or anything like them, if his report is anywhere near to the sensations which he received at the time, and to the account which he would have given at the time, then beyond question the bacchic rites are accompanied by miracle.

But such is not the case. The man does not know what he saw, and is not making any attempt to consult his memory and reproduce the record. The things which he did see, whatever they were, were *not* those which he now pictures, and did *not* make upon his mind the impression which, were the picture in the least degree true, they would have done. This, in his transparent candour, he allows us to see, and actually certifies, by one of those natural self-betrayals which are the most characteristic note of Euripidean art. He tells us that, at the preparation, he saw the bacchants draw water and wine, milk or honey, each at her pleasure, out of sticks and stones. And he adds that the sight of these things would have turned any one—Pentheus himself, for instance—into a convinced adorer of the Bacchic God[1].

---

deepened ; but the spirit is the same, and the plainest possible rendering would leave, in such phrases as πᾶν δὲ συνεβάκχευ' ὄρος, substantially the same sense.

[1] *vv.* 712 f.

ὥστ', εἰ παρῆσθα, τὸν θεὸν τὸν νῦν ψέγεις
εὐχαῖσιν ἂν μετῆλθες εἰσιδὼν τάδε.

Of course it would; it must produce in any human being, at least for the time, a profound respect for the Power by which such things could be done. And therefore it is quite certain that the man and his fellows, whatever he now may fancy, did not see them, because *then*, at the time of the supposed sight, they were not convinced, nor much impressed. If Pentheus had been there, he would have adored (says the man), and yet—

> Howbeit, the kine-wardens and shepherds straight
> Came to one place, amazed, and held debate;
> And one being there who walked the streets and scanned
> The ways of speech[1], took lead of them whose hand
> Knew but the slow soil and the solemn hill,
> And flattering spoke, and asked: "Is it your will,
> Masters, we stay the mother of the King,
> Agâvê, from her lawless worshipping,
> And win us royal thanks?"—*And this seemed good*
> *To all*[2].

That is to say, having seen the women served by their God with miraculous draughts, they immediately planned and unanimously resolved to make an attack upon them! Nor did the spectacle of the worship, though the mountain throbbed (we are told) and the wild beasts danced, bring at the time any change of mind; for it was then, after this performance, or rather in the midst of it, that the attack was actually made!

[1] "Who had tramped the town and had the knack of words" would be nearer to the tone. This passage is plainer in Euripides than in the translation, but the sense is the same.

[2] *vv.* 714 ff. (Murray, omitting rightly *v.* 716; see *v.* 667).

It would be absurd to frame in this way a story of miracle, which was to be accepted on the credit of the reporter. The man refutes himself. He shows that, *before the panic*, before the rout and the raid on the villages, he himself could and did witness a performance of the bacchic mysteries without any awful impression, without any impression beyond surprise and curiosity. He and the other clowns may have had fancies, and may have confirmed each other's fancies by "competing in report of novelties[1]." They were much excited; and here lies the cause of the rout which followed. But so vague were these fancies, so remote from conviction, that the sacrilegious proposal of the man from town was adopted without a dissentient voice. They ensconce themselves in hiding-places, and watch—doubtless with growing uneasiness—for an opportunity to make their attempt, which falls by accident to our excitable informant. Then ensues the panic. At the call of Agave, the wild women attack in their turn. The men, unprepared for this, fly—the narrator evidently among the first[2],—and the sequel, which we have already pursued, requires no further explanation. Terror breeds terror, until it is fairly established that a bacchant is proof against steel.

And now one of the fugitives comes, distracted between the fear of God and of man, to report the whole to his master. He expects the King's

---

[1] καινῶν λόγων δώσοντες ἀλλήλοις ἔριν v. 715 (C), a preferable reading, I think, to that of the other MS. (P), κοινῶν.

[2] See vv. 728–735.

displeasure; the story, however taken, is not to the credit of the King's servants; he begs that he may tell it freely in his own way[1]. And having got this permission, he launches forth into a description of bacchanal power, which represents not his know-ledge but his fright, and the desire to show that his fright had a cause. He paints the spectacle of the preparation and the mystery not as he saw them, but as he figures them, honestly and with full belief, after he and all his village have fled from the cele-brants. They bowed, as they must, as the King will have to bow, before the servants of the God,— before those who suckle wolves, make snoods of snakes, and thrill with their motion the rocks, and the trees, and the beasts of the field!

Though Euripides plainly shows, by the mouth of the narrator, that the story is throughout a dis-tortion of the truth, and, in the miraculous part, sheer fancy, he has nevertheless invested the whole, and the miraculous part especially, with wonderful beauty and power. This too is profoundly charac-teristic of him, and marks the peculiar turn of mind, which makes his work difficult for all, and to many a mere puzzle and offence. He never does pretend, as the way of poetry is generally to pre-tend, that "beauty is truth, truth beauty." He felt profoundly, painfully, he saw and is never tired of setting forth, the beauty, the treacherous and de-lusive beauty, that belongs and must belong to accepted falsehoods: the beauty *for which they are*

[1] *vv.* 664–671.

accepted, but which does not make them any the less false.   It is a beautiful and specious imagination that the self-devotion of a faithful wife should be rewarded by restoration from death, as religion falsely supposed in the case of Alcestis.   To glorify such a legend would be a natural exercise of piety and poetry; to satirize and degrade it, a common exercise of prosaic scepticism.   Euripides does neither, that is to say, he does both at once.   He turns the story into a bitter little realistic drama, sheer comedy in the plot and upshot, in which the resurrection, as matter of belief, is riddled with corrosive sarcasm ; but he does not blink, he paints with exquisite sympathy, the beauty of the sacrifice and the specious fitness of the reward.   It was a noble and winning imagination, which made Heracles, as a type of labour in the cause of humanity, into a figure triumphantly superhuman.   The truth is, nevertheless, that such labourers are only too human, notable in weakness as well as in strength. Euripides founds a tragedy upon this truth, showing Heracles as noble indeed, but insane ; but to the specious glory of the legendary conception he devotes a hymn which no piety could surpass[1].   So it is with him everywhere, and so it is here in the *Bacchants*.   It is a lovely imagination, responding to the deepest desires, instincts, cravings of spiritual man, that spiritual rapture should find an echo in

[1] I would refer to my essays on the *Alcestis* (*Euripides the Rationalist*) and the *Heracles* (*Four Plays of Euripides*).

the material world; that in mental communion with God we should find sensible communion with nature; and that, when the faithful rejoice together, bird and beast, hill and forest, should be not felt only, but *seen*, to rejoice along with them. It is not the truth; between us and our environment, whatever links there are, this link is wanting. But the yearning for it, the passion which made Wordsworth cry out for something, were it even the imagination of a pagan, which would make him "less forlorn," is natural to man; and simplicity leaps at the lovely fiction of a response. Just here is the opportunity for such alliances between spiritualism and superstition as are the daily despair of seekers after truth. Euripides rejects the fiction; but he does not commit the common, though suicidal, error of rationalism, by disguising or depreciating the loveliness.

Nor does he make another too common mistake of science, by pretending to know everything. Ignorant people explain strange things fancifully; but for all that, the world is full of strange things, and ignorant people do frequently see them. Many such things, and infinite, there doubtless are in the prospective dominion of psychology and physiology. What are the exact boundaries of spiritual and physical force, no one knows, nor knew in the fifth century B.C. Euripides does not pretend to know. It is impossible to gather, from what he puts into the mouth of the herdsman, whether, when the villagers of Bœotia saw the frenzied women do things apparently impossible in the way of carrying and balancing burdens[1], trick or fancy was, or was not, the whole account of the matter. Here and elsewhere the poet, following presumably the effect of his observations, leaves room for the unknown. In the meetings of the pious much was seen which did not happen; but much also might happen, which a wise man would not hastily explain.

And similarly in the description of the bacchic habits and ritual, though the man's imaginary recollection is wild and self-refuted, the grains of fact are not meant—at least that is my impression—to be exactly determinable. The bacchants could not create wine or honey by the wand; that is very certain. But as to the handling of snakes, the suckling of animals[2], and other things on the border-line of the credible, we are left to suppose what we please. We have been told before by the Chorus[3], and may well believe, that possessed women put live snakes in their hair. Here it is said that the worshippers of Cithaeron used snakes to gird their fawn-skins; but the context rather indicates that, whatever the narrator means, these snakes were in fact a ritual ornament, part of the costume[4]. The quaintest

---

[1] *vv.* 755 ff. [2] *vv.* 699 ff.

[3] *v.* 102. See the stories about Olympias, mother of Alexander the Great, cited from Plutarch (*Life of Alexander* II. § 5) in Sandys' *Bacchae*, Introduction p. xl.

[4] *vv.* 696–698

> νεβρίδας τ' ἀνεστείλανθ' ὅσαισιν ἁμμάτων
> σύνδεσμ' ἐλέλυτο, καὶ καταστίκτους δορὰς
> ὄφεσι κατεζώσαντο λιχμῶσιν γένυν.

The words σύνδεσμ' ἐλέλυτο point to an ornament, a snake-clasp; λιχμῶσιν γένυν suggests real snakes.

allegation, that serpents clean with their tongues
the faces of the faithful, appears only after the raid
and the return of the bacchants to their camp[1]; and
what happened then, the reporter, as his story shows,
cannot possibly know.   The trait is purely fanciful.

The news of this outbreak, and of the bacchic
victory, which, however interpreted, are sufficiently
grave, put the King and his adversary, the adept, in
a situation delicate for both, and precipitate the
crisis of their contest.   Pentheus, who though rash
and obstinate is neither a fool nor a villain, is struck,
as we shall presently see, by the testimony of the
herdsman to the good character of the sectaries, and
is not sure of his ground.   On the other hand, he is
furious at their " insolence,"—not the less so because,
in his very presence, and apparently among his
attendants[2], a voice is raised, respectfully but firmly,
in recognition of the new God.   His country, as he
conceives, is disgracing the Greek name[3], and his
first duty is to restore order.   For this point of
view there is much to be said, though Pentheus,
by his own fault, has not a good case, and

---

[1] *v.* 765 ff.   It looks like a misinterpretation of the phrase
λιχμῶσιν γένυν (*v.* 698) "*licking their* (?) *jaws*."   Such an explanation may very probably have been given by the rationalists.

[2] *vv.* 775–777.   The speech is assigned by the MS. to a
bacchant (XO.) but, as Prof. Norwood has observed, unsuitably.
If not given to the Chorus, it makes in this scene a fourth speaker
(with the Herdsman, Pentheus, and Dionysus), but that is no
difficulty, since we know that such exceptions were admitted.
Other traces of this speaker appear, I think, hereafter.

[3] *v.* 779.

wisdom would counsel him not to do anything
hastily.   However that is not his way ; he is, as
the herdsman has said, "too quick, sharp-tempered,
and imperious."   He gives orders that the Theban
forces, of all arms, shall instantly assemble for the
subjugation of the women[1].

Here however the bacchic leader interposes with
protests and proposals, which, though intelligible
perhaps if he be taken for a god, are certainly not
less so for those who regard him as a man.   He is
in truth scarcely less embarrassed than Pentheus.
We are nowhere told that he foresaw or intended
such an outbreak of the bacchants as has now taken
place, and must fairly assume the contrary, since
it compromises what was, for him, an excellent situation.   He cannot desire that the men of Thebes
should be led to battle against their rebellious
women.   He dare not let this happen, if by any
means he can prevent it.   He declares indeed, and
in his fanaticism perhaps believes, that, led by their
God, the women will rout the whole Theban army[2].
But, although the legend of Pentheus apparently
alleged such a miracle[3], the play of Euripides, which
is based on the real conditions of the world, rejects
and disallows it ; the legend, we are to understand,
presumably magnified some such occurrences as those
at Hysiae and Erythrae, where the bacchants successfully defy the casual weapons of a few villagers[4].
Manifestly this promises nothing for the result of a

----

[1] *vv.* 780 ff.   [2] *vv.* 789 ff., 798 ff.
[3] Aesch. *Eum.* 25.   [4] *vv.* 758 ff.

conflict with troops. Had it come to a fight, the
women, if not massacred (as Pentheus trucu-
lently threatens[1]), must, one would suppose, have
suffered severely. But suppose not, suppose a
feminine victory, a rout and slaughter of the men.
What sort of foundation, in the real world and the
real state of mankind, would this be for a new
religion? To common sense it is evident, that the
present success of the movement now depends upon
preventing a battle. To this therefore the adept,
since he too is no fool, now directs his whole
energies, pursuing it steadily and relentlessly by
one tack after another.

His first move, the suggestion that the bacchants, as a military force, are invincible, is brushed
aside by Pentheus with scornful impatience[2]. His
next, made with more urgency[3], is a practical offer,
specious and well worthy of consideration: he will

---

[1] *vv.* 796 f.

[2] *vv.* 787–801. There is a doubtful reading in *vv.* 789–792

ΔΙ.   οὔ φημι χρῆναί σ' ὅπλ' ἐπαίρεσθαι θεῷ,
       ἀλλ' ἡσυχάζειν· Βρόμιος οὐκ ἀνέξεται
       κινοῦντι βάκχας εὐίων ὀρῶν ἄπο—

ΠΕ.   οὐ μὴ φρενώσεις με.

So the MS., which I would follow, supposing an interruption by
Pentheus. "Bromius will not permit that, *when he brings his
votaries to battle* from their sacred hill, [you and your soldiers
should oppose him with success]." In κινοῦντι *move*, the verb
has its strategic sense. The insertion of σ' (Lenting) after
βάκχας is admissible, but not necessary; κινοῦντι should not be
changed.

[3] Note at *v.* 802 the change of metre from couplets to single
verses.

himself put an end to the disorder which he has raised, by bringing the women home :

The Lydian.   Sir, sir, it is still possible to settle this matter in a good way.

Pentheus.   By what way? Submission to women who are my subjects !

Lyd.   I myself without arms will bring them to this place.

Penth.   Ha! Now you begin to plot treachery against me.

Lyd.   Treachery! When I would use my own arts to save you.

Penth.   It is a plan, to which you have pledged yourselves, for the continuance of your rites.

Lyd.   No, a pledge, believe me, that I have now given to the God[1].

Pentheus replies by calling for his arms, and commanding the proposer to say no more.

This refusal, the turning-point of the tragedy, is an error : the gravest, after the original one of persecuting the sectaries upon an unproven estimate of their character, which the King commits. His suspicion, that behind the preacher's offer of assistance lies a conspiracy of some sort in favour of the new religion, is not unnatural, though apparently untrue.   But, " too impetuous and imperious," he does not perceive that, if this were so, it would be only a fresh reason for making terms with a movement, which, as Teiresias saw, cannot be broken by mere force.   It is however only fair to observe, that upon the vital question, whether the bacchanalia are an instrument of corruption, he is not yet satisfied ; and

---

[1] I accept the MS. reading, καὶ μὴν ξυνεθέμην—τοῦτό γ᾽ ἔστι—τῷ θεῷ, as punctuated and explained (*hoc quidem verum*) by Murray in his edition of the text.

moreover, that here he is not wrong. The rites are
dangerous, as the prophet has somewhat cynically
admitted; nor is the decency of the present performances very well established by such testimony
as that of the herdsman.

It is this doubt in the King's mind, and his
desire to assure himself, which lay him open to his
adversary. As he turns away to put on his arms,
the Lydian, now fairly at bay, arrests him with a
new proposal: Would he like to see the bacchanals
in their camp? He leaps at this with an eagerness
which surprises the proposer himself. He would
give anything, he says, for such a chance; the sight,
if he finds them drunken, will indeed be painful; but
even so, and on any terms, he will see. Secretly,
openly, anyhow he will go, and he is impatient to
start at once[1]. The subtle Asiatic perceives the
strength of his hold, and proposes further, that,
since a man detected in spying upon the rites of
the women will be in danger of his life, the King
shall disguise himself, in the bacchic dress, as a
female. Pentheus acknowledges the wisdom of the
caution, but shrinks from such a travesty of his
person—all the more when, at his request, the
stranger describes the details of the costume. Between these various impulses, to each of which in
turn the Lydian dexterously appeals, he hangs
uncertain, and finally, without deciding anything,
retires into the house, with his counsellor, for further
deliberation.

[1] *vv.* 810–820.

This dialogue, and the question of its effect and meaning, are of such importance to our problem, that it must be given, with the sequel, at length. I prefer, as a guard against prejudice, to use a version not my own, and select that of Mr Way, which, though unnatural (according to English habits) in its adherence to the form of alternate verses, is very close, and clear of any colouring.

Pentheus (to attendant). Bring forth mine arms! thou, make an
    end of speech.
Dionysus. Ho thou!
    Wouldst thou behold them camped upon the hills?
Penth. Ay—though with sumless gold I bought the sight.
Dion. Why on this mighty longing hast thou fallen?
Penth. To see them drunk with wine—a bitter sight!
Dion. Yet wouldst thou gladly see a bitter sight?
Penth. Yea, sooth, in silence crouched beneath the pines.
Dion. Yet will they track thee, stealthily though thou come.
Penth. Openly then!—yea, well hast thou said this.
Dion. Shall I then guide thee? Wilt essay the path?
Penth. Lead on with speed: I grudge thee all delay!
Dion. Array thee now in robes of linen fine.
Penth. Wherefore? From man shall I to woman turn?
Dion. Lest they should kill thee, seeing thee there as man.
Penth. Well said—yea, shrewd hast thou been heretofore.
Dion. Such science Dionysus taught to me.
Penth. How then shall thy fair rede become mine act?
Dion. I will into thine halls, and robe thee there.
Penth. What robe? A woman's?—nay, but I think shame.
Dion. Is thy desire to watch the Maenads dead?
Penth. In what garb, say'st thou, wouldst thou drape my form?
Dion. Thine head with flowing tresses will I tire.
Penth. And the next fashion of my vesture—what?
Dion. Long robes: and on thine head a coif shall be.
Penth. Nought else but these wouldst thou add unto me?

Dion.   Thyrsus in hand, and dappled fell of fawn.
Penth.   I cannot drape me in a woman's robe!
Dion.   Then in the fight with Maenads blood must flow.
Penth.   Ay, true:—first must I go and spy them out.
Dion.   Sooth, wiser so than hunt thee ills with ills.
Penth.   Yet, how through Kadmus' city pass unseen.
Dion.   By lone paths will we go. Myself will guide.
Penth.   Better were anything than Bacchants' mock.
[*Dion.*   I will pass in, and what befits devise.
Penth.   So be it. I am resolved: my path is clear.
        I go; for I must needs march sword in hand,
        Or do according unto thine advice.]   *Exit.*

In the last four lines, where there is a doubt respecting the cast of the parts, Mr Way adopts a cast, and in the words "I am resolved: my path is clear" he gives a translation, which are not commonly approved. Professor Murray represents a better alternative:

Penth.   Forward to my halls
       Within!—I will ordain what seemeth best.
Dion.   So be it, O King! 'Tis mine to obey thine hest
       Whate'er it be.
Penth.   Well, I will go—perchance
       To march and scatter them with serried lance,
       Perchance to take thy plan....I know not yet[1].

But in substance both versions agree. Nothing is yet decided, or even advanced towards decision. The whole issue, as developed in the foregoing

---

[1] *vv.* 843–846

   Πε.   ἐλθόντ' ἐς οἴκους . . . ἂν δοκῇ βουλεύσομαι.
   Δι.   ἔξεστι· πάντῃ τό γ' ἐμὸν εὐτρεπὲς πάρα.
   Πε.   στείχοιμ' ἄν· ἢ γὰρ ὅπλ' ἔχων πορεύσομαι
         ἢ τοῖσι σοῖσι πείσομαι βουλεύμασιν.

scene,—the King's first plan, to march against the bacchants in force, and the proposal of the stranger, that he should first see the camp, and the question of disguise,—all is yet open, and reserved for deliberation within.

Here the King goes within, and the Lydian, turning to his associates, exclaims in triumph :

> Women, the man sets foot within the toils.

Now (he says) shall Dionysus take away his reason, shall madden him, and so make him do, what sane he never would do,—put on the female attire, and, thus degraded, go where his own mother shall execute upon him the vengeance of the long-suffering God.

> Dionysus, play thy part now ; thou art near :
> Let us take vengeance.   Craze thou first his brain,
> Indarting sudden madness.   Whole of wit,
> Ne'er will he yield to don the woman's robe :
> Yet shall he don, driven wide of reason's course.
> I long withal to make him Thebes' derision,
> In woman-semblance led the city through,
> After the erstwhile terrors of his threats.

"I go," says he, "to dress him for death":

> And he shall know Zeus' son
> Dionysus, who reveals at last a godhead
> Most terrible, yet kindest unto men.

With these words, he follows the King into the palace.

After an interval, filled by the religious comments of the Chorus, the Lydian appears, and imperiously

summons forth Pentheus, who comes—a total wreck
in body and mind, dazed, drunken, idiotic, wearing
with delight the garb of his subjugation, the helpless
and servile victim of his conqueror. Dionysus has
done his work.

But how then has he done it? What has passed
within the palace during this interval in the action?
How are we intended to fill up, by imagination, the
scene which is withdrawn from our eyes?

We are to suppose, it is said, that the stranger,
man or god—for this alternative is here indifferent and
may be dismissed from consideration,—has exerted
the superhuman, or at all events mysterious, force
of his will, and thus, by his fiat or influence, has
reduced Pentheus from the state in which we see
him before his exit to that in which we see him
return. By miracle or mesmerism, by some efficacy
purely psychic, he has converted the man who goes
from us to deliberate into a creature incapable of
thought.

Now I ask the reader to consider, carefully
and without prejudice, by what right or with what
reason this interpretation can be imposed upon the
facts which the dramatist has exhibited, and the
text which is our sole authority for his meaning.

If we ourselves desired to present theatrically
an operation of this kind, a mesmeric operation, in
which one person, by the force of his will and without other instrument, takes away the rational and
even the sensory faculties of another, reducing him
from sanity to insanity and something beyond, to the

double imbecility of an intoxicated lunatic,—how should we show it upon the stage? Surely by showing it upon the stage. On the stage, in the presence of the spectators, the operation should be carried, if not to the end, at all events to a decisive point. But why not to the end? The power, upon this supposition, is independent of place, and needs no other opportunity than the presence of the sub-jugator and the subjugated. This freedom, this independence of occasion and instrument, is the very essence of will-power in all varieties, human or superhuman, mesmeric or miraculous. And in the visible exertion of it must lie not only its value in a spectacle, but its persuasive reality as a fact. Withdrawn from sight altogether, the process will hardly be realized; and it cannot be realized, it cannot convince the imagination, if, after witnessing an infinitesimal part of it, the spectator is asked to suppose the rest. How is he to suppose adequate, for the attainment of a given end, a force which, before his own eyes, and in all the conditions proper to success, either remains inactive, or acts without approaching the end?

Now it is in this incomprehensible way that Euripides, according to the hypothesis which we are disputing, exhibits the reduction of Pentheus to insanity by the will of the stranger. The insanity of Pentheus is evidently, as the subjugator tells us himself, a condition necessary for the execution of his plan to disguise the King as a woman and betray him to the bacchants. "Sane, he will never con-

sent[1]." So we are told, and so we see. From the
moment therefore, when this plan is conceived[2], to
make Pentheus insane must be the purpose and will
of the operator. And if by his will he can do it,
why does he not do it, then, there, and before the
audience? Why is it still to be done, when, after a
long colloquy with the subjugator, the patient retires
into the house? That it is then still to be done, we
not only see but are expressly told:

> O Dionyse,
> *This is thine hour* and thou not far away.
> Grant us our vengeance!—First, O Master, stay
> The course of reason in him, and instil
> A foam of madness[3].

"*Now*, Dionysus, to work!" But why now, and
not before? If to expel reason and instil madness
is a thing which the speaker can accomplish by
merely willing it, why is it not already performed?
So long as the victim remains without, the hour of
Dionysus has not struck; it begins with his entrance
into the house. Are we to understand then, that
the will-power of the deity is not operative, or less
operative, in the open air?

---

[1] *vv.* 851 f.

ὡς φρονῶν μὲν εὖ
οὐ μὴ θελήσῃ θῆλυν ἐνδῦναι στολήν.

[2] *v.* 810.

[3] *vv.* 849 ff. (Murray)

Διόνυσε, νῦν σὸν ἔργον· οὐ γὰρ εἶ πρόσω·
τεισώμεθ᾽ αὐτόν. πρῶτα δ᾽ ἔκστησον φρενῶν,
ἐνεὶς ἐλαφρὰν λύσσαν.

The stress thus laid by the operator upon this move, as making his opportunity, would be remarkable, and hard to reconcile with a mesmeric interpretation of the performance, even if, in the colloquy which precedes, some approach to the end had been actually achieved. Even then, the interruption of the process, the change of conditions, and the plain intimation that this change is momentous, would be contrary to the supposed nature of the business. But it is not the fact that Pentheus, before he leaves the stage, and by the effect of the colloquy, is seen to be approaching the condition in which he comes back. He comes back *mad*, mentally and physically insane, talking nonsense and seeing what is not there. He goes out uncertain of his intentions, unable, as yet, to decide between certain courses, each of which he has reason both to favour and to dislike, and proposing to consider them further. This is not madness, nor any approach to it. It is a condition common, in circumstances of difficulty, to the sanest. It may even be (and it is in Pentheus) a mark of improvement in wisdom and sobriety. It gives us no ground for supposing that if, as we will for the moment assume, Dionysus has achieved this much by the exercise of his will, a further exercise of the same power, when the scene is transferred to the interior of the palace, will deprive the King of his senses.

But again, it does not appear as a fact, that the hesitations and uncertainty of Pentheus prove, as far as they go, a mysterious ascendancy of will in the other party to the conversation. They are produced, or rather fomented, by the simple and common means of throwing out rapidly a string of suggestions, and objecting to every choice. "*Will the King, before slaughtering the bacchants, at least see them?* He is eager for it. *But his life will be in danger.* That is true. *Then he must go as a woman.* Revolting! Impossible! *But to fight is to shed blood.* Again too true." By such curves we return to the starting-point, and Pentheus, to talk it all out, naturally... takes his adviser into the house. From the triumph of the stranger upon this move (which he first suggests[1]), we learn that he has manœuvred for it,—and therefore that his project, needing the move, is something quite different from mesmeric influence. His manœuvres are dexterous, but not at all mysterious, and to put this colour upon them we must aid the poet by alteration. This is how Euripides should have written :—

PENTHEUS (*turning from him*).

Ho, armourers! Bring forth my shield and sword!— And thou, be silent!

DIONYSUS

(*after regarding him fixedly, speaks with resignation*).

Ah!—Have then thy will!

[*He fixes his eyes upon Pentheus again... ; then speaks in a tone of command.*]

Man, thou wouldst fain behold them on the hill Praying!

[1] *v.* 827.

PENTHEUS

(*who during the rest of this scene, with a few exceptions, simply speaks the thoughts that Dionysus puts into him, losing power over his own mind*).

That would I, though it cost me all
The gold of Thebes[1]!

And so on. Prompted so, we may find mystery everywhere. But put beside this English the original Greek, or the English of Mr Way:

PENTHEUS (*to attendant*).

Bring forth mine arms!—thou, make an end of speech.

DIONYSUS.

Ho thou!
Wouldst thou behold them camped upon the hills?

PENTHEUS.

Ay—though with sumless gold I bought the sight.

To this version, as to the Greek, the stage-directions of the other cannot be applied. How should "Ho thou!" be spoken "with resignation"? The Greek interjection (ἆ) signifies an excited protest, something like our "No, no!" or "Stop!" It is surely no equivalent for the English *Ah!* as a sign of acquiescence, nor is it interpreted, in Euripides, by any such addition as "Have then thy will!" Nor

---

[1] *vv.* 809–812 (Murray)

Πε. ἐκφέρετέ μοι δεῦρ᾽ ὅπλα, σὺ δὲ παῦσαι λέγων.
Δι. ἆ.
       βούλῃ σφ᾽ ἐν ὄρεσι συγκαθημένας ἰδεῖν;
Πε. μάλιστα, μυρίον γε δοὺς χρυσοῦ σταθμόν.

can it have been easy to give "a tone of command"
to what, in the Greek, is not a command, but a
question,—"Wouldst thou behold them?" But if
we make it an affirmation—"Thou wouldst fain
behold them"—and prefix to it a peremptory voca-
tive, "Man,...", then we see how the tone comes in.
And if the suggestions of Dionysus, beginning thus,
end upon a note of obscure menace—

PENTHEUS.

What of the city streets? Canst lead me hence
Unseen of any?

DIONYSUS.

Lonely and untried
Thy path from hence shall be, and I thy guide![1]—

then so much the better for the mystery. And
contrariwise, if he says merely

By lone paths will we go. Myself will guide[2].

In short, Professor Murray (I would submit) com-
poses the scene, as Euripides, if it were to be
construed and acted as a victory of supernormal
faculty, should have composed it, but did not.

But since in truth, if we follow Euripides, we
cannot suppose that the stranger, having got Pentheus to confer with him in the palace, makes an
idiot of him by merely so willing,—how is it done,

---

[1] *vv.* 840–841 (Murray)

Πε. καὶ πῶς δι' ἄστεως εἶμι Καδμείους λαθών;

Δι. ὁδοὺς ἐμήμους ἴμεν· ἐγὼ δ' ἡγήσομαι.

[2] Way.

and how is the manner of it explained, as of course
it must be, to the audience ?   Possibly that may not
now be discoverable.   The text of a dramatist,
shorn of the action and not interpreted by directions,
is but too likely to present, as the Greek tragedians
do, some problems not determinable.   But there are
some indications, all pointing one way, which, so far as
I know, have not been considered, and perhaps have
not been noticed.   Whether they are sufficient, it is
for the reader to decide.   I submit them for what
they may be worth.

Foremost, because most conspicuous, may be set
the fact that, when Pentheus comes forth demented,
the first symptom of his state is an affection not
at all mystical, but bacchic in the most vulgar
sense :

> Aha ! me seemeth I behold two suns,
> A two-fold Thebes, our seven-gated burg ![1]

In plain terms—and the style of Euripides is
even plainer than that of Mr Way—the man is
drunk.   He sees double, like any toper reeling out
of a wine-shop.   Now surely it was a blunder in
the dramatist, a mistake of judgement and taste, to
put in this trait, unless he really means that the
victim is intoxicated, and has taken something, some
drink or drug, such as would naturally do the work.
Assuming this, the trait is, in the circumstances,

---

[1] *vv.* 918–919 (Way)

καὶ μὴν ὁρᾶν μοι δύο μὲν ἡλίους δοκῶ,
δισσὰς δὲ Θήβας καὶ πόλισμ' ἑπτάστομον.

tragically horrible, the more so because of its brutality; otherwise we should not count it, nor, I think, is it commonly counted, for a happy thought. It may fairly put us on the enquiry, whether, as a fact, the subjugator is shown to have used such a means.

There is certainly nothing improbable either in the conception itself, or in such an application of it by Euripides. The stranger comes from Asia Minor, a home of poisons and poisoners[1]. As an adept in ecstasies, a communicator of secret delights, he is not likely to be without experience in drugs. That, however sincere in his religion, he is not scrupulous about the means of advancing it, we have already seen. He has told us himself that, to forward his plans, it is now necessary to destroy the King's reason, and that it shall be done. And done it is, with a promptitude for which, apart from miracle, only poisoning, intoxication, will account.

Let us ask then next: has he an opportunity? While he is in the house with the King, has anything passed between them, to make poisoning possible? Yes. There has been an excellent opportunity, arising naturally out of the situation. We are told so by the dramatist, if we read him as given by tradition. Pentheus and the stranger, having now made an alliance or truce, have pledged each other, as usual, *in drink*.

---

[1] So Andromache (*Andr.* 157) is charged, as an Ἠπειρῶτις, *woman of Asia*, with using φάρμακα to produce sterility; Medea poisons the wreath of Creusa, etc. The adept of the *Bacchants* may be classed for such purposes among women.

After the unseen interview, the first to re-enter is the Lydian, who calls forth Pentheus in words which the translators give thus—

> Thou who dost burn to see forefended things,
> Pentheus, O zealous with an evil zeal,
> Come forth before thine halls[1].—

and thus—

> O eye that cravest sights thou must not see,
> O heart athirst for that which slakes not! Thee,
> Pentheus, I call[2].—

representing the text as it has been printed from the Aldine edition (1503) down to this day:

> σὲ τὸν πρόθυμον ὄνθ' ἃ μὴ χρεὼν ὁρᾶν
> σπεύδοντά τ' ἀσπούδαστα, Πενθέα λέγω,
> ἔξιθι πάροιθε δωμάτων[3].

But the MS., the only one which preserves this part of the play, gives not σπεύδοντα but σπένδοντα. The Aldine editor substituted σπεύδοντα, catching at the verbal affinity of σπενδ- σπουδ- and the obvious simplicity of "zealous with an evil zeal[4]," and assuming that σπένδοντα, "pledging libation," was unintelligible. Changes of this kind, made in the dawn of scholarship, are like the step over the edge of a steep. We slide to the bottom, and there stay. For nearly four centuries Musurus was followed apparently without enquiry.

---

[1] Way.   [2] Murray.   [3] *vv.* 912 ff.

[4] This affinity and simplicity are arguments rather against than for the conjecture. They would have protected the reading σπεύδοντα, had it been original, from alteration to σπένδοντα in this place. Nor indeed is the confusion of ν and υ, so far as I have observed, a common error of the MS.

Nevertheless he was wrong. His correction is scarcely even plausible, as was at last observed by a scholar of the present day, Professor Tyrrell. "Eager to see what is forbidden *and* desiring what is not to be desired" is a tautology; and Euripides has not deserved, few writers less, to be accused of tautology by a corrector[1]. Professor Tyrrell therefore, to escape Musurus, would accept from him the reading σπεύδοντα, but nevertheless eject, as spurious, the verse so corrected,

σπεύδοντά τ' ἀσπούδαστα, Πενθέα λέγω,

noting truly that, without it, the sentence is not really defective[2] and yet might easily be thought so. But a readier and more legitimate way of escaping Musurus is to refuse his gratuitous conjecture.

For not only may σπένδοντα be the right word, but it demonstrably is. It is confirmed by the next speech of the Lydian. The intoxicated Pentheus sees horns upon the head of his guide—whether in imagination or because really he has put on those Bacchic emblems—and demands explanation of them. The God, he is told, is his companion, who "before unfriendly, *has now pledged his peace to us*":—

ὁ θεὸς ὁμαρτεῖ, πρόσθεν ὢν οὐκ εὐμενής,
ἔνσπονδος ἡμῖν.

---

[1] See the criticism attributed to him by Aristophanes (*Frogs*, 1154), to which Dr Sandys alludes, in his critical note on our passage.

[2] See Eur. *Hel.* 546, Soph. *Ant.* 441.

The use of *us*, not *thee*, is of course ironical, the speaker affecting to identify the interests of himself and his captive; it is between Pentheus and the deity that there has now been made "truce by libation" (σπονδαί). *Libation* then, and the drinking from the cup which was part of the ceremony, there has been; and when Pentheus is described as "making truce by libation (σπένδοντα)," we have simply another reference to the same fact.

It is natural and necessary that such a ceremony should be performed between Pentheus and the servant of Bacchus at this point; and we have been prepared for it by a train of suggestions. The adept, in the previous scene, has pretended a desire to serve the King's interest in the difficult situation created by the raid of the women from Cithaeron, and has offered, among other things, to give him an opportunity of seeing the objects of his suspicion. When the King accepts this offer so far as to invite the stranger to a conference in the palace, and consents to discuss the proposal that he should stake his life upon the fidelity of his adversary, it is natural and necessary that this truce and trust should be pledged in form. They have drunk together, with libation. The libation of Pentheus was doubtless not poured, not formally, to the new god: that would be premature. But a *truce* with the god (σπονδαί), and in this sense a *libation* to him, he has made. He has done this in order that he may see the bacchants; and since this desire, as the adept believes, is impious, he describes the King, so soon

as he safely can, as "eager to see what is forbidden,
and *making libation (truce) not fit to be desired*,"

πρόθυμον ὄνθ' ἃ μὴ χρεὼν ὁρᾶν
σπένδοντά τ' ἀσπούδαστα.

The libation of Pentheus, in so far as it can be said,
bitterly and with irony, to be offered to Bacchus, is
the sign of his defeat and subjugation. He has
purged his rebellion. "He rejects me from *libations*"
says the deity of the prologue[1] (σπονδῶν ἄπο ὠθεῖ
με). "*Make libation* and worship him" (σπένδε
καὶ βάκχευε), says Teiresias in his expostulation[2].
And libation, says his conqueror, he now makes.

Here then, in the cup from which he pours and
drinks, is the poisoner's opportunity to do that which
must be done. It is indeed a hideous and revolting
opportunity, open only to treachery and—which, the
cause considered, may appear worse—to sacrilege.
But such are the ways of fanaticism. To make the
King insane, and so bring him to destroy himself, in
appearance, by his own act, is the only sure and
safe means of preventing the military project which,
however it may result, must be disastrous to the
propaganda. For such an end, and to punish an
enemy of religion, an enthusiast like the adept will
violate any pledge, and profane all rites, not excepting
his own. And we now see why the house is "a

---

[1] *v.* 45.
[2] *v.* 313. See also *vv.* 284 f.

οὗτος θεοῖσι σπένδεται θεὸς γεγώς,
ὥστε διὰ τοῦτον τἀγάθ' ἀνθρώπους ἔχειν,

a tragic irony, when we know the sequel.

trap" for Pentheus[1], and why his retirement thither,
and his invitation of the adept to a conference[2], are
hailed with triumph as sealing his fate.   There
and there only can be done what the minister of
Dionysus means to do.

In retrospect therefore, by the symptoms of the
victim and the allusions of the victor, the nature and
means of the conquest are declared ; and this may
be enough for a reader.   But in the theatre, for the
information and excitement of an audience, it would
seem desirable, or even necessary, that the purpose
should be in some way foreshown. A plain declaration
in words, whether before or after, is prohibited by the
situation.   To the attendants of the King, however
ready to acknowledge Dionysus, the adept could not
safely have revealed that their master was to be
poisoned. He must necessarily pretend, as he does,
that the mind of Pentheus is to be disorganized by
divine and miraculous intervention: "Dionysus, now
to thy work!"   But the spectators, who, if they have
followed with understanding the course of the play
and the scene itself to this point, must instantly
perceive that the man's confidence rests upon something more material than faith, may receive from his
action all the further enlightenment that they can

---

[1] *v.* 848.

[2] *v.* 843

ἐλθόντ' ἐς οἴκους...ἂν δοκῇ βουλεύσομαι.

The retention here of the dual ἐλθόντε (Murray), "*We* will go
into the house, and I...," is, I think, clearly right, as against ἐλθών
γε (Nauck).

require. "Dionysus, now to thy work,—*for thou art not far away.* Let us punish him. *But madden him first, and put in him light frenzy.*" The means to do this must be near indeed ; it must—there is no other possibility in the situation—be upon the person of the speaker. Let him then but put his hand within his dress, and we, those of us who are not expecting Euripides to show us a miracle, shall have evidence enough. He carries about him, as from his nationality and profession we should naturally suppose, an intoxicating drug, an excitant of imagination and illusion. For a frenzy, he will proportion the dose.

The scene would thus explain itself, even if we were to assume that, in connecting the efficacy of Dionysus with a drug, Euripides was here taking an original line. But this, in my opinion, is most improbable. In such a time as the fifth century B.C., when both the study of medicine and rationalistic speculation upon the origin of superstitious beliefs were powerful movements, proceeding from the same Ionic centres of thought, and thus brought naturally into contact, the connexion of enthusiasm with intoxicants must have been notorious ; and it must, I should suppose, have been applied, long before the date of the *Bacchants*, by those who occupied themselves with such conjectures, to explain some of the performances attributed by legend to Dionysus and his votaries. The Athenian audience, the educated part of it, would probably expect the exhibition of a drug to figure as an element in a Bacchic story presented by Euripides. But even without this, the scene explains itself, before as well as after the accomplishment of the adept's design, supposing only, at the earlier stage, such interpretation by gesture as the words and situation imply. To those who could not or would not see, the choice of a miraculous interpretation was here, as elsewhere, left open. But it is not natural, and it is not Euripidean.

Whether by a divine act, a miraculous act, such as Aeschylus or Sophocles would probably have supposed in such circumstances, the situation would be made more tragic, is a question which we need not debate. Tragic it would be, no doubt, that a Being of superhuman strength and pride, opposed to pride and strength only human, should reduce the adversary to idiocy by a mere fiat. But in what sense is it less tragic, that, in the world as we see it, there are found such beings as the adept, appalling compounds of devotion, cunning, and cruelty, men who, to serve their God, would put venom into a cup of communion ? These are two tragedies, different in kind ; and the last, not the former, was the kind which interested that "most tragic of poets" who made his art out of "the things we handle and among which we live."

The fact that the madness and subjugation of Pentheus are produced by a drug will explain, if I am not mistaken, a later passage in the play, which has been regarded as desperate. For, when all is over, when the sanctified means has achieved the

end and the triumph of the cause is secure, the
Asiatic women, in their exultation, describe the
instrument in terms which, given the fact, are transparent, and, without the fact, are not intelligible at
all. The point is important; for we thus learn what,
in the bare text and without the action, does not
previously appear,—that these barbarians are accom-
plices of their compatriot, and understand, when the
adept predicts to them "the work of Dionysus," in
what manner that work is to be done. Being adepts
themselves and familiar with his operations, it is
natural that they should understand him; and their
consciences, as we see everywhere, are enslaved to
his direction. Whatever they know, they of course
must not reveal anything, placed as they are, of a
mystery so little attractive to proselytes. During
the ode which follows the retirement of Pentheus
and the adept into the house[1], and that which is
sung after their departure to the camp[2], the singers
may not even be alone; during the second they
probably are not alone, for the departure is witnessed
(as we are led to suppose) by some of the King's
subjects, and there is no reason why these should
immediately disperse[3]. And even if the women
were alone, the door of the palace is no place for
proclaiming that the master of it has been cheated
of his life by means not more sublime than those of
the vulgar murderer. They cannot with prudence
utter it even after the accomplishment, and in
strictness of reality perhaps they would not. But it

---

[1] *vv.* 862 ff.   [2] *vv.* 977 ff.   [3] See hereafter.

is conceivable, even in reality, that in their exultation
the truth should slip out, especially since now, for
the first time perhaps, they are left without auditors[1];
and in the theatre a declaration to this extent, one
reference in plain terms, would be desirable, if not
necessary, to complete the effect. And this we have.
The triumph of the bacchants over the death of
Pentheus finds expression, naturally enough, in a
reminiscence of the crisis which decides his fate, and
a series of allusions to the scene of his subjugation.
In part, but in part only, these allusions are intelligible, if we ignore the means by which the subjugation is effected :

> Let us in chorus extol our God, and raise our voices to cele-
> brate the fall of Pentheus the serpent-born, who took the woman-
> garb and the thyrsus-wand..., and with the Bull to guide him
> went to his fate[2].

These are simple references to the facts and the
language of the scene which we are considering.
But to the words " who took the thyrsus-wand " the
bacchants append the comment, that the wand, the
narthex as they here call it, was a *pistos Hades*

---

[1] See *vv.* 1148 f. The other slaves, if any are present, no
doubt follow the example of the speaker.

[2] *vv.* 1153–1159

> ἀναχορεύσωμεν Βάκχιον,
> ἀναβοάσωμεν ξυμφορὰν
> τὰν τοῦ δράκοντος Πενθέος ἐκγενέτα·
> ὃς τὰν θηλυγενῆ στολὰν
> νάρθηκά τε...
> ἔλαβεν εὔθυρσον,
> ταῦρον προηγητῆρα συμφορᾶς ἔχων.

(νάρθηκά τε, πιστὸν Ἄιδαν, ἔλαβεν εὔθυρσον). It is impossible, most interpreters think, to find in this expression any meaning consistent with the facts as they have hitherto been conceived, or indeed any meaning at all. The wand of Pentheus was his "death," but not "faithful," or "trustworthy," or even —if we might so press the word—"trusted." A string of conjectures, of which none has found acceptance, shows that, from this side, the phrase defies explanation. But it becomes transparent, when we know that the King was poisoned by a drug in his wine. It was remarked by Professor Tyrrell[1], that the word *pistos*, merely as Greek and apart from a context, is ambiguous, meaning either *faithful* (πείθομαι) or *potable* (πίνω), and that *pistos Hades*, merely as Greek, might mean "potable death, death by a potion[2]." Not only might the words have this meaning, but, in themselves and apart from a context, they could bear no other. "Faithful death," or even "trusted death," is an expression barely conceivable; "death in a drink" is an expression perfectly simple ; and native ears, to which both senses of *pistos* were equally natural, must take the epithet, at least primarily, in the obvious way. *Pistos Hades* signifies poison taken in a draught, and could hardly signify anything else. And still more obvious, more inevitable, is this interpretation, when the phrase is appended, as an explanation, to the word *narthex*. This word,

---

[1] Critical note *ad loc.*

[2] See Aesch. *P. V.* 480, where πιστόν is a drinkable medicine.

meaning properly the *hollow stalk* of a certain plant, was extended, by metaphor, to various objects, such as the bacchic wand, made from or comparable to such a stalk. None of its meanings are common in literature; but one of them must, in daily life, have been only too well known. In the lack of glass, a short piece of hollow stalk, stopped at the ends, offered the readiest way to make a *capsule* or *case* for things small, precious, and requiring careful protection, such as scrolls, unguents, etc. Hence the word *narthex* came to signify such a *capsule*[1]; and in this sense, but no other, it admits naturally the explanation *pistos Hades* or *death in a drink*. Strictly, of course, it is to the contents of the *narthex*, the drug itself, that the explanation applies; but, in the language of poetry, such compressions of phrase, by way of metaphor or transference, are habitual and almost regular. Thus, when the triumphant Chorus put into the phrase νάρθηκα εὔθυρσον, *thyrsus-wand*, the explanation πιστὸν Ἄιδαν, *death in the drink*, they are making a fierce and horrible jest, which doubtless on the stage they would deliver with the proper laugh. They play upon two senses of *narthex*, which they signify by giving first one interpretation (πιστὸν Ἄιδαν) and then the other (εὔθυρσον). The circumstances, the facts to which they refer, are such that they could hardly name the "wand" without thinking of that other *narthex*,—the little deadly thing which did "the work of Dionysus," and which, when the adept

---

[1] For references see Liddell and Scott s.v.

promised such work[1], they must have divined, even if he did not show it to them, to be within reach of the promiser's hand. But although the equivocation is thus prepared and obvious, to use it as a jest, and by way of comment upon the bloody narrative of the murder, would perhaps be impossible to any human beings not hardened by the singular astringence of religious hatred and religious devotion. It proves, as nothing so well could, the temper of their steeled fanaticism.

Thus, here and in the scene of the subjugation, the traditional text defends and justifies itself by mutual support. When we bring the points together, and perceive their relation, it is surely impossible to believe, that in one place the equivocation *narthex* (*pistos*), and in the other place the allusion to the *spondai* or libations which have passed between Pentheus and his guest[2], are the casual, unconnected, and unconscious product of a blundering pen. Unless we will say this, we shall allow, upon the assurance of the poet, that, according to his intention, the conquest of Pentheus is achieved by means of a drug.

Whether the word *pistos*, as well as the word *narthex*, is equivocal,—whether, that is to say, the phrase *pistos Hades* can have a meaning, if *pistos* be taken in the sense *trustworthy* or *trusted*,—is a question which I must for the present leave open. No such inference can be drawn from the passage of Euripides, because the sense *potable*, in this connexion

---

[1] *vv.* 848 ff.   [2] *v.* 913, *supra* p. 110.

obvious, is sufficient.   But if there was such a secon-
dary meaning, if " trusty Death " was a known expression, religious and bacchic, the more easily would
the jest have occurred to the poet's mind, and the
sharper would be its point.   And as a mere conjecture, it seems possible that the phrase was known to
religion.   Although in this play, as we have before
remarked, nothing, or at least nothing explicit, is
said of prospects beyond the grave, we can scarcely
doubt that, according to the type of religions cognate
to the Bacchic—the Orphic mysteries for example
and (probably) those of Iacchus at Eleusis,—we are
to suppose such prospects and assurances as part of
the more intimate revelations which are occasionally
mentioned[1].   The initiate was not only strengthened
for this world but also armed for the next.   The
bacchic emblems and costume were thus not only a
sign of fraternity, but also, in the religious sense, a
viaticum, a preparation for the great journey.   Indeed
we may, I think, fairly see a suggestion of this in
the language which the adept is made to use, when
he goes to dress the King in the attire " wherein he
shall depart to the house of Death (Hades)[2]."   If
bacchants, like some orders, invested their dead
with the religious costume, as an emblem of protection and promise, putting the fawn-skin upon the

---

[1] *vv.* 73, 471 ff.

[2] *vv.* 857–859

ἀλλ᾽ εἶμι κόσμον ὅνπερ εἰς Ἅιδου λαβὼν
ἄπεισι, μητρὸς ἐκ χεροῖν κατασφαγείς,
Πενθεῖ προσάψων.

body and the wand in the stiff hand, then we should have here a ferocious sneer quite appropriate to the behaviour of the preacher at this crisis. It is not necessary so to suppose, but I find the supposition plausible[1]. Now in connexion with such a habit, the phrase *pistos Hades*, "Death that is trusted" or "that may be trusted," strange as it is, would have a meaning. To the initiate, the King of the Dead is an object not of terror but of confidence. To the question

Wilt thou trust Death or not?

the initiate, like the scholar in Browning, can answer "Yes." And thus when the women describe the *narthex* (*wand*) of Pentheus as a *pistos Hades*, a sign of *trust in death*, they would not only be making their own bitter jest upon the poison, but also echoing the sneer of the adept at the significance, in this case, of the protective investiture. That this is so, I do not say. To prove it, the phrase *pistos Hades*, in the religious use supposed, must be not conjectured but actually found; and I repeat, that the passage of Euripides, being complete in sense without any reference to this meaning of *pistos* (πείθομαι), cannot be cited as, by itself, supporting that reference. I would merely signalize the possibility to the investigators of mystic phraseology[2].

---

[1] Possibly too this may throw some light on the strange phrase ἐν τέλει in *v.* 860. It may have meant, in this connexion, "at the hour of death."

[2] The translation "sure to kill," which has sometimes been forced upon πιστὸν ῞Αιδαν in our passage, is not to be thought of. As Tyrrell and others have pointed out, it is not derivable from

There is another passage in the play, which has been found difficult, and with reason, so long as we have not remarked that the madness of Pentheus is effected by poison, but becomes simple when that is perceived. The sermon of warning, which Teiresias addresses to the King, concludes with a dark suggestion: "No argument of yours shall persuade me to fight against deity. For you are mad, most miserably mad. Medicine will not cure your ill, *and medicine has helped to make it*[1]." The last words are muttered perhaps rather than spoken, and no further notice is taken of them. But to the speaker himself, and to the reader, they must have a meaning; and their only natural meaning is that Teiresias already suspects some one of having practised, by charms or spells or other such means comprised in the term *pharmaka*, against the sanity of the prince[2]; this appears to the prophet the most charitable explanation of his behaviour. But more than one critic has found this suspicion irrelevant, and has proposed to alter the text; and it is not easy to see,

the meaning of πιστός. The words νάρθηκα, πιστὸν Ἄιδαν, ἔλαβε might conceivably mean "he took the wand which *he could trust* to kill him"; but that is nonsense. They could not mean "he took the wand which was (in itself) destined to kill him." However, as I have said, there is no proof that πιστός (πείθομαι) has any bearing on the passage at all.

[1] vv. 326–327

> μαίνῃ γὰρ ὡς ἄλγιστα, κοὔτε φαρμάκοις
> ἄκη λάβοις ἂν οὔτ᾿ ἄνευ τούτων νοσεῖς.

[2] A supernatural influence, that of a god, would not come, I think, within the meaning of φάρμακον. But see Tyrrell's note.

from a dramatic point of view, why the point should be brought in, unless it bears in some way upon the story. But when we know that, in the end, it is by a *pharmakon*, in the strictest sense, that Pentheus is made literally insane, we see why Teiresias should be made to express a suspicion, which, from the nature of the case, can be aimed only at the King's enemies, the bacchants. It is a point calculated for the second hearing or second reading. That Teiresias should attribute dark powers to the new religious sect, is not unnatural, nor that he should charge them, in his own mind, with having used some such power upon their persecutor. But the reason why he is made, somewhat abruptly and obscurely, to throw out the hint, is that we, readers informed of the story, may remark how much nearer than he knows his apprehension strikes at the character of the King's adversary. By "medicine" indeed it is, that the adept of Dionysus will quench the light of reason in a resisting mind, but not by any such remote and mysterious medicine as the prophet seems to imagine. The *pharmakon*, with which Dionysus operates, is of that kind which can be carried in the purse and dropped into the cup.

In the pitiable and repulsive scene[1] which exhibits the degradation of Pentheus—the masterful man, headstrong but not ill-meaning, suddenly converted into a vain and vicious child—there is one trait which, as I have always thought, is intolerable, if we suppose his vanquisher to be a deity inflicting

[1] *vv.* 912 ff.

punishment for the refusal of worship. The mind
of the victim is not only enfeebled, but fouled. He
becomes beastly. This at all events, until the
poison unmans him, he is not. It may be, that, by
charging the women-converts with misconduct of
which no proof appears, he suggests, to a strict
judgement, no very favourable estimate of his own
purity. But in his anger at their supposed behaviour, and in his desire to resolve his doubts
by seeing what they do[1], there is no mixture, none
apparent in his language, either of malice or of
prurience. Considering who these women are, and
that among them are his nearest kinswomen and his
own mother, it would, no doubt, be monstrous that
he should find pleasure either in the suspicion itself
or in the prospect of proving it. But he finds pain[2].
In the background of his thoughts there may conceivably lurk some baser element of curiosity, as in
every human thought and feeling base elements do.
But that he cherishes, or consciously follows, any
such impulse, he has hitherto nowhere betrayed.
Now, morally as well as mentally, he is dissolved
into a brute. The suggestion of his leader, that the
virtue of the bacchants will be to him a delightful
surprise, awakes no response : the miserable wretch
is more interested in learning just how he should
hold his thyrsus[3]. He pictures the worst discoveries
with chuckling anticipation[4]. He can cite the names
of his mother and her sisters, for the silly purpose of

[1] *vv.* 812 ff.   [2] *v.* 814.
[3] *vv.* 939–942.   [4] *vv.* 957 f.

getting a compliment upon the finish of his female disguise, without hint of shame or apprehension[1]. He is vile. And the author of this "change of mind" notes it with pleasure and gratulation![2] Even in a man, provoked by violence and blinded by a fanatical devotion, such callous wickedness touches the limit of what is credible or acceptable. How would it be, if, according to the poet, this murderer were the true object of such worship as that of the Hymn to Holiness?

The Dionysus of this episode, and of almost all the play, is, like the Aphrodite of the prologue to the *Hippolytus*, and like all the gods of the Euripidean theatre, not a possible object of adoration. In most cases, as in that of Aphrodite, the obvious answer to the question so raised, is that the deity, the personal embodiment of a passion or a force, being in no way required by the mechanism of the story, will naturally be dismissed (by those who, like the poet, so incline) as a revolting and needless imagination. Here, in the *Bacchants*, the person of the adept is the very hinge of the story. But that he is superhuman, he never gives us any reason to think; and now he has disproved it. Poison is a human weapon, not superhuman, and the adept, however fiendish, is no fiend in respect of his power.

Before quitting this scene, we must notice a small but not insignificant question, respecting the number and parts of the performers. It is not probable that the entrance of the adept and his

[1] *vv.* 925 f.   [2] *v.* 944.

victim from the palace, and their departure for the
mountain, are witnessed by no one except the women
of the Chorus.   The poisoner, in forecasting his
triumph, declares his intention to make the captive
a spectacle to his own subjects[1]; and we should
expect a corresponding performance.   The conversion of the King's servants—the fact that they are, as
a body, now convinced by the report from Cithaeron
that the stranger is supported by miraculous arms—
is necessary to the development of the situation,
since, without this, they would attempt some inter-
ference.   And it is but natural that, when the King,
after his private interview with his new counsellor,
sets forth, so terribly transformed, upon his fatal
journey, fascination should lead some of his awe-
struck household to follow him beyond the door.
We should presume therefore that they do so, and
express by their behaviour the terror which the
adept has inspired, and which is essential, as a condition, to his success.   The sequel makes this
certain ; for by one man at least Pentheus and his
guide are followed all the way to Cithaeron, and by
this one at least they are doubtless followed when
we see them depart from the stage.   It is from
him that the Chorus, and the audience, receive the
story of the King's horrible end.   His narrative—

When we had got beyond the villages of Thebes and had
passed the river Asopus, we entered upon the bare slope of
Cithaeron, *Pentheus, that is, and I, who kept with the master*, and
the stranger who was to bring us to the spectacle...[2]—

[1] *vv.* 854 ff.   [2] *vv.* 1043 ff.

suggests, what we may well believe, that he was the only companion in whom fascination prevailed over terror so far. But at the beginning the attendance would be more numerous.

Among those who follow from the palace, one (the future reporter) should be supposed to distinguish himself as leader by his action, thus preparing the audience for his presence at the catastrophe. But this preparation, a thing important to the coherence of the drama, has been already begun, and more effectively, in the previous scene. There, as we saw[1], upon the conclusion of the herdsman's narrative, a bystander, whose language marks him as a servant of Pentheus, gives voice to his belief in the divinity and power of Dionysus. And to the same speaker we should assign an unappropriated verse which, at the close of the scene, occurs between the exit of Pentheus and the following speech of the Lydian:

Pentheus. We will go within, and I will decide as seems best.
The Lydian. As you will. In any event I am at your service.
Pentheus (leading the way)[2]. By your leave. Perhaps I shall take
    arms and march, and perhaps I shall adopt your advice.
                                                        [*Exit.*

[1] See *vv.* 775 ff. and *supra* p. 93.
[2] *vv.* 845–9.

   Πε. στείχοιμ' ἄν· ἢ γὰρ ὅπλ' ἔχων πορεύσομαι
        ἢ τοῖσι σοῖσι πείσομαι βουλεύμασιν.
   <Θεράπων.> ἥξει δὲ βάκχας, οὗ θανὼν δώσει δίκην.
   Δι. γυναῖκες, ἀνὴρ ἐς βόλον καθίσταται.
      Διόνυσε, νῦν σὸν ἔργον· οὐ γὰρ εἶ πρόσω.

The MS. assigns *v.* 847 (so placed) to *Dionysus*, but no one now accepts this, the third person (ἥξει, δώσει) being unsuitable. See the commentaries.

(*A Servant.*)   And he will go to the bacchanal camp, there to
    pay the penalty of his life.
The Lydian.   Women, he walks into the snare.   Now, Dionysus,
    to thy work !...

The servant speaks, as he naturally would, to his
fellow-slaves, and expresses the conviction which, as
believers in Dionysus, they doubtless share,—that,
whatever Pentheus may say, an irresistible might
will certainly conquer and destroy him.   The pre-
valence of this conviction is necessary to the sequel ;
and for this reason the expression of it, in these
interjectional comments, has a dramatic value, apart
from the more mechanical function which they perform, in presenting the speaker to our notice, and
preparing us for his part as reporter of the catastrophe.

To the scene of his report, passing over for the
present the choric interlude which covers the time
of the event, we may now proceed.   The brief
dialogue, which passes between him and the Chorus-
leader[1], brings out the notable point, that the man's
submission to Dionysus has no resemblance to what
we call, and the bacchants would call, a religious
conversion of the heart.   Far from sharing their
exultation, he can scarcely bear it with patience[2].
To superior power, however exerted, he bows, like
the slave that he is, without protest and without

    [1] *vv.* 1024–1042.
    [2] *vv.* 1032–1040.   The supposition of a loss to the text at
v. 1036 is unnecessary.   It is natural that the bacchant (*v.* 1037)
should interrupt the man, whose meaning (*v.* 1036) is sufficiently
expressed.

approval[1], without moral question of any kind ; and his natural horror at the event which he has seen and describes is in no way affected by his regarding it as the work of a god, and presenting the incidents according to this persuasion.

But indeed the situation gives little scope for colouring. In the state to which Pentheus is reduced, it needs no miracle to accomplish his destruction ; nor, without a determined expectation, could any miracle be found in what occurs. The bacchants are discovered in a glen or torrent-bed, "walled with rocks and overshadowed with pines[2]." The King and his conductor, approaching quietly by a grassy glade, reach a place from which the women are visible ; but Pentheus, complaining that he does not see well enough to "observe their mal-practices properly[3]," proposes to climb into a tree. Thereupon the stranger, "with superhuman force[4]," pulls down a pine, and having placed Pentheus upon it, releases it so as to leave him seated. At this moment the stranger "is no more to be seen," and a voice "from the air" calls the bacchanals to avenge themselves and their god. They rush to the place, and, perceiving their victim, attempt first to reach him with missiles from a rock opposite ; but, finding that he is beyond their range, they assail the tree, using boughs as levers to the roots, and

---

[1] *vv.* 1150 ff.
[2] *vv.* 1051–1052

  ἄγκος ἀμφίκρημνον...πεύκαισι συσκιάζον.

[3] *v.* 1062.   [4] *v.* 1069.

finally "plucking it out of the earth." Pentheus comes to the ground with it, and, vainly supplicating, is instantly torn to pieces.

Such are the facts. They are reported and, as it were, annotated by an observer so possessed by superstitious expectancy that even the disappearance of the Lydian is translated into a prodigy, and invested with the forms of a divine ascension :

For scarce was my master visible in his perch above, when *the stranger was no more to be seen, and from the air a voice—doubtless the voice of Dionysus—*cried, "Women, I bring you him that has made a mock of you, and me, and of my rites. Take vengeance on him." *And as he spoke, between heaven and earth there rose a wondrous blaze of fire*[1].

Comment, analysis, would surely be wasted upon testimony so naive as this. The performance of the Lydian at this moment, occurring in the circumstances depicted, could not appear wonderful to any rational mind ; and in view of this incident, if the rest of the story were filled with prodigies, they might and should be rejected without examination.

But in fact, except where the stranger is concerned, our informant sees no prodigy ; and what he relates concerning this awful personage is refuted, so far as it transcends nature, by himself. When the Lydian pulls down a pine, upon which to place his victim, the act is described in a manner which, if we take it for truth, is indeed stupendous :

And here it was that I saw the stranger do that thing miraculous. Grasping a pine's top branch sky-high, he dragged it down,

[1] *vv.* 1076 ff.

and down, and down to the ground, bending it round as the moving-spring is bent, when the running circuit of a wheel is drawn by the lathe[1]; even so did the pull of his arms bow to the earth that mountain-branch, with more than mortal might. Then, setting Pentheus on the pine, he let the tree rear itself again, loosing his grasp gently and with care not to fling the rider, till it rose right up into the air, with my master seated atop[2].

This is stupendous, if true,—if the tree was, as the man would have us conceive, a great tree, erect and firm. But, seeing who and what he is, why should we suppose any such thing? In a place like that which is described, upon the broken edge of a watercourse, one may find in abundance pines of such size and so hanging, that a man may use them as the Lydian does this one. If he could pull it down, it was such and so placed as to make that possible. So would say common sense, even if the narrator did not presently prove it. We turn to the assault of the bacchanals, and we read—

And when they saw my master seated upon the pine, first they tried to pelt him with battery of stones, from a rock-tower opposite on which they mounted, and with pieces of pine-wood for javelins, and some with their wands, which through the air they launched at their miserable mark, yet reached him not; for the wretch, though helpless to escape, was perched too high for their purpose. So presently, *with branches which they broke*(?) *from the trees and*

---

[1] For the most probable explanation of this simile, see the description of a primitive lathe by Mr Robertson, cited in Tyrrell's note. The exact reading however is doubtful. I would follow the MS., except in writing $\mathring{\eta}$ (for $\mathring{\eta}$) in *v.* 1066: literally, "it was rounded like the bow (spring) *in the engine* (*way*) *by which* a wheel draws the course of its circuit." The relative $\mathring{\eta}$ refers loosely to τόξον.

[2] *vv.* 1063 ff.

used for levers, they set them to tear up the roots[1], till, as this labour did not bring them to their end, Agave said, "Come, Maenads, *stand about the young tree* and lay grasp thereon, that so we may catch the mounted quarry, and he may never tell the secrets of the God's dance." *So they put a many hands to the pine, and plucked it out of the earth. And down from his seat above came Pentheus dashed to the ground, lamenting sore, for he saw that his fate was near.* Then, as his mother, arch-priestess of the sacrifice, fell upon him, he dashed the coif from his hair, that she, alas!, might know and spare him, and softly put his hand to her face, and said, "See, mother, it is thy son[2]."...

In all this (be it observed) the narrator finds nothing that calls for comment. Nor is there anything. The picture, as presented here, is consistent and self-explanatory. The pine has become a *sapling* (*ptorthos*)[3], a word apparently not applicable to a tree of any great size. And small indeed the tree must be, since Pentheus, falling with it, is not even stunned. And it stands so, it is so precariously attached, that the women can think of uprooting it with "branches," and, after so loosing the roots, do actually "pluck it out of the earth,"—although, as appears in the failure of their first attack, their powers are neither superhuman nor even remarkable. All this is natural, credible, consistent. But how does it

---

[1] It is worth note that in Prof. Murray's version this incident is inadvertently dropped. Upon the assumptions implied in describing the act of the stranger (*vv.* 1063 ff.), such a proceeding would be unintelligible. The word given as *broke* (συγκεραυνοῦσαι) is dubious, but does not materially affect the sense.

[2] *vv.* 1095 ff.

[3] *v.* 1107. The βλάστημα of *v.* 1071 *may* be the top branch, not the whole tree, though the ambiguity is notable.

compare with the miracle attributed to Dionysus? If the tree is such as these women can disroot, why in the world, without miracle, should not the Lydian bend it down for a moment?

The case is transparent. In the view of a person like this slave, the mysterious and wonder-working stranger has now acquired such a glamour, that he *cannot* do anything simple. His acts are miraculous *per se*. If he ceases to be seen, he has vanished. What his arm achieves *must* be more than human strength could perform, though the same, and more, may be done by others without exciting surprise. The story of the death of Pentheus, in so far as it purports to be miraculous, is self-refuted, and in this respect agrees with the method of the author throughout. The fact that, among such a band of furies, the victim is literally torn to pieces, does not impress even our reporter as in itself supernatural. The part of Agave, taken strictly as he relates it, exceeds perhaps, as he supposes, even the power of madness:

Then gripping the wretch by the left arm, and planting her foot against his side, *she rent away the shoulder*, *by divine permission doing beyond her strength*[1].

[1] *vv.* 1125–1128

λαβοῦσα δ' ὠλένης ἀριστερὰν χέρα,
πλευραῖσιν ἀντιβᾶσα τοῦ δυσδαίμονος
ἀπεσπάραξεν ὦμον, οὐχ ὑπὸ σθένους,
ἀλλ' ὁ θεὸς εὐμάρειαν ἐπεδίδου χεροῖν.

The first line lacks a caesura. But note that a similar verse is used by Aeschylus (*Eum.* 26) in alluding to the death of Pentheus—λάγω δίκην Πενθεῖ καταρράψας μόρον. One may suspect them to be quotations from some older work.

But it would be idle to weigh, as matter of evidence, the details of a description like this, which, from the nature of the case and the situation of the witness, must be the work rather of fantasy than of observation. The trait is however worth notice, as confirming, by a dexterous stroke, the impression previously conveyed,—that, up to this point and in their assault upon the tree, the bacchants have *not* exhibited any remarkable power. If the pine which they "pluck out of the earth" had been such as it is made to appear when the Lydian lowers it, the act of Agave, compared with such a feat, should pass for matter of course.

Such, if considered as testimony, is this story— part of it, all that surpasses nature, visibly untrue. But here again, as in the report of the herdsman[1], we are to note that Euripides makes no confusion between truth and beauty. The man's tale, in all that relates to the stranger, is a travesty and work of imagination, but it is none the less sublime. The same blind awe, the same tense expectancy, which make him a bad witness, make him an excellent vehicle of sensation. He is possessed, materially and grossly perhaps, but profoundly and sincerely, by the terrible apprehension of contact with the Power of Life and the World ; and seldom has this kind of emotion been more thrillingly put into words :

> And there he set the King,
> And slowly, lest it cast him in its spring,
> Let back the young and straining tree, till high
> It towered again amid the towering sky;

[1] *vv.* 677 ff., *supra* pp. 89 ff.

And Pentheus in the branches! Well, I ween,
He saw the Maenads then, and well was seen!
For scarce was he aloft, when suddenly
There was no Stranger any more with me,
But out of Heaven a Voice—oh, what voice else?—
'Twas He that called! "Behold, O damosels,
I bring ye him who turneth to despite
Both me and ye, and darkeneth my great Light.
'Tis yours to avenge!" So spake he, and there came
'Twixt earth and sky a pillar of high flame.
And silence took the air, and no leaf stirred
In all the forest dell. Thou hadst not heard
In that vast silence any wild thing's cry.
And up they sprang; but with bewildered eye,
Agaze and listening, scarce yet hearing true.
Then came the Voice again. And when they knew
Their God's clear call, old Cadmus' royal brood,
Up, like wild pigeons startled in a wood,
On flying feet they came[1].

Here, so far as concerns the main purpose of
this essay, the story ends, though the most tragic
part of the spectacle, or the most horrible, is still to
come, in the appearance of the mad mother bearing
the head of her murdered son. Even the fanatics

---

[1] *vv.* 1070 ff. (Murray). In *v.* 1077, καὶ τὸν ξένον μὲν οὐκέτ᾽
εἰσορᾶν παρῆν, the version, "There was no Stranger any more *with
me*," perhaps suggests a disappearance *seen*, if we may so say, by
the narrator. The original does not. The narrator, as is implied
in *v.* 1076, was watching Pentheus, and simply *missed* the
stranger when he looked for him again. But the translation, as a
whole, is not less faithful than beautiful, and attains the highest
point (*vv.* 1084–1085) precisely with the poet himself. No
"great Light" is to be found in the Greek of *v.* 1080; but it
leads admirably to the fancied flame of *v.* 1083. If Euripides
had thought of it, he might well have put it in.

from Asia have pity for Agave[1], and upon this point
their silence is even more expressive than their
speech :

> Kadmus, for thee I grieve. Thy daughter's son
> Hath but just doom—yet bitter doom for thee[2].

Of the justice meted to the daughter they say
nothing, and what could they say? Moreover
respecting Pentheus and respecting Cadmus—whose
conversion or submission, such as it is, they treat as
meritorious,—their opinions are their own, and not
commended, so far as appears, by the dramatist[3].

But indeed, so far as concerns Euripides and his
play, the question, whether the fates of Pentheus and
Agave, if inflicted as a divine punishment for sceptical
contumacy, would be just, is one which we need
not discuss, because, according to the play, their
fates are not so inflicted. The deity of the prologue
(if we should or may take his remarks as dramatic)
announces no such design, nor any design against
the King more definite than "proving upon him
and all Thebans the divinity" of Dionysus[4]. And
the "Dionysus" of the drama evidently has no such
plan, when he makes to Pentheus, unconditionally
and without any demand of religious submission,
his offer to bring the women back to their homes[5].
Indeed, to do him justice, we have no warrant from
the dramatist to suppose that he would have chosen
the path of assassination, though he takes it without

---

[1] *v.* 1200.   [2] *vv.* 1327–1328 (Way).
[3] As to Cadmus, see *vv.* 1330–1362.
[4] *v.* 47 f.   [5] *vv.* 802 ff.

scruple, when it appears conducive to the triumph of his religion. The design to poison Pentheus and betray him to the bacchants is formed, on the spur of the moment, before our eyes[1], as an expedient to forestall the possibility of his resorting to military force. It has not exactly the form or aspect which one would associate with the counsels of Providence.

However, such as it is, so, as we have seen, it is executed. Neither the mad exultation of Agave nor her sober laments raise directly the question, whether her destroyer is a personage human or superhuman. Of her laments, as the play once contained them, a part is lost,—though whether this is a loss to art, or even to the completeness of Euripides, is perhaps open to doubt. The remains of Pentheus, other than the head, are collected and brought home by Cadmus. There is external testimony[2] that, as the play was known and acted in antiquity, the mother, when the body had been put together, bewailed it in an elaborate and formal piece of rhetoric, "taking the limbs in her hands one after another, and expressing her sorrow in respect of each." This testimony is confirmed by our defective MS., which exhibits in one place[3] what looks like the preparation for such a speech, and in another place[4] what may be the beginning

---

[1] *vv.* 810 ff., *supra* p. 97.

[2] See text and commentaries at *v.* 1300 and at *v.* 1329.

[3] *v.* 1300.   Ἀγ.   ἦ πᾶν ἐν ἄρθροις συγκεκλῃμένον καλῶς;

[4] *v.* 1329.

of it.   At one of these places it has doubtless stood, and, as between the two, critics have differed in opinion.   For myself, if it be legitimate, I would gladly think that the uncertain indication of the MS. as to the place of this speech is a sign that it was variously placed in different texts ; from which, if such were the fact, one might fairly conclude that it was a recognized insertion, and not part of the work as it was left by the author.   A posthumous production is naturally open to such additions or variations, which are conspicuous (for example) in the *Iphigenia at Aulis*.   To judge the speech properly, we should see it ; but I can hardly suppose that it was dramatically appropriate, or anything better than an unfortunate concession to the lower sort of theatrical demand, going farther in this direction than any other example in the extant works of the poet,—a surmise which is not disproved by the special attention which the speech seems to have received from rhetorical students and expositors. It should be added however, that, in one sense, the *Bacchants* was certainly finished by the author, that is to say, he had composed the *finale*.   The scene or epilogue between Dionysus, Cadmus, and Agave, which follows the god's oration *ex machina*, is manifestly his, and there is nothing to suspect in the surviving fragment of the oration itself.

That the spectacle should be adorned with such an apparition and address—a divine epilogue answering to the divine prologue—is, according to the method of Euripides, a matter of course.   In the

injury of our copy[1], the entrance of the god has been
cut away, so that the precise manner of it cannot
be ascertained :—whether, that is to say, it was so
staged as to suggest a real scene, in which the
Lydian of the drama personates the deity, or whether
frankly as an impossible and theatrical exhibition,
with a figure suspended in the air and other like
accessories. The first way, in this play, would be
conceivable, since there is a human performer capable
of the function ; but analogy decidedly favours the
other, and so does the tone of the dialogue. Dionysus, when we find him, is addressing Cadmus, to
whom, in the usual way and with the usual frigidity,
he is revealing the sequel of his career according to
legendary prescription :—

> ...Thou to a serpent shalt be changed: thy wife
> Harmonia, Ares' child, whom thou didst wed
> When man, embruted shall to a snake be changed.
> Thou with thy wife shalt drive a wain of steers
> Leading barbaric hordes, Zeus' oracle saith,
> And many a city with thy countless host
> Shalt sack : but when they plunder Loxias' shrine,
> Then shall they get them bitter home-return.
> Thee and Harmonia shall Ares save,
> And stablish in the Blessèd Land your lives.
> This say I, of no mortal father born,
> Dionysus, but of Zeus[2].

So, very faithfully, Mr Way. From Professor Murray
the god gets a richer style—"griefs and wonders in
the winding years"..."she whom thou didst bring
Of old to be thy bride from Heaven afar"..."a wild

---

[1] *vv.* 1329–1330.   [2] *v.* 1330 ff. (Way 1331 ff.).

array of orient spears"..."back driven on stormy
ways and steep,"—and he is made to declare himself
"Son *confessed* of no man but of Zeus," a position
for which one would not easily find support in the
scene of Euripides. Not even Cadmus[1], though
doubtless a believer, makes any such acknowledgment to the deity of the machine, and Agave not
only treats him "almost with disdain[2]," but expressly
renounces, for herself, the practice of the triumphant
religion[3].

The revelations of Dionysus, regarded as an
appendix to the foregoing drama, are as futile as
they are dry. Between the world of Euripides and
that of mythology there is no possible continuity;
and the perfunctory recital of legends, here as in
other parallel situations, has inevitably the effect of
mockery. Cadmus forsooth is to become a snake,—
the Cadmus of this tragedy! Nor is it of any use
to tell us that he and his Harmonia—a personage
with whom the play has no concern—are to come
eventually, either as snakes or human beings, to the
Land of the Blest. The beauty of that picture, as
a tempering consolation for the horrors of Theban
story, is known to many readers in the lyrical version
of Matthew Arnold. If properly developed, and
linked to a play suitable in colour, it might well
serve, in the theatre, as a final repose for the
imagination. We may guess that before Euripides,

---

[1] It is Cadmus who responds to Dionysus in 1344–1348, not
Agave. So the MS., and Murray in his recent text.

[2] Murray.   [3] *v.* 1387 Βάκχαις δ' ἄλλαισι μέλοιεν.

perhaps by Aeschylus, it had been so used with sympathy and good effect. But in the mouth of this Dionysus, the meagre statement,

> Thee and Harmonia shall Ares save,
> And stablish in the Blessèd Land your lives,

rings as false as the rest; and we are not surprised, when Cadmus, after commenting bitterly on his immediate prospects, dismisses the promise of Paradise with a sneer: he is to be denied even the quiet of the dead![1]

The plain truth is that, apart from the mechanical requirements of the Athenian theatre and a popular audience, Dionysus, such as he appears in this epilogue, has no interest for Euripides or his reader. About Cadmus and Agave, and about other matters more important, such as the future of the Bacchic religion at Thebes and in Hellas, the drama itself foreshows us all that we want,—a sequel in which there is no place for human serpents. One question indeed we might like to put, but not to a Dionysus— whether anywhere, at Thebes or beyond, a suitable reward awaited the zeal of the Asiatic apostle.

The play, as we have it, concludes with the peculiar choric "tag"—found also in the *Alcestis*, *Medea*, *Andromache*, and *Helena*,—which describes "the event of this action" as a surprise: "That which was expected comes not to pass, and for what is not expected Heaven finds a way; and such is the end of this story[2]." As I have said elsewhere, I see

---

[1] *vv.* 1360 ff.   [2] *vv.* 1388 ff. πολλαὶ μορφαὶ κ.τ.λ.

no reason to suppose that this is not the genuine work of the poet, and authentic in each place where we find it.   It marks very well—and it was presumably so intended, used, and understood—the discordant, irrelevant, mythical *finale*, which Euripides, for obvious reasons, almost regularly appends to his realistic and anti-mythical plots.   So understood, it is perfectly appropriate, as we have just seen, to the *Bacchants*, the *finale* of which, with its absurd theophany, is not less inconsistent with the purport of the action than that of the *Andromache* or the *Medea*.   If the tag was appended to this posthumous tragedy by the exhibitors or actors, we may approve their intelligence and acquiesce in their judgement.

In the course of this survey, we have passed over, for the sake of clearness, certain portions of the play, as not affecting, directly at least or materially, our primary subject,—the poet's treatment of the supernatural.   Thus of the scene in which the apostle of Dionysus is brought before King Pentheus as a captive, and of the choric odes for the most part, we have taken little notice.   But since these are just the places where the preacher and sectaries are seen to most advantage, to leave these in the shade would be to ignore the sincerity and candour of the dramatist, and to disturb the balance of his work.

The *balance*—let us insist and observe.   It is not the way of Euripides to hold, as it were, a poetic

court, and deliver judgement on the persons and
transactions which he exhibits. It never can be the
way of those who seek first, as he did, to show men
and the world "as they are." It is not true that
characters, tendencies, movements can be classed as
good and bad. On the contrary, any strong and
marked disposition of mind will be good for some
purposes and bad for others. That, just that, will
be, humanly speaking, the final sentence upon it.
So it is with the religious enthusiasts of this tragedy.
Their unscrupulous cruelty is hideous. Their faith
in divine support, however genuine, is mixed in
the leader with fraud, and, in the assistant troupe,
with an abject and mischievous credulity. But for
all that, their creed is of a high and spiritual type,
their rites are pure and their morality exalted, and
they seek the conversion of the world with disin-
terested zeal and admirable courage.

Even the leader, detestable as upon the whole
he is, proves himself an ardent and brave devotee,
who, in the part of captive and martyr, confronts
the oppressor with a dignity which compels our
sympathy[1]. His mildness, candour, and trust in an
invisible protection contrast to great advantage with
the petulance, prejudice, and violence of the King.
Horace in a well-known passage, following probably
some Greek precedent, applies this scene as a Stoic
parable, to illustrate the serenity and independence
of the virtuous man, who, however threatened, has
always the power to die[2]. The comparison, though

[1] *vv.* 453 ff.   [2] Hor. *Epp.* I. 16. 73.

legitimate enough as such, cannot and need not be strictly pressed : we need not suppose Horace (or his authority) so to misunderstand Euripides, as to think that the prisoner of Pentheus, when he says

> The God himself will release me, whenever I will[1],

is contemplating a release by suicide. But the parable or comparison, though loose, is not without a bearing on the interpretation of Euripides. It does seem to imply that, in the scene of Euripides, the prisoner is presented for our admiration, and that his conduct is to be regarded as virtuous. And this, I think, is the natural impression, and seems to be, more or less, the general impression of readers.

Penth.	How is thy worship held, by night or day?
Dion.	Most oft by night; 'tis a majestic thing,
	The darkness.
Penth.	Ha! with women worshipping!
	'Tis craft and rottenness!
Dion.	By day no less
	Whoso will seek may find unholiness.
Penth.	Enough, thy doom is fixed....
Dion.	...What dire thing wilt thou do then?
Penth.	First shear that delicate curl that dangles there.

[He beckons to the soldiers who approach Dionysus.

Dion.	I have vowed it to my God; 'tis holy hair.

[The soldiers cut off the tress.

Penth.	Next yield me up thy staff!
Dion.	Raise thine own hand
	To take it. This is Dionysus' wand.

[Pentheus takes the staff.

Penth.	Last, I will hold thee prisoned here.
Dion.	My Lord
	God will unloose me when I speak the word[2].

---

[1] *v.* 498 λύσει μ' ὁ δαίμων αὐτός, ὅταν ἐγὼ θέλω.
[2] *vv.* 469 ff. (Murray).

485

It is natural to think, and readers do generally think, that this angelic behaviour, this patience, faith and courage, is conceived by the dramatist as genuinely virtuous and admirable. But surely, to view it so, we must suppose that the prisoner is in danger. If he is merely playing the martyr, if his talk of trust in God is a mockery, if he himself, as God, commands and is ready to use such weapons as fire and earthquake,—what is there to admire? I conceive that he really is in danger, that the King's denunciations of torture and death[1] are no idle threats, and that, were it not for the ascendancy which the man has acquired over the servants of Pentheus, and strengthens by his demeanour in the King's presence[2], he might at least have lain long in the lightless dungeon to which he is sent[3]. And I find this reading of the scene not only more interesting, but more obvious, than that which makes the captive omnipotent and his submission a merciless trick.

In the women of the Chorus, their character and opinions, and the estimate of them which the play should be taken to recommend, we have a branch of enquiry where we feel especially our lack of external information. Even for contemporaries, nay, even for the poet himself, their case may have been ambiguous. But we increase our difficulties gratuitously, if we assume that everywhere, or anywhere, they speak, directly and precisely, for Euripides.

---

[1] *vv.* 241, 356.
[2] *vv.* 434 ff., 504 ff.   [3] *v.* 510.

No dramatist has suffered more than he from the practice, never legitimate and always perilous, of construing dramatic language in this inartistic and arbitrary way. It is true that the Greek Chorus, being in some respects an adjunct to the drama rather than part of it, could be used as a mouth-piece more easily and less improperly than ordinary personages of the action. But it is not true of Euripides, that he was in the habit of identifying himself with the Chorus in particular; and I think it perfectly clear, that he does not mean to be represented, generally or at all, by the Chorus of the *Bacchants*. Their part throughout, including the choric odes, is strictly relevant to the drama, and there is nowhere any sign that they speak otherwise than properly for themselves. A large portion of their sentiments,— for example, their exultation, both before[1] and afterwards[2], over the horrible fate of Pentheus—is plainly not shared by the dramatist. This being so, we have no reason anywhere to hear his voice in what they are made to say. If they are consistent with themselves, if their feelings, doctrines, acts are natural or conceivable as a whole, the dramatist, as such, is quit of any further responsibility.

Nor again are we bound, or entitled, to seek any precise harmony between the Chorus and other personages in the play, not even those who may be counted, more or less, as upon their side. Their quality is different even from that of the master whom they serve. Moral elevation is more marked in

---

[1] *vv.* 977–996.   [2] *vv.* 1153–1164.

them than in him[1],—perhaps a distinction of sex ; and
he, perhaps as a man, is of a more ruthless temper.
We cannot say whether they, unprompted, would have
devised or executed his crimes against Pentheus, or
whether he would share their pity for the mother.
Much less, and almost nothing, have they in common
with Cadmus or Teiresias. Of the chasm—it is
more than a rift—which divides them from the
prophet, we have already spoken[2]. Between what
they preach as the religion of Dionysus, and what
Teiresias receives, there is hardly any resemblance
beyond the name.

It is this last point especially which should be
remembered, in considering the connexion and
bearing of the *Hymn to Holiness*[3]. This ode immediately follows the scene between Pentheus and
Teiresias, upon which, in the natural course, the
Chorus must be supposed to comment. If we realize
the dubious and embarrassing position in which the
missionaries are placed by the declaration of the
prophet, we shall not be surprised that their comment is in part obscure. It is equally impossible
that they should reject his support of their cause
and that they should pass without question his
astonishing glosses upon their doctrine. They pru-
dently do not name him, and direct open censure
only against Pentheus. But Teiresias is not less
in their thoughts, and much of what they say is
designed for him, either by way of agreement or of
dissent.

[1] *vv.* 370 ff.   [2] *Supra* pp. 48 ff.   [3] *vv.* 370 ff.

It is to meet the views of Apollo's prophet that they here dwell twice upon a topic which elsewhere they hardly touch, and plainly do not regard as vital to their religion,—the connexion of their God with the vine, the grape, and the gift of wine[1]. Teiresias makes this fundamental, and uses it, after his fashion, to couple Dionysus with Demeter, Goddess of the Earth and giver of food[2]. The Chorus, who otherwise ignore his harmonistic combinations, support him on this point to the extent—it is little enough —of praising " Him who amid wreaths and good cheer rules the happy hour, to whom belongs the dance inspired, the sound of laughter and pipe, and rest from care, when the grape-juice comes at the feast of gods, and merry men ivy-wreathed win sleep from the mantling bowl," and again, " the Son of Zeus, *who, though glad to make merry, yet loveth Peace, Peace that giveth store and children fair. Equally to rich and to less he grants delight of wine that bringeth no pain*[3]." Between these passages, and immediately before the latter, stands the emphatic reference to Macedonia, as the best seat for the true religion, which we have noted

---

[1] *vv.* 378 ff., 417 ff.   See *supra* p. 42.

[2] *vv.* 274 ff.

[3] *vv.* 417 ff.   ὁ δαίμων ὁ Διὸς παῖς
χαίρει μὲν θαλίαισιν,
φιλεῖ δ᾽ ὀλβοδότειραν Εἰ-
ρήναν, κουροτρόφον θεάν.
ἴσα δ᾽ ἔς τε τὸν ὄλβιον
τόν τε χείρονα δῶκ᾽ ἔχειν
οἴνου τέρψιν ἄλυπον.

before[1]. We remark that the women, if they praise
the cup, are firm for temperance,—no quarrelling, no
waste, no luxury. In this doubtless they speak as
women, and also perhaps as admirers of Macedonia.
That name does not indeed suggest temperance ; but
the drunken Macedonian of history is generally a
man of high rank. The force which, when the *Bacchants* was written, Macedonia was soon to put forth,
was never drawn from a people of sots ; and whatever
the sobriety of the men, the women, we may presume, did their best to maintain and strengthen it.
It is to "men" ($\dot{a}\nu\delta\rho\dot{a}\sigma\iota$[2]) that, in the first passage,
they assign the bowl ; nor is it clear that by "men"
they mean both sexes. In the repeated sarcasms of
Pentheus[3] the worshippers of Dionysus have good
reason to avoid the least appearance of a lax rule in
such matters for the woman.

To Teiresias again, and to his uncongenial
theology, the Chorus allude, when they deprecate
"that wisdom ($\tau\dot{o}$ $\sigma o\phi\dot{o}\nu$) which is no wisdom, nor
fit for the thoughts of a man[4]." In a short life, they
say, "he that pursues the great may miss the near,"
which is madness and mischievous. And to the same
vein they return in the conclusion, when they commend "the wisdom of keeping the heart and mind
from *men superfluous*" ($\pi\epsilon\rho\iota\sigma\sigma\hat{\omega}\nu$ $\phi\omega\tau\hat{\omega}\nu$), men who
exceed the mark. "What is held and used by the
many, the humbler sort," that, say they, is enough for

---

[1] p. 29.   [2] v. 385.
[3] vv. 221 ff., 260 ff.
[4] vv. 395 ff. $\tau\dot{o}$ $\sigma o\phi\dot{o}\nu$ δ' $o\dot{v}$ $\sigma o\phi\dot{\iota}a$ $\kappa.\tau.\lambda$.

them[1]. All this is irrelevant to the present issue between the preachers and Pentheus, whose crude notions of order and sense are as far as possible from excessive speculation. It is aimed obliquely at what is repugnant to them in the attitude of the prophet, at his ingenious conciliations of new and old, at his evasive subtleties and rational mythology, at the policy of a hierarchical tradition, to which all faiths are fundamentally indifferent, at the philosophy which disdains to fight against a doctrine when you can so easily explain it away! To a vital faith, plain hostility is less disagreeable than this. And best of all, say the women, is the simplicity of common folk, who are not too proud to believe what they can use.

How far Euripides, in his own mind, was ready to go with such religion, we have no means to determine, nor is it necessary for the appreciation of his play. Negatively, as against Delphi, such religion would probably please him well enough. He saw, at all events in Macedonia if never before, its beauties, its powers of spiritual energy, lovely imagination, passionate zeal. He saw also its moral and intellectual dangers, its hunger for miracle, its ferocious and sanctified hate. He saw these things and excellently painted them; and as a dramatist he is committed no further.

We cannot pass from this ode without touching, by way of curiosity, on the question whether, in the

---

[1] *vv.* 427 ff. σοφὰν δ' ἀπέχειν κ.τ.λ. Note here the coincidence, in the word φωτῶν, with the language of *v.* 401.

second strophe[1], the women should be understood
to express a special affection for the seats of the
worship of Aphrodite—Cyprus, Paphos, and (according to one explanation[2]) the Egyptian Delta with its
famous temple at Memphis. If they do, why do
they, and how is it proper to the situation? Nothing
of the sort occurs elsewhere, either in this ode or in
the play. It is characteristic of their zealotry, that
they show no care for any gods or rites but their
own. And of all deities in the Pantheon, Aphrodite, one would suppose, is the last whose patronage,
at this moment, they would desire to claim. That
their worship is in fact paid to the goddess of sex, is
the very charge which Pentheus repeatedly alleges as
the ground of his severities[3]; and this is the sole
connexion in which her name is found. Why then
should the women, who are repudiating this charge,
wish themselves at Paphos, and in what honest
sense could the wish be understood? It is no
explanation to say that with the worship of Aphrodite that of Dionysus was sometimes associated, as
it also mixed, truly or nominally, with most forms of
pagan polytheism. These women show no taste
for such alliances, and this is the very alliance
which they have here most reason to renounce or to
conceal. Do they intend a defiance to the King's
accusation, and mean that, *even* at Paphos, their
religion would be practised with purity? They do

[1] *vv.* 402 ff.

[2] See Tyrrell *ad loc.*, with whom so far I agree. See *infra*
p. 156.   [3] *vv.* 225, 459, etc.

not so explain themselves; and moreover, since they are alone[1], the defiance could have little point. Is it a self-betrayal, an inadvertent confession of weakness? In the situation, this is hardly conceivable. From every point of view, such language seems inappropriate and incomprehensible.

And further, they proceed in the next sentences to declare for "Pieria" (Macedonia) as the chosen home of their cult, and this distinctively, exclusively: "thither," they say, "thither would they be led, *there* may the bacchant duly celebrate her rites." To preface this by a cry of yearning for Paphos and Memphis appears something worse than irrelevant.

Some years ago I suggested, as an escape from these difficulties, that the sentences expressing affection for Aphrodite might be understood, with the help of inverted commas, as attributed by the women to the "mad men ill-advised," of whom they have just before spoken, so that, for themselves, they would be rejecting, not adopting, the sentiment. Several critics[2], while admitting the difficulty, have demurred to this solution, and I must admit that it is artificial and unsatisfactory. But the difficulty, and the need of a solution, I feel more strongly than ever.

And it should at all events be observed, that the

----

[1] Though the exit of Pentheus at *v.* 369 is not indicated, nor his re-entrance at *v.* 434, to keep him on the scene seems extremely unsuitable. See especially the reference to him in *v.* 373.

[2] E.g. Professor Norwood in *The Riddle of the Bacchae.*

accepted reading, which gives the sense " O, to be in Cyprus ! " (ἰκοίμαν ποτὶ Κύπρον), is not traditional but conjectural.   The MSS. give

ἰκοίμαν ποτὶ τὰν Κύπρον,
νᾶσον τᾶς Ἀφροδίτας,...

but this no one accepts.   It is unmetrical and un-grammatical.   The common remedy of omitting τὰν[1] is facile, but has no other merit.   For grammar it is not even sufficient, nor does it well account for the tradition.   And considering further that it produces no satisfactory meaning, surely upon the whole it is not entertainable.

The context, the whole position, demands, I think, that the speakers should disclaim any desire for Paphos ; and the only question open is whether and how this meaning can be recovered from the confessedly false tradition.   Now there is some reason to think that the name " Cyprus " comes from an annotator, not from the poet.   To the description "the isle of Aphrodite" (τὰν νᾶσον τᾶς Ἀφροδίτας), the addition of the name is, for poetry, needless and somewhat flat.   Omitting it, we are left with

ἰκοίμαν ποτὶ τὰν
νᾶσον τᾶς Ἀφροδίτας,

which, though not acceptable, does perhaps suggest an acceptable correction :

ἰκοίμαν—τί ποτ’ ἂν τὰν   [Κύπρον]
νᾶσον τᾶς Ἀφροδίτας,
ἵν’ οἱ θελξίφρονες νέμον-
ται θνατοῖσιν Ἔρωτες

[1] Elmsley.

Πάφον, ἄν¹ θ' ἑκατόστομοι
βαρβάρου ποταμοῦ ῥοαὶ
καρπίζουσιν ἄνομβροι;
οὗ δ' ἁ καλλιστευομένα
Πιερία μούσειος ἕδρα,
σεμνὰ κλιτὺς Ὀλύμπου,
ἐκεῖσ' ἄγε με, Βρόμιε, Βρόμιε, κ.τ.λ.

"I would seek—Ah, why should I seek the isle of Aphrodite, where in Paphos dwell the Loves that make weak the hearts of men, or why that isle², which the strange river with its countless mouths makes fertile without rain? Nay, where in Pieria rises majestic Olympus, noblest seat of song, thither would I be led"…

Here, from the first, the main thought is "O, to be in the land of true religion (Macedonia)!"—ἱκοί-μην τὴν Πιερίαν. Revolted both by the hardness of Pentheus and by the coldness of Teiresias, the women long to be with the simple folk of the North. But, recalling the accusations of the King³ and the dubious exculpation of the prophet⁴, remembering that Pentheus has asserted, and Teiresias not denied, an affinity in practice between the rites of Dionysus and those of Aphrodite, they are seized with anger, and burst into a disclaimer which is the more effective because it suspends and deflects the course of the period. But this irregularity, unless explained by punctuation, might easily defeat the reader; and ΙΚΟΙΜΑΝΤΙΠΟΤΑΝΤΑΝ, written so, might well be remodelled into the ΙΚΟΙΜΑΝΠΟΤΙΤΑΝ which we find. Of course this cannot be demonstrated, and, were I printing the

¹ Retaining in *v.* 421 ἴσα δ' ἔς, the reading of the MSS. This however is a separate question.
² ἄν τε (νᾶσον). The Delta (?).　　³ *vv.* 225, 236.　　⁴ *vv.* 314 ff.

text, I should merely mark the tradition as faulty. But the modern vulgate—ἱκοίμαν ποτὶ Κύπρον—I find inexplicable. Enough however, and perhaps too much, of a question which we may be content to leave unanswered.

The enthusiasm of the Chorus for Macedonia finds expression again in the next ode[1], where indeed they seem to imply that the religious destiny of the country was marked (like that of Parnassus according to Aeschylus[2]) by the most ancient names of its geography. For we can hardly doubt that when they speak of the river *Lydias* as "Father[3]," they have in mind their own Lydian origin ; and, in view of this, we should find a like import in the sentence before, which declares that their God "shall pass the *Axios* to bring (ἄξει) the whirling women of his dances." It is not likely that Euripides invented these expositions, which for him would have little attraction or meaning. He adopted them rather from what he was told in the country itself.

Except the *Hymn to Holiness*—where a certain obscurity is produced by the necessity of caution in criticism of Teiresias—the choric odes are clear in drift and, for the most part, even in detail. The finest, and the most dreadful, is that which fills the time while "the work of Dionysus" is being done upon the body and mind of King Pentheus[4]. It is a

---

[1] *vv.* 565 ff.   [2] See *Eum.* 11 with my note there.

[3] *v.* 571.   The arrangement of this passage, which is adopted by Murray from Wilamowitz, seems the best.

[4] *vv.* 862 ff. ἆρ' ἐν παννυχίοις κ.τ.λ.

passionate outpouring of hope and trust, punctuated
with a terrible refrain of victorious exultation, which
reminds us of passages in the *Psalms*. Indeed the
whole piece, though remote from us in form, in
substance resembles exactly the most familiar types
of religious composition :—the rescued believer
compared to a fawn that has escaped from the snare
into happy pastures[1],—the strength of Heaven slow
but sure[2],—the air of simplicity (" How little it costs
to believe !"[3]) combined with a staggering confidence
(dissent is "madness," and belief is obedience to
"the law"[4]),—the world a sea and the church a
haven[5],—all is in the typical strain of popular faith,
the quintessence of its strength and beauty. That
all this exalted feeling is devoted, for the moment,
to the praise of a perfidious assassination,—this too
belongs to the type. Doubtless the Te Deum for
the massacre of St Bartholomew was sung with
ardour, and the prayers which accompanied the
slaying of Sharp were more than commonly
fervent.

From a dramatic point of view, in distinction of
character and essential relation to the plot, the
Chorus in the *Bacchants* is an uncommonly successful
attempt to naturalize this accidental and precarious
form of art. There is real cause for their presence,
and true propriety in the expression of their feelings
by dance and responsive song. There remains
indeed a note of conventional fiction in the im-

---

[1] *vv.* 866 ff.   [2] *vv.* 882 ff.   [3] *vv.* 893 ff.
[4] *vv.* 887, 891.   [5] *vv.* 902 ff.

munity with which, in spite of threats[1], these loud and voluble disturbers of the peace must, from theatrical necessity, be permitted to exercise their freedom in the teeth of the imperious oppressor. But this is a trifle compared with the objections to which the average Chorus is liable. Served as he is, Pentheus finds it more than enough to deal with the principal, and the case of the subordinates may well be supposed to stand over.

We have now touched summarily, but for the present purpose sufficiently, upon those parts of the play which do not directly concern our question, and, returning to that, may draw to a conclusion. Comparing the *Bacchants* with other extant works of Euripides, what we should find new in it is neither the tone and method of the play, nor the opinions, so far as any opinions are implied, of the author. The range of imagination, the pitch of the characters, are the same as elsewhere, realistic, limited by observation and experience. The conventional forms of Athenian tragedy are used exactly as he had used them before. What is new and unique, not only in Euripides, but in the classical literature, as we possess it, of ancient Hellas, is the thing, the human phenomenon, observed and depicted, which is, in one word, *faith*, or a faith,—religion as we mostly now conceive it, exclusive in belief and universal in claim, enthusiastic, intolerant, and eager to conquer the world. To us the phenomenon has long been familiar; but we gather from the play that in

[1] *vv.* 511 ff.

Hellas it was hardly to be found, or at all events that Euripides, when he went out of Hellas, saw for the first time its genuine traits.

What he reports of it, if translated into mere prose, would seem to be this. It is a spirit which appeals chiefly to simple folk ; it is more congenial to women than to men, though a man possessed by it may gain, especially over and through women, an almost unlimited influence. It is rapidly infectious. It is highly dangerous to political and hierarchical authority, thrives by repression, and, if intemperately handled, may convulse and even destroy society ; but by temporizing, compromise, and the appearance of concession it may be weakened, absorbed, and even entirely dissipated. Though likely to breed disorder, it is not, in its essence, unfavourable to virtue, but, on the contrary, elevates and stimulates it. Of certain virtues it is especially productive, as of courage, both to suffer and to act. It bestows upon the faithful an exquisite happiness, a supreme sense of harmony and joy, so that, in comparison with it, all things seem light and of no importance. It is credulous, rich in imagination, and averse from control,—indifferent therefore or hostile to science and to rational speculation, but open to fraud and easily roused to frenzy. Its love is ardent, its hatred furious,—a hatred which can obliterate all other feelings, and, in regard to an enemy of the faith, can even extinguish every sentiment of honour and humanity.

And we may agree that he has seen far and said well.

NOTES ON THE *BACCHANTS*.

I ADD here remarks on a few passages which I have not had occasion to touch.

v. 506 οὐκ οἶσθ᾽ ὅτι ζῇς, οὐδ᾽ ὁρᾷς, οὔθ᾽ ὅστις εἶ.

This verse, though immensely emended, seems to me quite sound. Literally, "Thou know'st not what thy life is, nor seest, nor what thou art." In English this is awkward, because *nor...nor*, having no connexion, embarrass the ear. But in Greek, where the forms are different (οὐδέ...οὔτε) and cannot be connected, no such objection arises : οὐδ᾽ ὁρᾷς relates to οὐκ οἶσθα, but οὔθ᾽ ὅστις εἶ to ὅτι ζῇς. In smoother sequence the sentence would be οὐκ οἶσθα οὐδὲ ὁρᾷς οὔθ᾽ ὅτι ζῇς οὔθ᾽ ὅστις εἶ. The slight disturbance seems natural to an angry speaker.

vv. 661 ff.

    Ἄγγ.   ἥκω Κιθαιρῶν᾽ ἐκλιπών, ἵν᾽ οὔποτε...
             [λευκῆς χιόνος ἀνεῖσαν εὐαγεῖς βολαί.]
    Πε.   ἥκεις δὲ ποίαν προστιθεὶς σπουδὴν λόγου;

"Versum fictum ad aposiopesin tegendam censet Verrall : cf. *I. T.* 253 " (Murray, *ad loc.*). Compare also *Bacch.* 1027 f. ὥς σε στενάζω, δοῦλος ὢν μέν, ἀλλ᾽ ὅμως. [χρηστοῖσι δούλοις ξυμφορὰ τὰ δεσποτῶν], where, as all agree, a verse from the *Medea* has been imported to fill up a construction (ἀλλ᾽ ὅμως) which is really complete, though some reader did not understand it. And so also in other places.

V. E.   11

" I come from Cithaeron where never...*do the snow-
showers cease.*" Were this true (though Euripides
and all Athenians must have known that it was not),
it would be irrelevant here. The story, which is
laid in summer, has nothing to do with snow. The
genuine verse, if any there was, is lost. The sense
required is shown by the question of Pentheus:
"And *what* is the news which you make so urgent?"
The man must have shown or implied urgency, as
thus: " I come from Cithaeron, where never...were
such things seen before as I have to tell!" But
why then suppose any loss? Wild and breathless,
the herdsman would naturally finish his sentence by
gesture, throwing up his hands, or the like. For
want of efficient punctuation and stage-directions, this
baffled an ancient editor, who borrowed from somewhere a verse (really referring, as we may suppose, to
Cithaeron, and describing some particular occasion
in winter) to fill the supposed gap. The borrower
may be responsible for the unusual metre (ἀνεῖσαν
χιόνος Dindorf), though we need not think so. I
find this a clear and interesting specimen of a process which, in our copies, has doubtless gone farther
than we can trace it. If the *Medea* had been lost,
who would have suspected *Bacch.* 1028?

vv. 753–757

> ...ἐπεσπεσοῦσαι πάντ᾽ ἄνω τε καὶ κάτω
> διέφερον· ἥρπαζον μὲν ἐκ δόμων τέκνα,
> ὁπόσα δ᾽ ἐπ᾽ ὤμοις ἔθεσαν οὐ δεσμῶν ὕπο
> προσείχετ᾽ οὐδ᾽ ἔπιπτεν ἐς μέλαν πέδον,
> οὐ χαλκός, οὐ σίδηρος.

See Sandys' note: ὁπόσα, as he suggests, includes
the τέκνα, and we need not suppose the text defective. The full form would be ἥρπαζον μὲν ἐκ
δόμων τέκνα, ἥρπαζον δὲ καὶ ἄλλα, καὶ ἐπ' ὤμοις
ἔθεσαν· ὁπόσα δ' ἔθεσαν, οὐ δεσμῶν ὕπο.... The
compression of this, by leap from point to point, is
surely not surprising, but proper to a wildly excited
narrator. By "not bronze, not iron" is meant that
even heavy things of metal, utensils, weapons, etc.,
were so snatched up and carried. This also, with
deference to those who feel difficulty, I find natural
and simple.

THE FIRST HOMER[1].

THE discussion of Homer flows on, a noble stream, broadening and deepening with the accession of tributaries from prehistoric archæology and other sources. We admire the spectacle, but are not without apprehension that the volume may obliterate the channel, and that, like Father Thames in *The Critic*, the river may need a reminder to keep "between his banks."

In general, the very last thing that we get from disputants on either side is an exact construction and estimation of what, truly or falsely, is recorded about the history of Homer. The tradition, such as it is, is hardly ever even correctly represented. The most punctilious of scholars (Grote, for example) are in this matter not to be trusted. It is the internal evidence which, on both sides, furnishes the main artillery; the tradition, when it gets a turn, is treated with little respect, and, what is less justifiable, is construed with little attention.

It is not surprising if, in these conditions, we make little progress towards agreement. Internal

---

[1] Reprinted (by permission), with modifications, from *The Quarterly Review* of July, 1908.

evidence about the history of a book, if not controlled
by record, is liable to infinitely elastic interpretation.
From a given phenomenon, such as a discrepancy in
the narrative or an inconsistency of manners, different
conclusions will be drawn with equal legitimacy,
according to the circumstances of the time at which
we know, or may suppose, the composition to have
been executed. If these circumstances may be
placed anywhere in the course of some three or four
centuries at least, about which we know almost
nothing except that they were a time of profound
changes—and this is, in effect, the licence which we
are apt to assume in discussing the problem of
Homer,—how can we expect that we shall produce
any mutual impression? But, before we accept these
conditions of debate, we should exhaust, by the most
scrupulous construction, the possibilities of such
external testimony as may exist. We cannot but
think that the ancient tradition about the origin of
Homer suffers unfairly from certain prepossessions,
which all would disclaim, but which are more easily
disclaimed than abandoned.

For us modern readers it is scarcely possible,
whatever we may say and however we may try, not
to take the name " Homer " as meaning, *prima facie*
and presumptively, a book consisting of the *Iliad*
and the *Odyssey* as we possess them, or the author
of such a book. Nothing else of importance bearing
that name has been extant since the revival of
learning; and of the far larger mass which originally
bore it, and which, if we believe what we are told,

was extant long after the Christian era, nothing of importance, except the *Iliad* and *Odyssey*, was accepted as "Homer" in the learned ages of antiquity—that is to say, from about 300 B.C.—or, after that date, was commonly read or even studied. It is natural therefore, plausible, and inevitable, that we should not only use "Homer" as a compendious expression for these two poems, but, if we raise the question of authorship and origin, should put it to ourselves in the form "What was the origin of the *Iliad*, or of the *Odyssey*?", assuming these as the starting-point for discussion.

Nevertheless we must not so begin if we would study the tradition fairly. If we do, we practically forestall some of the most important conclusions which we have to verify. As a matter of record, and apart from inference or hypothesis, this "Homer" of ours, comprising the two poems in their extant form, appears as an artificial product of scholarship, the result of a critical process; and the validity of this process is precisely one of the principal things which we have to consider. Nor must we presume, before proof, that the *Iliad* or the *Odyssey*, meaning the poems as we have them, had either of them an independent beginning at all. Upon the record, they first appear neither as constituting Homer nor as independent, but as parts of Homer. Whether, and in what shape, they existed before, is matter for inference and investigation, but cannot be investigated to much purpose if we begin by assuming an answer.

The history of "Homer" as a definite book, with a fixed extent and content, begins, upon tradition, in the middle or latter part of the sixth century B.C., and at Athens. Then and there, but not before, nor at that time elsewhere, we have testimony to the existence of a definite book or collection commonly entitled "the Poetry of Homer." Possibly it bore also, as we shall see, another and a better title, but this one it certainly bore. That it had a definite extent and content is proved by the fact that it was the subject, like our Bible, of official sanction and enactment. There were precise orders about the recitation and study of it, a thing impossible unless the book or corpus was itself determined.

Of any earlier "Homer" existing in these conditions, or any conditions of fixity, we know nothing from testimony; and what we do know about political and literary conditions generally is altogether against the presumption of such a fixture. It depends, not upon the use of writing—a matter which in some stages of this discussion has played too large a part—but upon the practice of reading. It is by readers, and the recognition of readers, that fixed and definite books are protected. We shall not here prove, but it will hardly be disputed, that a body of readers existed nowhere in Greece before the sixth century. At that time, and in one particular State, the nucleus or foundation of such a body was formed, by a revolution in the method of education not less momentous than any movement in history. The formation or collection of "Homer" is said—and we believe it—to have been a part or instrument of this movement. The book, or perhaps we should rather say, the library, was adopted, and (we are told) was arranged, as the material of improved education at Athens.

The movement itself, the novel development of education, and its immeasurable importance, would be known by inference, even if it were not recorded. The whole history of Athens and of Hellas is but the sequel and effect of it. The amazing and unprecedented success of the democratic experiment, in itself no novelty, which was made at Athens in the last years of the sixth century, is explicable by nothing else than a sudden and incomparable increase in the diffusion of intelligence and intellectual culture. Literature tells the same story, upon which it is needless to insist. It would be absurd, of course, to suppose a high standard of acquirement, or to think that in the sixth century, or in the fifth, Athens was, in the later and modern sense, a place of learning. But all things are measured by comparison. The population which embraced and realized the democratic conception of Cleisthenes, and achieved, as a people, in every department of life, the triumphs which Athens achieved between the birth of Æschylus and the death of Euripides, however far from erudition, had plainly an immense superiority of mind in comparison with their predecessors and contemporaries.

This lead, with all its consequences, the Athenians themselves, looking back upon their

great age from the less advantageous position of
the fourth century B.C., ascribed wholly to the better
education which, by the efforts and encouragement
of their successive governments, they adopted and
established in the sixth. Such is the language of
the statesman Lycurgus, in an eloquent passage of
his extant speech (§§ 102–107). He treats it not as
matter of theory, but of notoriety, that the whole
Athenian triumph, the repulse of the Persians,
Marathon and Salamis, the Athenian hegemony and
the Athenian empire, had a principal cause in the
studies which, in the previous generation, they as a
people had adopted and espoused. It all came, he
says in the plainest terms, from their familiarity with
certain literature, to wit, "the Poetry of Homer."

Nor is there reason to doubt that, under proper
interpretation, this view was as completely true as
any such simplification of history can be. The
success of Athens had many contributory causes or
occasions ; but the main cause clearly was that, in an
age when not even the elements of literary education
were yet diffused among any of the peoples with
whom Athens had to contend, those elements at
least, by energetic public efforts, were diffused in
Attica. Before the close of the sixth century the
Athenians were, what as yet no other people was,
generally familiarized with at least one great book,
and had the advantage of this mental stimulus.

We should remark, indeed, that it is not upon
the mental stimulus that the Athenian statesman
himself insists, but rather upon the moral instruction

which the Athenians derived from their studies. It
was by familiarity, he says, with the patriotic sentiments to be found in the Poetry of Homer that
the Athenians became eminent in patriotism ; and
similarly, we are doubtless to assume, in other
virtues there exemplified or inculcated. But, though
we need not deny this moral effect, and may well
suppose that, upon the whole, Homer was in this
way a means of elevation to a people starting from
the general level of Greece in the time of Pisistratus,
it is nevertheless, we think, plain, that, in insisting
exclusively upon this side of the matter, Lycurgus,
and the Athenian public opinion to which he appeals,
overlooked much, perhaps most, of the truth. The
mental advantage, immense when it was a singular
privilege, of being generally trained in the compre-
hension and exposition of some good literature, had
surely more to do with making the Athenians into
the leaders of Hellas, than the fact that more men
there than in the other cities could repeat the lines
in which Hector commends the sacrifice of self to
country. A not dissimilar question arises upon the
effects of the Protestant movement and the consequent diffusion of training in the Bible. Apart from
the moral lessons, this education enlarged the class
of readers, who discussed their reading, and who
thus became better thinkers and more competent
generally in all the business of life. The example of
Scotland is notorious. And similar, we may suppose,
mutatis mutandis, was the effect of the Athenian
book, simply as a book, widely taught in Athens at

a time when as yet no such teaching was common elsewhere.

By Lycurgus this whole educational movement, and the adoption of Homer as the basis of it, is attributed to the Athenians as a people, without distinction of persons or of any particular authority. By others (the testimonies are familiar and we need not cite them) the movement, and the operations on the book "Homer" connected with it, are attributed, now to one, now to another of the persons powerful at Athens in the age when the thing was done—to the sons of Pisistratus, especially Hipparchus, to Pisistratus himself, and even to Solon. There is no need to reject or suspect any of these ascriptions, which have presumably the same measure of truth as the connecting of the Reformation now with one and now with another of the princes or statesmen of the sixteenth century. Hipparchus in particular is described (by no late or contemptible author, but by an Athenian whose work could be attributed to Plato) as extraordinarily and almost fanatically active in the diffusion of intellectual culture (*Hipparchus*, p. 228 B). That the movement was zealously supported by authority may safely be assumed from its rapid success ; and that we know little or nothing of the methods, probably very simple, is no reason for doubting the fact of official activity. And as to the making or collection of the educational book, "the Poetry of Homer," it cannot possibly have been completed, as we shall see, in any very short time, and may well have extended over the forty or fifty years (say 570–520 B.C.), which would include all the names traditionally associated with it.

By both the above-mentioned witnesses, and elsewhere, stress is laid upon one particular ordinance respecting the national book or literature, namely, that it should be regularly and publicly recited at the great festival of the Panathenæa, celebrated in every fourth year. The emphasis laid upon this, as a proof of respect, is very proper; but we should observe, as having an important bearing upon the question, what was the nature and content of the collection, that neither in those places nor (we believe) anywhere is it suggested that this occasional recitation was the principal use or design to which the books were applied. The practical effect of such performances could hardly be anything; and we should attribute nonsense to Lycurgus, if we supposed him to ascribe the greatness of Athens to the fact that an Athenian might hear Homer for a few hours, upon perhaps some ten or a dozen occasions in the course of his life. But this is not said or suggested. In Lycurgus, the whole context, and in particular the comparison which he makes between the Athenian use of Homer and the instruction of the Spartans, shows that by the "hearing" of Homer he means the habitual hearing, by all in the course of education, and by many subsequently in recitation and reading aloud. He speaks of "hearers" where we should say "readers," because instruction and literary communication generally, in

the times of which he speaks, was mainly oral. In
the Platonic treatise, and what is there said about
Hipparchus, the reference to education, and to
Homer as an instrument for that purpose, is
explicit.

From this Athenian Homer of the sixth century
our extant Homer is unquestionably derived, and
probably with little or no other change than common
accidents of transcription. Directly or indirectly,
the Athenian texts, diffused from Athens as the
source and ruler of learning—until, as was said, all
Greece, as Athens first, had been "educated by
Homer"—were the principal, and, it would seem,
the only important factors in forming the texts which
we read to-day.

What then was the determinate book or collection, which at Athens, in the sixth century, was
called "the Poetry of Homer"? That it consisted
of the *Iliad* and *Odyssey*, or that these poems had in
it any distinctive mark, there is, so far as we know,
no evidence whatever. There is some direct
evidence, and much indirect, for the opinion (no
new one, though not established) that the Athenian
"Poetry of Homer" was substantially identical with
what is otherwise known as the "Cyclus," the
"Circle" or "Round"—either with the whole of it
or with some part. This was a sort of history, in
epic verse, beginning with the beginning of the
world, and carried down through the heroic age of
the Theban and the Trojan wars until the end of
the latter and the return of the Greeks. It is known

to us mainly by a partial abstract, dating probably from the fifth century A.D., when it is said to have been still extant. It was at all events extant and notorious, though little read, in the flourishing ages of ancient learning. It is described as a narrative continuous from beginning to end. The *Iliad* and the *Odyssey*, such apparently as we possess them, were parts of the story, standing in their proper places. The exact dimensions of the whole are uncertain, but were certainly vast, much larger than the two extant poems put together. We are positively told[1] that the whole, the "Circle" as such, was regarded as the work of Homer by "the ancients," a statement which can mean nothing but that it was so regarded in the sixth century; for before that time there was no history of literature or established opinion about such matters, and for all later times we have proof that part, and most, of the "Circle" was not generally accepted as "Homer." Moreover, in the sixth century, when the legends were still regarded as matter of fact, the compilation of such a poetical history, if there were material for it, would command interest, whereas in later times it would have been futile and out of date. In short, unless the Athenian Homer of the sixth century was the "Cycle," we cannot conceive how the Cycle came into existence, or was preserved, or got, as it did, the name of "Homer."

---

[1] Suidas. The statement, like every part of the tradition about Homer, has been explained away, but, as we think, without reason.

Further, this supposition at once explains and accords with the tradition, that the Athenians of that age not merely adopted or compiled, but "arranged" their collection. This detail does not appear in the authorities chronologically nearest. Neither Lycurgus, for instance, nor the Platonic " Hipparchus " says so ; they speak merely of adoption and collection. But their language in no way excludes an arrangement or redaction, as alleged by others, principally by Cicero in the first century B.C., and by Pausanias in the second century A.D. These statements, that Pisistratus arranged the poetry of Homer, have been treated by some, in the modern controversy, with a kind and degree of scepticism which, if applied impartially, would make astonishing holes in ancient history, chiefly because they have been supposed (quite unnecessarily and erroneously, as we hold) to apply directly and specially to the *Iliad* and *Odyssey*, and, if accepted, to prejudice the question how those two poems were composed. But the statements relate to "the poems" or "poetry of Homer," by which, if they are well-founded and descend from the sixth century, must be meant what was then so accounted and called. We see no reason to doubt (though the wildest expedients have been adopted in order to avoid the conclusion) that they do descend from the natural source, the Athenian antiquaries of the fourth and third centuries, who were in touch, by a solid train of literary tradition, with the time of the alleged arrangement.

In some sense, indeed, in order to be made, the Cycle must have existed earlier, since it is never said that the Athenians actually composed their Homer. But the situation and the operation are not hard to conceive in a natural way. We can readily understand and explain them up to, or rather down from, a certain point. The material was poetry, in the conventional epic style, which had been composed, and hitherto diffused, by professional reciters or story-tellers, principally, it would seem, in Ionic Asia. The subjects were taken from a common stock of popular and more or less harmonious legend. If we assume the creation of some specially successful and authoritative poem—an *Iliad* or a *Thebaid*—embodying a part of the story, the production of other poems closely related to it, prefaces, continuations, and supplementary incidents, would be the natural course of things in the circumstances, the natural effect of a double desire in the story-tellers to give their audiences something novel yet easily intelligible. Such a process, given the assumed nucleus or nuclei, would produce a mass of poems tending to constitute, though not actually constituting, such a history as the Cycle was. If they were collected, it would not be difficult, by selection, some correction, adaptation, and a little composing of connexions and completions, to make up a total having as much consistency (far from perfect) as the Cycle seems to have had. But, for the actual production of the history, the arrangement or redaction would be an indispensable factor. It could not actually come into existence as a complete thing, and much less could it be preserved, under conditions conceivable (to say nothing of evidence) in the seventh century or earlier. The Athenian educational movement supplied, it appears, what was requisite for the production, and the public sanction of Athens what was requisite for the preservation.

All this process, however, assumes, as a starting-point, the authoritative and stimulating nucleus or nuclei; it assumes, for the Trojan part of the Cycle, the existence first of something like an *Iliad* and something like an *Odyssey*. Assuredly neither of these poems, such as they now are, could be produced, by such operations as are attributed or attributable to Pisistratus, out of pieces having originally no other connexion than a general agreement in the story and a similar conventional style. In both, the artistic unity, the ruling conception, is far too strong for this. But, let us once more observe, the Greek authorities do not say, though they are frequently discussed and criticized as if they did, that Pisistratus "arranged the *Iliad*" or "the *Odyssey*." The thing arranged, and in a sense constructed, by the Athenians was "the Poetry of Homer," by which we at all events understand the "Cycle," and, with this understanding, have no difficulty in accepting the tradition. It is perfectly consistent with the tradition to suppose that the *Iliad* was adopted, as a part or a chapter in the Cycle, exactly as it previously existed and was originally created by a single author. Whether this was so, or was not, must be determined not by the tradition, but by the internal evidence of the poem.

But, before we turn to this, let us say a word or two more, first of the Cycle and its title or titles, and then of the critical process which evolved from it the later and modern conception of "Homer" as consisting of the *Iliad* and the *Odyssey*. The poetry out of which the Cycle was made seems to have been generally recited and circulated, all of it, as anonymous. In the absence of libraries, histories, biographies, and scholarship, it is likely that the audiences of the reciters were little interested in the question of authorship. If any name was given, Homer, author probably of some determinant nucleus, an *Iliad* or *Thebaid*, had the credit of all. The collection, therefore, as a whole, bore his name, at all events in popular parlance, as "the Poetry of Homer." But we must not presume that the collectors either believed in the single authorship of the collection, or even warranted the name.

For anything that appears to the contrary, the appellation "cycle" or "circle" may be as old as the thing; and, though this is not generally supposed, we think it probable, for this reason. The attempts to explain the name "circle" from the content or form of the work appear to us altogether unsatisfactory. A thing is not "circular" because it is large, or full, or compact, compendious, complete. Such applications of the name are cited, but can be explained only by false analogy, from resemblance, in the points noted, to something which was called "circle" for some better and proper reason. Such a reason, for the Athenian collection, exists, not in the book itself, but in the purposes for which it was used and intended. It was to be taught and to be studied as a course of reading; and the course, we presume, when finished, was to be begun again. It was "the circle" in which study was to revolve. And similarly perhaps with the recitation at the Panathenæa. More than one of our authorities, in mentioning this, specifies that the recitation was "by way of resumption," one recitation beginning where the last ended. This detail, otherwise unimportant, is essential if the ordinance originally referred to the Cycle, of which only a small part could possibly be given upon a single occasion. Here also the proceeding was to be "circular"; successive parts were to be taken, until all had been taken, and then *da capo*. Such, we suppose, may have been the original design.

But neither these uses of the Cycle, nor the ascription to Homer, could long survive the effects, infinitely greater than can have been foreseen, of the educational movement. The literature, which, under the new stimulus, was produced at Athens in a single century, was alone sufficient to exclude from general notice, by competition, so vast a body of antique story. And criticism, even the most rudimentary, as soon as it existed, must demur to the attribution of all to a single authorship. In Herodotus, about a century after Hipparchus, we find that the cutting down has already gone far. The allusions of Herodotus to the subject are just what we might expect

them to be, if, *prima facie* and apart from criticism,
" Homer" was the Cycle.   He gives, just incident-
ally, a reason why the "Cypria" (part of the Trojan
story in the Cycle) should not be reckoned as
Homer's—namely, a disagreement with the *Iliad*.
Why it might be, he does not think necessary to
specify.   He speaks as if it *was* in "Homer," as
" Titus Andronicus" or " Henry VI." is in "Shakespeare."   Already, for Herodotus, the *Thebaid* itself
(or part of it) is doubtful " Homer"; and, in short,
we are well on the way to the point at which common
opinion stopped—that the *Iliad* and *Odyssey* only,
or almost only, are " Homer."   It is noticeable that
Herodotus pretends to no external information about
authorship ; and it is, to say the least, doubtful
whether any trustworthy discoveries of that kind
were made later.   No such supposition is needed to
explain the result.   The *Iliad* and the *Odyssey* were
left to Homer because they were the best parts of
his putative work.   No more was left to him, because
this was quite enough to assign to one man.   Rejection went no further (though some wished to go
further and divide the two poems) because the two
together did not seem clearly too much.

The next step, as might be expected, was to
distribute the rejected mass among supposed authors.
This we need not and cannot here follow out.   The
attributions are extremely suspicious, for reasons
which have often been stated.   The very names of
the alleged poets are not mentioned, none of them,
we believe, in any extant work of the fifth century,

when the poetry afterwards assigned to them was still popular. This may be explicable, but it is odd. The assignations vary, and were never generally established. We are probably best advised if we follow the more cautious critics of antiquity, and treat as anonymous all parts of the Cycle which we do not choose to call " Homer."

Such, in very brief and summary statement, is the tradition as we understand it. And now to the main question. When the Cycle was collected, arranged, and made up, what, if anything, was done to the *Iliad*, or to the *Odyssey*? Possibly nothing, or nothing of importance. So say the "defenders of unity"; and the tradition proves nothing to the contrary. If we hold otherwise, as most at present do, it is because the poems, both of them, or at all events the *Iliad*, exhibit a profusion of peculiarities for which, as we think, nothing will fairly account except an artificial and rather violent process designed to accommodate them, as parts, to such a quasi-historical compilation as the Cycle was.

We take an instance from the *Iliad*, a familiar instance, though we shall state it partly in our own way. The Greeks, for want of Achilles, are defeated and driven to their ships, to which the Trojans are actually beginning to set fire. At this crisis Patroclus persuades Achilles to let him lead the Myrmidons to the rescue. The scene is a turning-point in the story, and the narration of it vivid and unforgettable. We proceed. Patroclus, after some triumphs, is slain, and the armour of Achilles, which he wore, is lost. To replace it, Thetis obtains new armour from Hephæstus, to whom, in making her request, she naturally recounts the loss and the cause of it, the sending forth of Patroclus by Achilles (*Iliad*, xviii. 446). But to our surprise she relates this, not as we were shown it before, but with utterly different circumstances. According to her, the Greeks were beleaguered, and so hard pressed that they could not go out or sally from their camp. Thereupon certain elders approached Achilles with entreaties and gifts. He refused to give aid himself, but armed Patroclus and sent him with a strong force to the war. The two accounts are manifestly not discrepant merely, but absolutely different in conception. Both are clear; both give effective situations; on the one side the extreme crisis of firing the ships, the entreaty of Patroclus, and the sudden rush to the rescue; on the other side the beleaguerment and the solemn embassy. In either way the thing might well happen, but by no possibility in both at once.

Now, if the " Making of the Armour " was designed as a sequel to the " Sending of Patroclus " —as of course it was if our *Iliad* was shaped as we have it by one author—why do they not agree? It is surely idle to plead negligence or a lapse of memory. Lapses are common, but not of this magnitude or kind. Why should the narrator forget completely a scene which no reader can forget, a principal moment in his story? Why should he reconstruct it? What put into his head the new scene and the impossible embassy? Nor can it be a case of interpolation. The second account is no loose or inaccurate or garbled version of the first, but a complete and self-consistent reconstruction, with new circumstances and a different purpose. Nor does it help at all merely to make a distinction of authors, and assign the " Making of the Armour" to a new hand. If the new hand meant his work for a continuation of the other's, he would have told the previous incident as he found it. He would be even less likely to reconstruct the scene than the original narrator, because more conscious of his obligations as a continuator.

Twist the matter as we may, the obvious and natural supposition is, that the "Making of the Armour" was composed by some one who had before him, or rather behind him, the "Sending of Patroclus" described as he describes it. The "Making of the Armour" should be part of an *Iliad* in which the "Sending of Patroclus" was told according to the "embassy-version" (so to name it), and not, as in the extant book, according to the "fire-version." And the question is, here and repeatedly elsewhere, when, by whom, and above all why, was a compound made, which takes the "Sending" from one version and the "Making of the Armour" from another, and combines them without reconciling.

Another example, recurring throughout the work, is the ever-changing aspect of the Greek camp, now not fortified, or fortified at most with a ditch, now with a rampart hastily run up in consequence of the defection of Achilles, and now again with a wall so solid as to rival that of Troy—the three pictures not successive and connected by explanation, but assumed and dropped and reassumed with tacit indifference. Neither for one composer nor for a plurality of composers is such treatment natural or (to us) explicable, if the composer or composers were free to design, and actuated only by the motives of an artist.

The more conscious we are of the unity of the work and the dominance of one general conception, and the more we are convinced that all parts of the actual story (with perhaps some trifling exceptions) must have been designed as parts of a story closely similar, the more puzzling is their imperfect adaptation. Who was the composer, and what can have been his motives, who took these freedoms with his materials, and took no more ?

Now the alleged Athenian collection and arrangement of Homer afford an answer, so suitable to the internal evidence that, if we had not such a tradition, we must have invented it. That is to say, we can, quite probably, suppose the Athenian redactors to find this part of the Cycle—the *Iliad*—in such a condition or conditions that, in their situation and with their purposes, they would make of it what we have.

Take the case of the double " Sending of Patroclus.'' Be it supposed that (never mind when, in the tenth century B.C., or the thirteenth, if any one pleases) Homer composed the *Iliad* with what we called the "fire-version" of this incident, the version of it which is first narrated in our book. Let us call this *Iliad* A. Might it not presently occur to a reciter-poet, stimulated by the example, that the "embassy-version" would also be a good one, giving a different opportunity? But the "embassy-version" requires a fortified camp, in which the Greeks are beleaguered and unable to sally, but otherwise act at leisure. Accordingly our second composer (B) fortifies the camp, which (we will suppose) A did not, and remodels accordingly those scenes of the story where the camp is actually assailed. Also (suppose for simplicity), this same B invents the "Making of the Armour," and, of course, there narrates the "Sending of Patroclus" according to his own version, with the embassy. Subject to these changes, he adopts A bodily, as why should he not?

Now suppose (we simplify the case, intending merely to show the general nature of the process assumed) that these *Iliads* A and B, verbally identical for the most part, but totally different in the "embassy-version" and certain connected episodes, come both, from different quarters, into the hands of the Athenian collectors. What should they have done with them, and (a different question) what were they likely to do? "Keep both as they are," we should now say, and so would have said Cicero, or Aristarchus, or Aristotle—any one in the ages of erudition. "Both are mere fictions, and each good in its way." But in the sixth century the stories could not possibly be so estimated. This view was to be afterwards evolved, by Thucydides and others, products of the movement which the collectors were initiating. To the sixth century, the Trojan war, heroes, gods and all, was a reality, which the Homeric poems more or less exactly represented. Probably, before the collection, no one was clearly conscious of the divergences. And what the collectors made and wanted was a book to be learnt, to be the basis of national instruction, a history compiled from the epics, with the *Iliad* as a part of it. What then more natural and proper than to combine the versions in a harmony, supposed to represent the truth, or the nearest approximation to it obtainable in the circumstances?

Upon these principles, between two totally incompatible versions of the same incident, you must choose. For the "Sending of Patroclus" we take the version of A, the "fire-version," discarding that of B, the "embassy." But this would be no reason for discarding the "Making of the Armour," an episode of many hundred lines, which, as a whole, is equally compatible with either version of the "Sending." It goes in therefore as we find it; and by an oversight, such as is sure to occur in constructions of this kind, and does occur in harmonies far more skilful and elaborate than could be commanded by Pisistratus, it is allowed to carry with it the half-dozen lines (xviii. 446–452) in which the "embassy-version" of the "Sending" is summarily related by Thetis.

Further, if we turn to the "Sending" itself

(xvi. 112 foll.), we see that, though based mainly on
the conception (A) that the resistance of Achilles
is overcome by the firing of the ships, it contains
passages which are not easily attributed to a poet
possessed by that conception.   Let the reader peruse
what passes, or is related, in our *Iliad* between the
moment, when Achilles descries the fire, and the
outrush of Patroclus and his men (xvi. 130–256),
especially the incident of the cup, libation, and
prayer (*ib*. 220 foll.), and consider whether this is
the way in which the thing would naturally be
imagined, upon the supposition that the ships are
now burning.   All is fine poetry, but is it all proper
to the situation ?   Does it not ignore the urgent and
desperate crisis, and assume, on the contrary, that
there is no need for haste?   But according to Thetis
and her "embassy-version," there was no need for
haste.   We suspect therefore strongly, that here
also, along with the version of A, we have elements,
as much as seemed possible, incorporated by a
harmonist from the version of B.

From B, or a closely related version, comes also,
we may naturally suppose, Book ix., the embassy to
Achilles, the difficulties of which, within itself, and in
relation to the rest of the work, are well known and
generally admitted.   It lacks connexion, it seems to
be forgotten, and there are other doubts.   Moreover, though this is not so generally admitted, we
ourselves agree with those (for instance, Dr Leaf[1])

---

[1] See, in his edition of the *Iliad*, the Introduction to Book ix.,
and the notes to ix. 168 foll., and elsewhere.

who say that the book itself exhibits imperfect harmony. We have sometimes two ambassadors, but
also an ill-connected third (Phœnix) who, it would
certainly seem, did not originally figure here. All
this is the more perplexing because both the general
conception and the parts (if they would but fit) are
magnificent. But whence and why did Phœnix
come in? To this question we have not seen any
satisfactory answer. We would suggest that he is
one of the elders who, according to Thetis, went
as ambassadors to Achilles and procured the sending of Patroclus. The version B, or some version
closely related, contained two embassies, one (that
which forms the bulk of Book ix.) to which Achilles
conceded nothing, and a second, comprising Phœnix,
to which, as related by Thetis, he granted the sending of Patroclus. The first could be adopted in the
harmony without offence, and accordingly was; the
second was plainly inadmissible; but, upon the
common principles of harmonists, some of it, as
much as seemed possible—the presence and speeches
of Phœnix—was amalgamated with the first, "though
not without leaving clear traces of the joints."

We cannot here work this out, nor do we
pretend that it could be worked out to any precise
distribution of A and B and other letters. But upon
some such hypothesis we can account to ourselves
for the actual relations between Books ix., xvi., xviii.
of the *Iliad*; and we cannot account for them upon
any hypothesis which does not somewhere import
a harmonist—no poet, but the compiler of a history.

To this operation we should attribute, not exclusively but mainly, those peculiarities in which, as it seems to us and to many, the two epics, or at all events the *Iliad*, are unique. We cannot here illustrate the matter any further. But this, we think, is the cause, for instance, of the strange fluctuation between different conceptions of the scene (the Greek camp). Manifestly this discrepancy, if present in the contributory sources, could not be eliminated without thorough and bold recomposition, which was not (as we apprehend) within the design, or perhaps the powers, of the harmonists. And above all, to this cause we assign that characteristic of the *Iliad* which, though some can ignore it, we cannot ignore. The main design is masterly, the parts are almost all admirable—yet they do not fit. Repeatedly the thread seems to break, the track to be lost; and we arrive, after some wandering, at a stage of progress already reached before. Such is the natural, the inevitable effect of a harmony. And (to repeat this essential point) if it is asked why the harmony should have been attempted, and why it was possible, we reply, " Because the contributory versions were, each with each, to a large extent, not only concordant in matter, but verbally identical." Therefore they could be united ; and the historic impulse, natural though mistaken, gave the motive for such a combination.

It cannot be proved that the harmonizing was the work of the Athenians, or connected with the redaction of the Cycle. It may conceivably have

taken place elsewhere and earlier. Only this seems
a gratuitous supposition. We have no tradition
suggesting it. The required conditions of purpose
and mental attitude are not, we think, so likely to
have existed anywhere or at any time as in the city
and age of Pisistratus.

Whoever made the harmony, he or they had
doubtless not the least intention to suppress or
replace the versions, or any expectation of this effect.
They made such an *Iliad* as they wanted for a new
purpose, presuming, if they considered the matter,
that others would circulate as before. How could it
be foreseen that in no long time the new education
would make an altered world, would create a polity
and society never before imagined? That Athens
would for ages rule the teaching and supply the
books of all civilized peoples, as in some degree she
does to this day? That in a few generations the
"rhapsode," the reciter of Homer, would be an
extinct profession, and epic poetry, all but a small
reserve, a drug in the market? In the events
which happened, the Athenian Homer of course
obliterated and extinguished whatever competitors
existed. Nor indeed do we suppose that it had
much to compete with. Respecting the diffusion
and influence of Homer before the Athenian
movement, much more is sometimes asserted or
assumed than the evidence warrants. But of this
we cannot here speak. We suppose, and we think
it natural, that when, some centuries later, text-
criticism arose, all sources for Homer, except those

directly or derivatively Athenian, had long disappeared.

The silence of the ancient text-critics respecting the Athenian operation, or rather the fact that apparently they did not use the tradition as a ground for analysis, and anticipate the modern treatment of the Homeric question, has been taken by some as disproving the operation, or indicating that it cannot have been important. We do not see this. It is quite likely that the Alexandrian scholars, knowing what we do about that operation, knew little or nothing more. They seem to have assumed that the Athenian *Iliad*, their *Iliad*, was substantially the work of one author, descending, in the manner of transmission familiar to themselves, from a remote prehistoric antiquity. If they so assumed without warrant, they only did what has been done by many moderns far more experienced than they in research and criticism.

With respect to the *Odyssey*, we admit of course that the traces in it of a harmonist, if any, are far fewer and less convincing than those in the *Iliad*. Were it not for the *Iliad*, they would hardly have been suspected. Nevertheless, the analysts of the *Odyssey* do seem to have proved that, at least in some places, the treatment of materials is harmonistic. There are some mere patches, notably in the "Slaying of the Suitors" and the exchange there of the bow for the spear. As to a common authorship for *Iliad* and *Odyssey*, or rather for *an Iliad* and *an Odyssey*, that is a matter beyond the scope of this article.

Now it will be seen, and we would specially insist, that the question we have been considering, whether the actual state of the epics, or either of them, is partly the result of a harmony, has no necessary bearing whatever on many of the issues which students of Homer debate. It is on this point especially, we think, that controversy tends to confusion and prejudice. A harmonistic theory of the *Iliad* implies nothing whatever, *per se*, as to the date and origin of the supposed components, or the value of any part, or of the whole, as evidence upon customs, culture, and other such topics. If it were ever so completely proved that our book was made in the sixth century B.C. by a mechanical, or partly mechanical, amalgamation of versions, all the versions, and every substantial part, might none the less be as ancient and as nearly contemporaneous as we please to suppose. We ourselves think it probable (so far as, in conditions almost wholly unknown, one thing can be more probable than another) that the components of the *Iliad* do mainly belong to a time more narrowly limited than some analysts would suggest, and that what we called the variant "versions," those that lasted and determined the eventual product, all followed at no great distance upon that of Homer, the original designer. At all events this may be so; and the question between unitarian and harmonist ought not to be affected, as it frequently is, by arguments or theories about date. For example, the different views about the Homeric armour, and whether it represents a reality or a

conventional confusion, are all of them consistent
with a harmonistic theory respecting the genesis of
the existing text.

Indeed there is no inconsistency, in strict theory,
between the view that our text is a harmony and
the view that all parts of it, all the materials, are by
one author. And in the circumstances, such as we
should imagine them, of poetic composition in the
age of Homer, it is quite possible that some variant
versions, or variant episodes, of the story were actually
composed by the original designer. To attribute
to one hand so much variation of treatment, as the
existing combination seems to require, would be a
rather violent conjecture; nor do we see the need of
it, or the difficulty of supposing a few successors
to the designer, perhaps nearly contemporaneous,
who, stimulated by his example and using the same
conventional style, could achieve as near a resemblance to his manner as, for our part, we find
between different portions of the *Iliad*.

Nor again is our view inconsistent with what is
called, or should properly be called, "expansion" of
the original story, that is to say, the insertion of
episodes, freely composed by poets, which really
were intended to fit without discrepancy into the
original frame. We do not, for the present purpose,
either assert or deny such expansion; still less do
we assume that expansion, if such there was, extended over a long period. What we say is that,
expansion or no expansion, the extant *Iliad*, at all
events, exhibits the phenomena of a harmony, the

quasi-historical combination of versions partly incompatible and not designed for union. Whether the versions were narrowly or widely separated in time of origin is a distinct enquiry. And the nearer they were, and the more concordant therefore in natural and conventional colour, the easier and the more tempting would be the operation of the harmonist. For this reason, and for others, we doubt, as we said before, whether the development of versions, or of those versions which lasted and contributed to the final result, can have been distributed over so long a time as some would assume.

The proof of the harmonistic operation depends of course on the number of "sutures"—plain breaks in the context, and discrepancies such as no free composer could be tempted to make or to pass. However plain these may be, we cannot expect, as a rule, to determine precisely what the harmonist has done, and what was the scope of the material which he has not preserved. Of this we can have a glimpse, only if in any case the rebelliousness of the materials, or the maladroitness or timidity of the operator, has led him to include matter absolutely irrelevant to his composition and explicable only by what he has omitted. Considering the literary inexperience, which we may or must attribute to harmonists of the sixth century B.C. or earlier, instances even of so gross a handling may be expected to occur, as in fact they do. One such instance we propose to investigate in the following essay, to which this will serve as an introduction, explaining our point of view.

As we have spoken with more respect than is common of what some would call "the Pisistratean legend," we will repeat that there is no necessary connexion between the demonstrable dislocations of our *Iliad* and the hypothesis that the Athenians were wholly or mainly responsible for them. Contempt for the Athenian tradition is fortified, unfortunately, by the authority of many excellent scholars; but the texts, as we have said, are not treated fairly. It would be much if the defenders of unity, and controversialists generally, would perceive that there is room within the record for them all. If it could be shown that the internal evidence of the *Iliad* favours the hypothesis of single authorship, there is nothing against it in Cicero and Pausanias. For anything they say, or the rest say, Pisistratus may have done nothing to the *Iliad*, separately and as such, except to purchase and have copied a MS. dating from the days of the original poet. Only, we say, somebody must have done to the *Iliad* what no one is so likely to have done as the Athenians of the sixth century. We think, indeed, that some operations have been assigned to that epoch, which go beyond the likelihood. We do not suppose that any considerable modification of the text was made in the interest of Athens or her princes. The "sycophant of Pisistratus," as the Athenian operator has been derisively called, is, we rather think, a fictitious personage. But the tradition is not

responsible for him.   Indeed the tradition, fairly
read, has no essential concern with the personal
action of Pisistratus.   If his name be displeasing
(though we respect it), let us say, with Lycurgus,
that the Athenians conceived and carried out the
profoundly important educational movement, in connexion with which—as others say, who may well
have known—they arranged, as well as collected,
their " Poetry of Homer."   That they did things
with it altogether novel and, in the circumstances,
stupendously effective, is proved by all history to
this day.   Having new purposes, they may naturally
have made a new book.   We believe them to have
made in good faith a quasi-historical harmony of
certain ancient poems, which were in such condition,
and so related, as to invite the operation.   If, new to
the business, and taking the first stumbling steps
towards the foundation of European learning, they
did some mischief which we could have taught them
to avoid, it is due mainly to them and their Homer
that we have any learning at all.   It is possible to
feel a mild resentment when one reads of " the Pisistratean legend."   We should ourselves as soon speak
of the "legend" that the authorized version of the
Bible was a product of the Protestant Reformation.

However we have no quarrel with any one, and
we expect no immediate agreement.   It has been
said by some that there is a reaction coming against
expansionists, harmonists, and all such.   It may be
so.   But the sutures of the *Iliad* are there, and will
be seen whenever men look.

THE MUTINY OF IDOMENEUS.

A LOST BIT OF HOMER.

THE origin and composition of the *Iliad* passes with some for a problem too indeterminate to yield any results. Granting (they say) that the existing book has features not commonly found, more discrepancies in the story and a less straightforward progress, there is no evidence, properly so called, to show how these features were produced. A single authorship (unitarian view), development by successive hands (expansionist view), the artificial combination of divergent versions (harmonist view) —all these hypotheses, with various modifications, are equally possible; and the choice, resting in the last resort upon purely subjective impressions, is no profitable matter for debate.

To those who are of this mind—now perhaps a minority among students—the following pages are not addressed. In my opinion, the harmonist view, not excluding but not demanding "expansion," has been proved over and over again[1]; and I cannot suppose that I shall move in this direction those

---

[1] For a summary statement of it, see the preceding essay.

who remain immoveable after studying (for example)
the commentary of Dr Leaf.   But to those who are
satisfied that the harmonist view contains at all
events some part of the truth, I would submit an
illustration of the process supposed, which may be
found interesting and perhaps suggestive.

No portion of the *Iliad* exhibits the natural effects
of the harmonistic process more strongly, perhaps
none so much, as that portion which lies between
the retreat of the Greeks to their camp and the
consent of Achilles to lend them the aid of his men
under the delegated command of Patroclus (Books
xii—xv).   The reason for this, upon the principles
here assumed, is obvious.   Among the divergences of
incident, introduced by the fancy of poets, or a poet[1],
rehandling the common theme, one of the most
important was the fortification of the camp by a wall,
a condition profoundly modifying the course of the
narrative.   Which version, with the wall or without
it, was the older, may not be now ascertainable, and
may at all events be left indeterminate without
prejudice to the assertion, that the extant story
sometimes assumes and sometimes ignores such a
fortification, and therefore (since no narrator, composing with natural freedom, could plan a story
ambiguous in such a particular) must have been
produced by combining artificially a version or
versions, in which the wall existed, with another or
others, in which it did not.   The motive for such a
combination was the only possible motive for a

---

[1] On this point see preceding essay, p. 193.

harmony, the motive which has produced other harmonies, such as those, once popular, of the Four Gospels. The harmonists, accepting all the stories as representing, each partially and imperfectly, an underlying truth and common basis of historical fact, endeavoured to reproduce this truth by the method— still common in popular criticism, and expelled but recently, if it has been completely expelled, from the procedure of the learned—of putting together so much of all versions as could be united without sheer contradiction. In the case of Homer, we know of one occasion upon which such a process may naturally have been used,—the collection and arrangement of Homer by the Athenians of the sixth century B.C.

Now at the end of the existing Book XI, the story of the *Iliad* has reached a point at which, between *wall* and *no wall*, the embarrassments of the harmonist must culminate. The Greeks have been beaten to their camp; and presently, at the end of Book XV and beginning of XVI, their ships upon the shore are to be fired by the pursuing Trojans. Between, if anywhere, must come a taking (or takings) of the wall, and a fight in the walled enclosure. Yet if these were to find a place within a frame not meant to embrace them, distension and confusion were inevitable. And in fact both distension and confusion are visible and enormous. The huge and erratic combat here inserted must be supposed, according to the existing narrative, to be covered in time by an incident (the errand of

Patroclus[1]) grossly incommensurate even in its actual and extended form. So much for the distension. And the confusion is also plain. Even an inobservant reader, a reader for pleasure, in passing through this part of the poem, will become aware of its impediments in a general way. He will sometimes, not seldom, be unsure of the line on which he is supposed to be moving, unable to say where he is, what precisely is happening and what may be expected next. The experiment is not very often tried; for in truth, to read the *Iliad* continuously is less common, especially after the first reading, than might conventionally be assumed. To fix upon definite points or grounds of objection requires of course not mere reading but examination. The results, the decisive results, of such examination have been often stated. The narrative abounds with dislocations, signs of patching and forced connexion, not the less certain because for the most part the breaches are not violent, the points of juncture not always conspicuous and sometimes not precisely determinable.

That is to be expected. In tacking together two or more narratives actually parallel, that is to say, treating with variations the same stage of a common story, there could be no necessity or temptation, generally speaking, to make very violent connexions. What could not come in, except on such terms, would naturally be omitted. But it is to be expected, unless the harmonist were more

----

[1] xi 611 ff., xv 390 ff., xvi 1 ff.

expert than the harmonists of the *Iliad* can possibly have been, that sometimes the breaks, sutures, mechanical connexions, will deserve the name of violent. Sooner or later the harmonist will grasp at more than, upon his principles, he can properly hold, and will bring in an episode, or a portion of it, which admits of no attachment even plausible to the ear, with the result that, after the juncture, the narrative will be, for some space, unintelligible. Our present concern is with a juncture of this kind, a violent juncture, and its consequence, a piece of narrative unexplained and unintelligible. What I propose to show is the cause of the phenomenon, and why the harmonist has here made a connexion manifestly not justifiable or plausible. It was because he was compelled, by the nature and relation of his materials, to begin a new extract, a large extract which he was unwilling to discard, so as to include in it the termination of a certain episode, for which, as a whole, the harmony afforded no place. From certain passages of the extract, irrelevant and meaningless in the existing connexion, we can divine the general course of the episode suppressed ; and we may confirm our conjecture by reference to other parts of the *Iliad*, which are obscured by corresponding suppressions, and by corresponding restorations can be made clear.

The case shall be stated as briefly as possible, and without elaborate argument. The merits of such a case, if it has any, must lie in its appearing, upon statement, fairly obvious. The facts alleged in support should be seen to meet together, so to speak, of their own accord. Moreover, as to the facts themselves, the separate items of the construction, proof is already accessible. The observations upon discrepancies and difficulties in the existing story, which are here used, have, in general, all been made and often repeated by students, from the authors of the Greek commentaries downwards, who did not suspect any connexion between them[1]. This at least is in our favour. We take, as they are given, points fixed and recognized, and have only to add that they lie, if we may use such a metaphor, upon a certain symmetrical curve.

The dislocation, from which we start, is found in Book XIII, at the place (*v.* 206) where the story recurs to the person of Idomeneus, King of the Cretans. It marks the entrance of that hero upon the well-defined battle-scene in which he, with his squire Meriones, plays the chief part,—the *Aristeia of Idomeneus*, as it is called. The scene extends back from this point to *v.* 136, and forward through the greater part of the book. It is free in the main from interior difficulties, but exhibits traits, such as the participation of chariots, which are surprising, to say the least, when the action is supposed,

---

[1] To Dr Leaf's commentary, in particular, I should be understood to refer for all observations upon the text, which do not involve explicitly the supposition of a suppressed episode. In general, I follow him closely, though I do not repeat this on each occasion, nor notice shades of difference which are of no importance to our present subject.

as its place in our *Iliad* requires, to be passing in
such space as could be included within the limit of a
wall and of a populous camp or rather military city.
To this peculiar situation the scene makes no allusion, so that, but for its place in the *Iliad*, all might
and naturally would be supposed to pass in open
ground. That will be worth notice hereafter, though
it is not the point on which we are first to fix our
attention. Within itself, the narrative is simple,
except a passage or series of passages extending
from the first appearance of Idomeneus until he and
Meriones go forth together to the battle (*vv.* 206–
294). All this, in its present connexion, is irrelevant
and unintelligible.

Before we consider it, let us recall the character
and relation of the personages. Idomeneus, King
of the Cretans, is one of the first figures in Homer,
and his special distinction is Meriones. No other
prince has a personal attendant so high in rank and
in prowess—a man of equal birth, his own nephew,
and a warrior equal to the best, attached to him as
servant and follower. Homeric princes have sometimes special and familiar companions, such as
Patroclus is to Achilles; they have household officers
with certain functions, heralds, cupbearers and so
forth, of various degree down to mere slaves; and
they have attendants. But they have not, as a
rule, attendants comparable in quality to Meriones.
Agamemnon himself has none such. Meriones, as
a person, is a match for any; he can himself, on
occasion, sit in council with the greatest; he is no

dependant of the King, but neither is he simply his friend ; he attends him though his equal. To us, who have kept with regard to royalty the spirit of the feudal ages, such a relation is not surprising. But it is remarkable in the *Iliad* ; and it not only marks the Cretan prince, whose personal merits are great, with a high note of dignity, but also sets in a strong light the connexion between the pair.

And now, returning to the *Aristeia*, let us fix the situation in our minds, both as it affects the combatants generally and with reference to Idomeneus in particular. The Greeks have been defeated, first in the plain (Book XI), and then at the wall, which has been carried by the Trojans (Book XII). Idomeneus is prominent, as he usually is, in both combats (XI 501, XII 117). Amid wild confusion, the beaten defenders of the wall have been rallied for a stand within the camp by the aid of the god Poseidon[1]. The fight has recommenced, but of Idomeneus we have not yet heard. And here[2] the narrative proceeds thus :

So he (Poseidon) set forth to go by the huts and the ships of the Achaians, to spur on the Danaans, and sorrows was he contriving for the Trojans.

Then Idomeneus, spearman renowned, met him on his way from his comrade that had but newly returned to him out of the battle, wounded on the knee with the sharp bronze. Him his comrades carried forth, and Idomeneus gave charge to the leeches, and so went on to his hut, for he still was eager to face the war.

[1] XIII 1–135.   [2] *ib*. 208.

Then the mighty Shaker of the earth addressed him, in the voice of Thoas, son of Andraimon,...[1]: "Idomeneus, thou counsellor of the Cretans, say, whither have thy threats fared, wherewith the sons of the Achaians threatened the Trojans?" Then Idomeneus, leader of the Cretans, answered him again: "O Thoas, now is there no man to blame, that I wot of, for we are all skilled in war. Neither is there any man that spiritless fear holds aloof, nor any that gives place to cowardice, and shuns the cruel war, nay, but even thus, methinks, must it have seemed good to almighty Kronion, even that the Achaians should perish nameless here, far away from Argos. But, Thoas, seeing that of old thou wert staunch, and dost spur on another man, wheresoever thou mayst see any give ground, therefore slacken not now, but call aloud on every warrior." Then Poseidon, the Shaker of the earth, answered him again: "Idomeneus, never may that man go forth out of Troy-land, but here may he be the sport of dogs, who this day is wilfully slack in battle. Nay, come, take thy weapons and away: herein we must play the man together, if any avail there may be, though we are no more than two. Ay, and very cowards get courage from company, but we twain know well how to battle even with the brave."

Therewith the god went back again into the strife of men, but Idomeneus, so soon as he came to his well-builded hut, *put on his fair armour about his body*, and grasped two spears, and set forth like the lightning....

And Meriones, his good squire, met him, while he was still near his hut—he (Meriones) was going to fetch him a spear of bronze[2]—and mighty Idomeneus spoke to him: "Meriones, son of Molos, fleet of foot, dearest of my company, wherefore hast thou come hither and left the war and the strife? Art thou wounded at all, and vexed by a dart's point, or dost thou come with a message for me concerning aught? Verily I myself have no desire to sit in the huts but to fight."

[1] A description of Thoas.

[2] From his own quarters. See XIII 168 οἰσόμενος δόρυ μακρὸν ὅ οἱ κλισίηφι λέλειπτο, where we also learn that he had broken his spear in fighting.

Then wise Meriones answered him again, saying: "Idomeneus, thou counsellor of the mail-clad Cretans, I am going to fetch me a spear, if perchance thou hast one left in the huts, for that which before I carried I have shivered in casting at the shield of proud Deiphobos."

Then Idomeneus, leader of the Cretans, answered him again: "Spears, if thou wilt, thou shalt find one, ay and twenty, standing in the hut, against the shining side walls, spears of the Trojans whereof I have spoiled their slain. Yea, it is not my mood to stand aloof from the foe when I war; wherefore I have spears, and bossy shields, and helms, and corselets of splendid sheen."

Then wise Meriones answered him again: "Yea, and in mine own hut and my black ship are many spoils of the Trojans, but not ready[1] to my hand. Nay, for methinks neither am I forgetful of valour; but stand forth among the foremost to face glorious war, whensoever ariseth the strife of battle. Any other, methinks, of the mail-clad Achaians should sooner forget my prowess, but thou art he that knoweth it."

Then Idomeneus, leader of the Cretans, answered him again: "I know what a man of valour thou art, wherefore shouldst thou tell me thereof? (*Here follows a long and eloquent eulogy of Meriones' courage: in no strait would Idomeneus desire a better comrade.*) But come, no more let us talk thus, like children, loitering here, lest any man be vehemently wroth, but go thou to the hut, and take thee a mighty spear."

Thus he spake, and Meriones, the peer of swift Ares, quickly took a spear of bronze from the hut, and went forth after Idomeneus, with high thoughts of battle[2].

Now, as far as I am aware, there is not any one, and perhaps there never has been since the beginning of Homeric studies, who maintains that this passage, as it stands, is satisfactory as a composition

---

[1] Better "near," σχεδόν. The point is that the quarters of Meriones are distant, not close by, like those of Idomeneus.

[2] XIII 208–294. Translation of A. Lang (slightly modified).

intended for this place. Nor can it be made so by correction. From first to last, in every part as in the whole conception, it presumes some totally different state of affairs. Each paragraph, and almost every clause, raises some new and unanswerable question. Why has Idomeneus disarmed, just when the wall has been carried, the triumphant Trojans are pouring through the camp, the Greeks rallying for a last resistance, and he (we are told) "is minded still to fight"? Why then has he disarmed? How is such a thing even conceivable? And if explicable, why is it not explained? Why is it not even stated as a fact? What relevance, in the given situation, has the language of Thoas (Poseidon)? Why does he reflect upon the behaviour of Idomeneus not as senseless and incomprehensible (which it is), but as disloyal (which, so far as we are shown, it is not)? And what, above all, are we to make of the dialogue between Idomeneus and Meriones? The two are inseparable companions, bound together not only as lord and liegeman, master and servant, but by the strongest affection. Meriones has urgent, instant need for a spear. The quarters of Idomeneus, which we should presume to be also those of Meriones, are close by. Why does the squire not take thence what he wants as a matter of course? Why must he go to his own quarters (*v.* 168), which, without explanation, we are to suppose distant? Why, upon meeting Idomeneus, does he change his mind? Are we to suppose that he is thus reminded of his

lord's existence ? If the loan of a spear must, or
could at such a moment, be matter of request, why
should Meriones frame the request with ceremonious
formality ? Why should Idomeneus pick offence
out of an expression (" if you have a spear left") in
which no malice is apparent ? Why is Meriones
equally sensitive ? Boast and counter-boast, retort,
reproach, and apology,—what is it all about?

Confronted with such a mass of riddles as this,
we have no right to attempt either justification or
mending. All is wrong, all out of place, not this
line or that speech in particular, but the whole.
Nor can we reach more tenable ground by attri-
buting the passage, as an original composition, to a
harmonist, the maker of a patchwork, desiring to
make a link between materials not designed for
combination. We do not see how such a purpose,
any more than that of a free composer, could require
or naturally lead to the creation of these difficulties.
A harmonist may be, and should be supposed, not
less rational than a poet, or any other man. Why,
to fill a place, should he compose what does not fill
it ? What reason had he to assume that Idomeneus
could here be found without his armour ? Or that
Meriones lived apart from him? Or that the friends,
in such a situation, could talk as they are made to
do? Why he, more than Homer, or than ourselves?

If any real explanation and solution is to be
found, it must start with this proposition : the
passage, in its original connexion, was natural and
intelligible. Nor is there any difficulty in so sup-

posing. The passage, as we have seen, is part of an episode—the battle-piece known as the *Aristeia of Idomeneus*—which was not made for its present place in our *Iliad*. The whole episode is no fight within the wall, as our *Iliad* makes it. It is a fight in open ground, taken from a variant version of the story, and put here (in the extant *Iliad*) because, for some reason, no better place could be found for it. So far, in substance if not in words, all will agree who are likely to pay attention to this essay. If then, within this episode, we find included a passage which (1) is not intelligible, and (2) commences with a breach of continuity, what should we infer? First, that the story or version, from which the episode is taken, comprised facts, precedent to the episode, which made our passage intelligible; and that, since these facts do not appear in our *Iliad*, they were excluded as not compatible with other versions which, in this respect, were preferred. And secondly, that part of these facts, or some reference to them, stood, in the original composition, immediately before the enigmatic passage, which owes the abruptness of its commencement, and its obscurity generally, to the necessary suppression of this reference.

The questions which thus arise are these. (1) What are the precedent facts to which the enigmatic passage points, or, in other words, in what conditions would it be intelligible? (2) Why were these facts rejected, when the episode was taken into the frame of our *Iliad*? And (3), since the explanatory facts were rejected, why was the enigmatic passage nevertheless retained? Now it is only too likely that these questions may be unanswerable. A harmony of versions, when the versions are lost, will present many such questions (and the *Iliad* does) to which, however sure we may be that there was an answer, no definite answer can now be given. But on the other hand, in a particular case, the true answer, or part of it, may be discoverable ; and our chance of discovery is manifestly the greater, in proportion to the bulk of the incompatible matter which the harmonizer, by the straits of his task, has been compelled to admit. The more glaring the difficulty, the more we may hope to solve it. And the present case is in this respect uncommonly promising.

What then (our first question) are the conditions, in which the unintelligible passage would be intelligible? This is no matter for argument. No answer can have any value, which is not obvious. But when the passage is studied from this point of view, some things do seem obvious.

First and chiefly, before this scene could occur, there must have been a quarrel, and a complete breach, between Idomeneus and Meriones. Meriones for some reason has actually renounced the service and company of his lord, has left their common quarters, and moved to another and a distant part of the encampment. Hence, when he wants a spear, however urgently, he must go for it to that distant place. He will not go, he does not think of going, to the lodge of Idomeneus, though that actually lies in his way.

But again, he there meets Idomeneus, who asks his errand. Thereupon he instantly changes his mind, and proposes to furnish himself, if permitted, from the quarters of the King. Why this change? What has he discovered? What has happened? This only, that Idomeneus (whom we first find at his quarters and without his armour, though a battle is actually raging) has put on his arms, is visibly on his way to the battle, and declares his purpose "not to sit in his tent, but to fight." This intention then on the part of Idomeneus is a new thing, a surprise to Meriones; and it elicits from Meriones an instant move towards the resumption of their habitual relations. Therefore the breach of those relations was due to what is now changed,—*the wilful absence of Idomeneus from his service as one of the Greek army*.

What we see, in the dialogue here passing between the two, is a hasty repair of the breach. Pointless and meaningless, unless the quarrel and the ground of it be presupposed, the scene, upon these conditions, becomes simple, vivid, and drama-tic. The two men, loving each other heartily, have parted and broken off intercourse, because Meriones would not follow his leader in a mutinous abstention from the field. The King, having come to a better mind, desires and expects to get his liegeman back; and naturally, being the offender and the superior, would fain achieve this by simply ignoring what has passed. "What brings you from the fight, friend?" he asks, as if nothing were amiss. "King of the Cretans," answers Meriones, surprised but eager to be satisfied, "I am going...to fetch me a spear from your lodge, if there is still one there (for me)." It is an acceptance and offer of peace. But the King's uneasy conscience suspects an insinuation: "Spears! There are scores at my hut, my spoils from the enemy! *I am not such a shirker*, but that spears may be found there, and all other weapons in plenty!" Wounded by the unmerited rebuff, the squire begins in the same tone: "Nor am I without spoils of my own, and lying at my quarters,—*which indeed are not near*. I too am no coward, but one that, when called to battle, am ever found in the front of it!" It is bitterly spoken, and with cause; but here, in spite of the provocation, the old affection prevails: "And if," continues Meriones, "there is one man in all the army, who should not have forgotten what I am, who knows what I am,—it is you!" Even the pride of Idomeneus is not proof against this, and he breaks into warm protestation: "Indeed and indeed I do know it. The bravest of men you are, and the best of comrades you are; none so much to be trusted, let the peril be what it will. In ambush none so steady,...," and so on and so on, with rising enthusiasm, till he is sure that all is well; then: "But let us be children no more; fetch you a spear, and follow me to the fight!"

Such is the substance of the scene; which surely is unmistakable as a scene of reconciliation, produced by the return of Idomeneus to the field after a time of wilful abstention. He has been following for a while the pernicious example of Achilles, and punishing the fault of Agamemnon at the expense of the common cause. Like Achilles too, he has held out personally even after permitting his men to serve ; for they are fighting, and he not armed, at the point where our mutilated passage begins. But he has already resolved to join them, moved perhaps partly by the wounding of a dear friend, the "comrade" who is mentioned in our text[1] and must have been named in the context originally preceding but now suppressed. With this purpose he is about to arm, when he is accosted by Thoas (Poseidon). Here we note, as fitting the situation so conceived, and as confirming what we have already deduced, the insulting tone of Thoas, and the meek and evasive answer which Idomeneus makes to his rebuke : "So far as *I* am aware, no one is *now* at fault[2],"—in effect a confession of past delinquency, though like most men, he prefers to accuse Heaven rather than himself[3]. His chief and very intelligible desire is that Thoas will carry his exhortations somewhere else[4]. But Thoas does not depart, for all that, without a denunciation of "the man that *wilfully* neglects to fight[5]," which surely no prince or man could hear with patience and without reply, unless he were both conscious and repentant.

[1] XIII. 211.   [2] *ib.* 222.   [3] *ib.* 225 ff.
[4] *ib.* 228 ff.   [5] *ib.* 232 ff.

But further,—and this is a point of great significance,—it is implied by the passage, if we consider
it carefully, that the inaction of Idomeneus, his
refusal of duty, has been something more than the
affair of a moment. It is not enough to suppose
that, in a fit of petulance or weariness, he has quitted
the fight now in progress. We might perhaps,—
supposing the battle-field not very near—account in
this way for his disarming, and for his behaviour to
Thoas, but not for the estrangement of Meriones.
The attendant prince has changed his quarters,
and removed from the encampment of the master
to a distant place. This he cannot have done in
the midst of a battle ; he could scarcely even know,
in such circumstances, that the retirement of his
master was deliberate. The King's revolt from duty
has been followed by a quarrel between the friends,
and this by a formal separation, for all which we
must suppose occasion and time. Nor (we may be
sure) was it here, in the midst of the battle-scene,
that all these facts were related by the composer of
it. They must have been related somewhere, but
not here, in that version of the whole story or of this
episode to which the battle-scene properly belonged.

Now it is obviously possible, and even probable,
that this version has been used by the harmonists,
the framers of the existing *Iliad*, elsewhere, and
that this battle-scene, the *Aristeia of Idomeneus*, is
not the only matter, peculiar to the version, which,
more or less successfully, they have incorporated in
their collection. And in any such matter there may

remain traces of the same incident, the mutiny of Idomeneus, which has left traces so deep in the *Aristeia*. Of course, since the incident was not admitted into our *Iliad* (why not, we shall see hereafter), references to it will have been suppressed, so far as possible. But traces not only may remain, but almost certainly will, if in fact such references were originally comprised within any piece which has been taken from the version into the harmony. From a composition designed for continuity it is, generally speaking, impossible to make any considerable excisions without leaving signs of the process, or so that the resultant residue shall seem altogether complete and satisfactory.

What we now propose to show is that the version or story in question, the same which contributed the *Aristeia of Idomeneus*, contained also Book x of our *Iliad* (the *Doloneia*); that in the earlier part of that Book the narrative is notoriously faulty, unsatisfactory, and imperfect; and that this imperfection is due to the excision there of what was originally and properly the principal theme of the narrative,—the beginning of our suppressed episode, the beginning of the mutiny of Idomeneus. Here again we shall build upon observations established and even ancient.

It will surprise no student of Homer, that elements, foreign to the main scheme of our *Iliad*, should be sought and found in Book x. The Book is visibly extraneous; that is a commonplace of criticism. But within itself it is, for the most part, singularly compact, continuous, and free from suspicion of flaw. That is indeed a chief part of its peculiarity. All of it belongs plainly to one and the same design; and there is scarcely another Book or equal portion of the poem, concerning which we can confidently say the same. But though all belongs to one design, that does not prove that the text, in its present form, contains all which the designer gave. The absence of insertions does not disprove omission.

It is true that on this side also the *Doloneia*, in one sense, may defy attack. The *Doloneia* proper, the portion of Book x which narrates the expedition of Diomede and Odysseus, the capture of the spy Dolon, and its consequence, the disaster of Rhesus, is in completeness, as in continuity, unexceptionable. These qualities, merely for themselves, would not in most compositions be noticeable. To pursue clearly and steadily a definite purpose is not in itself a distinction among story-tellers. They achieve it generally, the worse as well as the better. But in the stream of our *Iliad*, so smooth a reach is rare. All are aware of it, and it is a principal factor in theories about this particular Book.

But, as students and readers are also aware, the description is not applicable, without reserve, to the Book as a whole. From the moment when the nocturnal enterprise becomes the subject of debate, as soon as Agamemnon and his counsellors are brought to their meeting-place beyond the dyke, all is well. But the preliminaries, the steps taken to get the council thither, are not so well. They are spun out, that is to say, they raise expectations which the sequel does not satisfy. The council in the plain, regarded merely as a preface to the story of Dolon, impresses us as a device (to apply the formula of Aristotle) "possible indeed, but not necessary or probable"; and the impression is strengthened by the elaborated business of the summoning. Consequently the descriptive details, though appropriate, stand out in disproportionate relief. Critics of all shades are agreed in taxing the author of the *Doloneia* with these defects.

Let us however say at once, with the utmost clearness and emphasis,—for mistake would expose our method of criticism to just reprehension,—that there is nothing here, in the conduct of the story, which would by itself justify us in suspecting the solidity of the composition. A bit of spinning out is no astonishing phenomenon ; and to argue that, because the assembling of the council in the plain is somewhat unnatural, superfluous, and over-elaborate, the narrative is therefore likely to have been garbled, would be absurd. Only, in such a field as the *Iliad*, any irregularity becomes a point for enquiry. In ground which is known to contain ruins, the least mound is a place to be probed.

And first, before we probe, let us look at the shape of the mound, or, in plain words, let us summarize this episode, the council in the plain, as it stands.

We are here of course at a stage in the story of Achilles preceding that of Book XIII. The Greek camp is still intact ; but the Greeks, in consequence of the defection of Achilles, have already sustained

such reverses that Agamemnon, the cause of that
calamity, is discredited and almost desperate.   Wild
to try something, he is yet so conscious of impaired
authority, that he dares not give an order upon his
own responsibility.   It is night, but he cannot sleep.
The Trojans, eager for the morrow, have en-
camped outside their city, and he can see their fires
from his tent;—for the *Doloneia*, like the *Aristeia
of Idomeneus*, is one of those episodes of the *Iliad*
which takes no account of a Greek wall.   At last
he decides to consult Nestor, in the hope of some
helpful suggestion.   But while he is dressing, arrives
Menelaus, equally anxious and already up, who
suggests the sending out of a spy, though he adds
a significant doubt whether his brother will get any
one to undertake such a service.   Agamemnon
replies that, in their appalling situation, assuredly
they both want all the advice they can get.   "Go
now," he continues[1],

Run swiftly by the ships, and summon Aias[2] and Idomeneus.
I will betake me to noble Nestor, and bid him arise, if perchance
he will be fain to go to the chosen band of sentinels and
lay on them his command.   For to him above others would they
listen, since his own son[3] is chief among the sentinels, he and
the squire of Idomeneus, even Meriones, for to them above all
we entrusted this charge.

Then Menelaus of the loud war-cry answered him: "How
meanest thou this word wherewith thou dost command and
exhort me?   Am I to abide there with them, waiting till thou
comest, or run back again to thee, when I have well delivered to
them thy commandment?"

---

[1] x 53.   [2] i.e. the greater Aias.   [3] Thrasymedes.

Then the King of men, Agamemnon, answered him again: "There do thou abide, lest we miss each other as we go, for many are the paths through the camp."

Having further impressed on Menelaus that, in delivering his message and "bidding the men awake," he must be punctiliously courteous and even deferential, he dismisses him, εὖ ἐπιτείλας. Referring to this order later, in conversation with Nestor[1], Agamemnon says that he expects to find Menelaus, and those to whom he was sent, at the place without the camp, where the sentinels are posted, "for there I bade them assemble." We will assume therefore (for the moment) that the order is so meant and understood.

Agamemnon then proceeds to the quarters of Nestor, rouses him, and proposes that they together should visit and inspect the guards, who (he says) may probably be negligent. Nestor consents, but desires to be accompanied by others, in fact by all the chief leaders, Diomede and Odysseus, Aias the less and Meges, Aias the greater and Idomeneus. Agamemnon informs him that the last two are summoned already and will be found with Menelaus at the guard-post. Nestor, accompanied by Agamemnon, rouses in succession Odysseus and Diomede. The latter, protesting with friendly vehemence against the old man's activity, is sent to summon the remaining pair, Aias the less and Meges, whom he brings to Nestor[2].

---

[1] *vv.* 126–127.

[2] To Nestor, as we must understand, not to the post of the guards, for nothing is said to Diomede about the guards or the intention to visit them (*vv.* 159–179).

At this point[1] the scene is transferred to the guard-post, where we are to suppose both parties, that of Menelaus and that of Agamemnon (or rather of Nestor), to have arrived. The council then add to their number the two captains of the guard, Thrasymedes and Meriones, and, so augmented, go beyond the dyke to deliberate. Nestor, still taking the lead, proposes that some one should make a nocturnal expedition, to ascertain the intentions of the enemy. After a pause, Diomede offers, and asks for a companion, whom, readiness being now general, he is permitted to choose. He chooses Odysseus ; and the pair are equipped and set forth[2].

Now it needs no microscope to discover, why this scene of complicated preparation is viewed by critics and readers, as the fact is, with no favourable eye ; why holes are picked in it, with and also without much reason, and there is a general disposition to convict the composer of little faults. We feel that we do not want the thing, because, in plain truth, it comes to nothing. The purport of the scene, considered in itself, is clear, and vividly clear. It exhibits the conscious and perilous weakness of authority, in an army brought to the verge of ruin not merely by the error, but by the gross offence and misbehaviour, of the commander. The best military machine might in such a case get out of gear ; and the Greek host, a confederacy of clans and chiefs, is no such machine. It is not indeed yet broken. The sentinels, though distrusted, are found

---

[1] *v.* 180.   [2] *v.* 272.

to be doing their utmost[1]. The chiefs, as persons, are prompt, tireless, and courageous. But—no man ventures to give an order; that is the sum of the situation. The commander-in-chief is demoralized and self-effaced. To get advice and direction, from Nestor, from Idomeneus or Aias, from somebody,— that is his one hope. It has come to this, he says bitterly, that he and his brother, if they have a request to make, must carry it themselves, and be content, even then, to recommend it by address and humility[2]. A dangerous service is likely to be refused[3]. Even exhortation is a delicate matter, demanding the choice of an acceptable agent[4]. Having got Nestor, Agamemnon gets behind him and acts no more[5], except—a poor exception—when, by a transparent hint, he excludes Menelaus and himself from the list of possible comrades, which is left to the choice of Diomede[6]. Even Nestor will not command, nor advise, nor even inspect, without the concurrence of supporters[7]; and the chiefs, when assembled, demand nothing of anybody but themselves.

It is all natural enough, well imagined, and well drawn. But, as a factor in the story, it does not satisfy, for this reason, that nothing comes of it all. On the expedition which follows, all these fears and precautions have no effect. If Menelaus, the origi-

---

[1] *vv.* 98 ff., 181 ff.   [2] *vv.* 67 ff.

[3] *vv.* 38 ff.   [4] *vv.* 57 ff.

[5] See the proceedings at the guard-post and in council, *vv.* 190 ff.

[6] *vv.* 234 ff.   [7] *vv.* 108 ff.

nator of the plan[1], had simply proposed it to Diomede or Ulysses, or any fit agent, the result, so far as appears, would have been the same. Now to the possibility of the proceedings, as matter of fact, that is no objection. Useless machinery is in real action common enough, and nothing commoner than expectations and apprehensions, which in the sequel are neither fulfilled nor contradicted, but just drop. But not so in a story, where the whole bargain, as between narrator and auditor, is to show and perceive connexion. Here, if it is laboriously impressed upon us, that a certain person or persons have lost authority, something, we are bound to suppose, will be seen to come of that loss. If the royal brothers fear to be disobeyed, some one, we suppose, will prove disobedient. Our cue is to suppose so. And if nothing comes, if all are obedient, we are thrown out, and seem, as it were, to be cheated. For this reason the council in the plain is unsatisfactory, a clear mistake in machinery.

But before we dismiss it as such, we should make sure that we read it right, and that the meaning of the designer was unquestionably what we have assumed. Now in this direction we cannot look far without finding reason for doubt, and more than doubt. Agamemnon (we have said) conducts a party to the guard-post, where Menelaus brings others to meet him by his command. This command is an indispensable link in the chain. But that link is not to be found. No such command is in fact

[1] *v.* 37.

given by Agamemnon or received by Menelaus.
Here is what Agamemnon says[1]:

Need of counsel have I and thou, royal Menelaus....But go now, run swiftly by the ships, and summon Aias and Idomeneus. I will betake me to noble Nestor, and bid him arise, if perchance he will be fain to go to the post of chosen sentinels, and direct them. Him they are likeliest to obey, since his own son is chief among them, he and the squire of Idomeneus, Meriones; for to them specially we gave the charge.

Now here is a simple question. Would my reader write this, or could any one write it, to signify a command from Agamemnon, that Menelaus shall bring Aias and Idomeneus to meet Agamemnon at the guard-post? There is not a word of any such matter. Nestor, if he will, is to visit the guard-post. But that any one else is going there, or is to go, Agamemnon or Menelaus, Idomeneus or Aias, there is surely not a syllable to say or show. The words are perfectly clear, so far as they go, and signify that, when Agamemnon has done with Nestor (whom he proposes to send to the guards), he wishes to have an interview (for counsel) with Aias and Idomeneus, whom Menelaus is to summon for that purpose.

[1] *vv.* 43–59

χρεὼ βουλῆς ἐμὲ καὶ σέ, διοτρεφὲς ὦ Μενέλαε,...
ἀλλ' ἴθι νῦν Αἴαντα καὶ Ἰδομενῆα κάλεσσον
ῥίμφα θέων παρὰ νῆας. ἐγὼ δ' ἐπὶ Νέστορα δῖον
εἶμι, καὶ ὀτρυνέω ἀνστήμεναι, αἴ κ' ἐθέλησιν
ἐλθεῖν ἐς φυλάκων ἱερὸν τέλος ἠδ' ἐπιτεῖλαι·
κείνῳ γάρ κε μάλιστα πιθοίατο· τοῖο γὰρ υἱὸς
σήμαινει φυλάκεσσι καὶ Ἰδομενῆος ὀπάων
Μηριόνης· τοῖσιν γὰρ ἐπετράπομέν γε μάλιστα.

And so Menelaus understands, as appears by his
question, "Am I to stay there with them, waiting
till thou comest?", to which Agamemnon replies
"Wait there, lest we miss each other[1]." By *there*
is of course meant the place to which Menelaus is
sent, the quarters (which lie together[2]) of Aias and
Idomeneus[3]. Shall they await Agamemnon there, or
shall Menelaus return to Agamemnon, wherever he
then may be, and leave the others to follow and find
him? Agamemnon has left this alternative open, so
that the question is necessary; and his decision,
that they shall wait for him there, is best in the
circumstances for the reason given. All is clear
and natural. But if Agamemnon has appointed the
guard-post as a *rendez-vous*, and Menelaus so understands, what is the sense of his question?

When therefore presently we find Agamemnon
furnished with a couplet, which says, or at least is meant
to say[4], that he has ordered Menelaus (with Aias
and Idomeneus) to assemble at the guard-post, what
does that prove? He has not given any such order;
he has said nothing from which such an order is or
possibly could be extracted. On referring to what
he has said, we may indeed perceive, that, by scrutiny
and inference—by putting together (1) the mention

---

[1] *vv.* 60–66. [2] *v.* 113.

[3] See Leaf's note. He remarks truly that this is what we should
naturally understand, though the sequel (*vv.* 126–127) assumes
otherwise.

[4] On the strange syntax of *vv.* 126–127, see the commentaries
there, and remarks hereafter.

of Idomeneus as one of those whom Agamemnon wishes to meet, and (2) the remark that Nestor, as father of Thrasymedes, one of the captains of the guards, will have influence over them, and (3) the mention of "Meriones, squire of Idomeneus," as captain of the guards together with Thrasymedes—one may reach this conclusion : that Idomeneus, through Meriones, might have influence with the guards, and that some such thought might be (though there is nothing to show that it is) in the mind of Agamemnon. But that this obscure and remote suggestion of a conceivable motive for sending Idomeneus to the guard-post is Agamemnon's way of telling Menelaus to bring there Idomeneus and also Aias, and that this command is what the composer of the passage really meant to signify,—that is impossible to believe. No one ever wrote so, and no one could. The composer meant something quite different, and has made his meaning perfectly clear : Menelaus is to go to the quarters of Idomeneus and Aias, summon them, and wait there with them for Agamemnon.

What then, once more, does the subsequent couplet prove[1]? What can it prove, but that the story has been garbled and distorted by the author of the couplet? The author of the couplet, by implication, has put a false and impossible meaning upon the speech to which it refers. The misinterpretation suits, and is plainly devised to suit, the conception that the whole story tends merely and directly to the

---

[1] *vv.* 126–127.

assembling of a council at the guard-post. The misinterpretation is a device, presumably the least violent that could be found, for forcing the story, or portions of it, into this frame, when the true purport of the speech, and the course of things, evidently quite different, which the speech really contemplates, had become, for some reason, inadmissible. And it is but fair to suppose that, in its original form, as designed, the story responded better than it now does to the expectation which it raises, and showed some effect as resulting from the disintegration of authority in the Greek army, and in particular from the discredit and impotence of Agamemnon.

The natural effect, the effect which we should expect, is a mutiny. Some one will do what the royal brothers fear; some one will refuse obedience. And so in the original version it was, as we are going to prove. The relation has been excised, but must have been given in connexion with the unfinished errands of Menelaus and Diomede. Nestor, Odysseus, Diomede, are all compliant, as we are told in ample detail[1]. But here there is an abrupt change of style. The success of Diomede, who is sent for Aias the less and Meges, is recorded in a single verse[2]; "he went his way and he brought them." And of Menelaus, when Agamemnon has sent him to the quarters of Aias (the Telamonian) and Idomeneus[3], we hear nothing more till he is found among the council in the plain[4],

[1] *vv.* 73–178.   [2] *v.* 179.
[3] *v.* 72.   [4] *v.* 230.

—an elliptic method of narration (let us note in passing) which, even if the connecting movements were really foreshown and accounted for, is not in the epic manner, nor suitable to the apprehension of auditors. Among these four then, whose answers we do not hear, Aias the greater, Aias the less, Idomeneus, and Meges, we must look for those who refused; and the sequel shows us which they were. It is no easy thing, as we have remarked before, to trim a story with complete success into a shape for which it was not composed. *Suberunt vestigia.* We actually have, not in form but in effect, a list of those present at the council,—a passage which makes it unlikely that Meges was there, and certain that Idomeneus was not.

Nestor has asked for a scout, and, after a pause, Diomede, breaking the ice, has volunteered to go, if he may have a companion.

So spoke he, and they were fain, right many, to go with Diomede. Fain were the two Aiantes, comrades of Ares' company, and fain was Meriones, and right fain the son of Nestor, and the son of Atreus, Menelaus, spearman renowned, yea and the hardy Odysseus was willing to steal into the throng of Trojans, for always daring was his heart within him[1].

In short every one, the lead once given, is eager to redeem his hesitation; from gallant men we could expect nothing less. And in fact every one present is named. Even Agamemnon, though scarcely to be thought of for such a service, here puts in a remark[2], which, though the practical effect is to

[1] *vv.* 227–232.   [2] *vv.* 234 ff.

withdraw Menelaus, seems to include among the available not only his brother but himself. But of Meges and Idomeneus—nothing.

Now as to Meges, we might suppose inadvertence. Though a king with voice in council, he is not a very conspicuous personage. But Idomeneus has hardly a superior, either in rank or in personal qualities. How should he be forgotten, when Meriones, his satellite, is remembered and named? And in truth the presence of Meriones itself goes far to prove, in the circumstances, the absence of Idomeneus. Meriones is no ordinary associate of the councillor-kings, nor naturally could be: he is young, and he is subordinate, not an independent voice. In this very Book, when counsel is at a premium, neither Agamemnon nor Nestor proposes to consult Meriones. And if his chief were present, he is the last person whose advice could be wanted. But when the kings arrive at the guard-post, they take with them two supernumeraries, Meriones and his brother-captain Thrasymedes[1]. In our text, no reason is given for this irregular proceeding; but there was one, as we now can see. The kings, as a council, are short of two, because Idomeneus and Meges have refused. The captains of the guard are the readiest substitutes, and Meriones, if willing, specially appropriate as, in some sort, a representative of the absent Cretan.

All fits and converges to the conclusion, that on this occasion Meges and Idomeneus (severally and

[1] *v.* 196.

independently so far as we see) refuse their service.
The occasion is probable. Waked in the dead of
night, for no definite purpose, and at the call of a
commander justly detested, men better disciplined
than the Greek princes might rebel. Of Meges'
insubordination there seems to be, in our *Iliad*, no
further trace, and we may suppose that it was tran-
sient, ending perhaps as well as beginning with the
refusal to disturb himself, which he must have
conveyed through Diomede. If this were so, if he
returned to duty in the morning, there could not be
(as we shall presently see) any further note of his
conduct in the existing narrative. His part was
presumably thrown in, after the manner of skilful
story-tellers, to lend colour, by likeness and unlike-
ness, to the principal matter, the revolt of Idomeneus.
This, as we know, was a grave affair. From the
termination of it (still extant[1]) we have seen that
his anger survived the night, and more than the
night, and kept him for some time out of the field.
The suppressed matter, the bulk of the story, we
cannot reconstitute with precision. But one thing
we may note with interest and satisfaction, that
there was an encounter between Idomeneus and
Agamemnon, in which the King of men must have
heard truths; for in figuring the movements of the
night, we must of course follow the real sense of the
order given to Menelaus, and not that preposte-
rously put upon it by the extant version[2]. Menelaus

---

[1] XIII 210–294. See above.
[2] X 53–66, 126–127. See above.

goes to the quarters of Aias and Idomeneus, wakes them, and waits there, as arranged, for Agamemnon, who presently follows[1]. All is thus laid in train for the explosion. The temper of Agamemnon we see. His savage mortification, his accusations of heaven and earth (*v.* 15), have no affinity to repentance; even in preaching politeness to his brother, he shows how much he loathes and resents the necessity for such behaviour (*vv.* 67–71). That Idomeneus, his equal and scarcely less proud, would be, in the cir-

[1] What were the intermediate movements of Agamemnon in the original story, we cannot say, nor does it matter. The present text makes him change his first plan, and speak as if he meant to accompany Nestor to the guard-post (*v.* 97, 126–127); and it implies, without definitely asserting, that he does so. The plurals σφέας (140), ἀλᾶσθε (141) and αὐτούς (149) must include Agamemnon, who must therefore accompany Nestor at least so far as the quarters of Odysseus. Here we lose sight of him till he is found (*v.* 233) at the council. It is not impossible that, in the original also, Agamemnon followed Nestor to the guard-post, before proceeding to the quarters of Idomeneus as arranged with Menelaus (*vv.* 53–66). But this is not what, from that arrangement, we should expect; and even the present text is hardly consistent with the supposition. The singular βῆ (Nestor) in *v.* 136 is surprising, if such a companion as Agamemnon is to be included; and it is strange that, in the interviews with Odysseus and Diomede (*vv.* 137–176), such a person as Agamemnon should be present yet never noticed. It is perhaps more probable that Agamemnon really parted from Nestor either at Nestor's quarters or (at the furthest) at those of Odysseus, and that the present suggestion is due (as certainly are *vv.* 126–127) to the trimming of the reviser. However this question is of no importance. At some point, in the original story, Agamemnon left Nestor, and went to the quarters of Idomeneus and Aias, where they, and Menelaus, awaited him.

cumstances, neither gracious nor patient, we can well imagine; and the rest would follow of itself.

We have seen already, from the termination of the episode, that Meriones preferred the common cause to the quarrel of his chief[1]. The beginning agrees; for Meriones attends the council, although, upon the arrival of Agamemnon and his party at the guard-post, the breach with Idomeneus must have been patent and declared. And seeing how far the chief carried his quarrel, we cannot wonder that it led, as we saw, to a complete rupture between him and his servant. The scene of this rupture has of course disappeared; but one interesting incident of it is recoverable from a surviving allusion.

Since, in the examination of this, we shall insist upon a linguistic detail of that sort which some, who claim to defend Homer, are apt to depreciate as microscopic, we will take occasion to remark that, in the present enquiry as a whole, it is not to our case, but to that of the defence, that the term "microscopic," if a reproach, will apply. We rely upon observations large, obvious, and prepared for us from the beginning of criticism. It is to support the coherence of the existing narrative that the microscope must be used, and abused, in order to discover, in part of the composition, a meaning which is not there[2]. But it is a good instrument nevertheless, and a necessary. The harmonistic process, as it leaves big traces, leaves also some less

---

[1] XIII 240 ff. See above.
[2] See above on X 53–66.

big. Upon one of them we are now to turn the glass.

Let us go back to the end of our episode, to the reconciliation between Idomeneus and Meriones in Book XIII. Meriones, we remember, has broken his spear in the fight; he is going for another to his own distant quarters, when, at those of Idomeneus, the king, armed for battle, meets him and asks his errand. Upon this the squire, changing his mind, replies :

Idomeneus, bearer of counsel for the mailed Cretans, I am going to fetch me a spear from your lodge, if there is still a spear left there; for we broke the spear which I carried before, casting at the shield of proud Deiphobus[1].

"We broke,"—why *we* ? The plural jars the ear in English, and in the Greek is worse, because of the singular participle ($\kappa\alpha\tau\epsilon\acute{\alpha}\xi\alpha\mu\epsilon\nu\ldots\beta\alpha\lambda\acute{\omega}\nu$) which must be taken with it in spite of the intervening singular. We know of course that in some languages the first person plural may be used when the speaker is not referring to any individual except himself, as for dignity, or as a mark of function (*we* of authorship), or for other like purposes of which the shades do not here concern us. And in some styles, as in Latin for example and occasionally in Attic tragedy, this is carried far, so that such a plural may be

---

[1] XIII 255

Ἰδομενεῦ, Κρητῶν βουληφόρε χαλκοχιτώνων,
ἔρχομαι, εἴ τί τοι ἔγχος ἐνὶ κλισίῃσι λέλειπται,
οἰσόμενος· τό νυ γὰρ κατεάξαμεν, ὃ πρὶν ἔχεσκον,
ἀσπίδα Δηϊφόβοιο βαλὼν ὑπερηνορέοντος.

hardly distinguishable from a singular. But in no style will be easily found such a *we* as this of Meriones, gratuitous, misleading, and simply wrong. Moreover, to the Greek of Homer plurals of this class, even in proper conditions, are almost, if not absolutely, unknown[1]. *We* and *our* are in Homer plurals proper. With reluctance therefore, and under protest, do scholars assume, as our text requires, that *we broke* here means *I broke*. What it ought to mean, the only thing which in Homer it properly can mean, is that the spear was broken by Meriones and Idomeneus.

And this it did mean, according to the intention of the composer, now concealed from us by the addition of a verse[2], which, at the expense of a solecism, identifies the spear with that which Meriones has just broken in battle. Nor hitherto have we known of any occasion on which the breaking of a spear by the two friends can have occurred. But it did occur, as surely ought now to be plain, at the rupture of their friendship, when Meriones renounced the service of his mutinous lord, and quitted their quarters for a distant place. The breaking of a spear was a symbol, probably a customary symbol, of such a renunciation. Till then, the spears of Meriones, with all that was his, were kept of course in the common stock. Upon the quarrel, a spear of his was solemnly broken, in sign that, as the angry

---

[1] In the examples here cited, evidently without faith, by Leaf, a true plural sense is always admissible, and sometimes necessary.

[2] *v.* 258, ἀσπίδα Δηϊφόβοιο βαλὼν ὑπερηνορέοντος.

men then meant, the breach was final and the bond on both sides dissolved. Whether the weapon was broken literally between them, or by one of them for both, the act was mutual, and is properly described by the plural,—"*we* broke the spear, which I carried before."

When therefore Meriones says, "I am going to fetch me a spear from your quarters, *if there is one still left there; for we broke the spear which I carried before*," he means that he is ready to be reconciled and return to his allegiance, if (for in the surprise of the moment he is not sure), if that is really open to him, though Idomeneus has not actually said so[1]. The words "for we broke my spear" do not refer to "I am going…," as the text now assumes, nor do they merely convey the information that he seeks a spear because he is without one. They refer to the doubt "if there is a spear still left in your quarters," and, taken so, they signify what is in his mind,—"if, which from what passed between us I must doubt, there is still a place for me in your service." The ambiguity of expression, natural to an uncertain state of feeling, is devised, very skilfully, as an opportunity for the misconstruction put upon it by the conscious and suspicious Idomeneus[2]. And the mishap of Meriones in the battle[3], whereby he comes to want a weapon, is of course also arranged expressly for the purpose of this dramatic turn.

[1] See XIII 249–253.   [2] *vv.* 259 ff., see above.
[3] *vv.* 159 ff.

The history and state of the text here are peculiarly interesting. They give us a glimpse of the linguistic habits native to the harmonist. He, and his public, must have been familiar with loose uses of the first person plural. This trait is not Homeric, nor is it characteristic of Greek. But it was familiar to the ancient habits of Attic, as we still see in tragedy. Further, it is instructive to note that the text, as the harmonist left it, is so plainly unsatisfactory that it has barely escaped further mutilation. The formality of the address, "Idomeneus, counsel-bearer of the mail-clad Cretans," is grotesquely unsuitable to the situation as supposed in our *Iliad*, and it makes one verse. Hence, as far back as we can trace, there have been votes for omitting this verse[1]. But in the true situation such an address was proper, not only because the man is not sure how he stands with his master, but because it touches precisely, after the manner of Greek invocations, the thoughts which are passing through his mind. The *counsel-bearer* (βουληφόρε) glances at the beginning of the quarrel, when Idomeneus refused his duty as councillor, which devolved upon Meriones. And *mail-clad* marks the new and essential fact, that the prince, like his subjects, is now in arms.

We may add then, to our relics of the suppressed episode, the fact that, when Meriones renounced Idomeneus, the rupture between them was signified by the breaking of a spear. And with this we reach the limit of what, so far as I see, is ascertainable,

[1] *v.* 255 is absent in many MSS.

and have completed such answer as can now be given to our original question,—What are the presumptions which would make intelligible the end of the episode, the reconciliation-scene of Book XIII?

We were next to ask, why this episode, the mutiny of Idomeneus, was excluded from the frame of our *Iliad*. The answer is obvious and simple. The episode was incompatible with other versions, which, in this part of the story, the framers of the *Iliad* were compelled by their scheme to prefer. The mutiny of Idomeneus occurred, as the place and purport of our Book x show, before the crisis of the story, the driving of the Greeks to their ships[1]. The conclusion of the episode, the battle comprising the *Aristeia of Idomeneus*, was part of the crisis itself, as presented in that version; and Idomeneus was there represented as inactive during the earlier part of the day's fight[2]. But in the version which furnishes the main outline of the *Iliad*, the version which some Homeric scholars distinguish as "the *Achilleis*" and regard as the original, there was no room for this inactivity. Idomeneus was active and conspicuous in the battle of that morning, as we see in our Book XI[3]. And this was confirmed by that version, or those, which equipped the camp with a wall. (The "*Achilleis*" recognized perhaps no fortification at all; the mutiny-version, so to call it, has a dyke but no more[4].) When the Trojans

[1] How long before, we cannot exactly say. The allusions of Book XIII seem to require a lapse of at least one day.

[2] XIII 210 ff.   See above.   [3] XI 501.   [4] See Book x.

carried the wall, Idomeneus was active in the defence[1]. Now in Book XI the story of the critical day is carried up to the very last point to which the taking of the wall, if it is to come in, can be deferred, —indeed rather beyond that point. To the taking therefore, and the fights within the wall, we here proceed[2], discarding necessarily the abstention of Idomeneus, and therefore the whole of his mutiny.

It is likely that this necessity was rather agreeable than otherwise to the makers of the harmony, if (as we have every reason to think) they were those who collected and arranged the Athenian Homer of the sixth century. The purpose of that collection was educational, and in Athens at all events, even at a much later date, Homer was popularly esteemed as an instructor in war, useful in forming the minds and morals of warriors. For this purpose, self-will and insubordination (it might be thought) were quite sufficiently represented in the story by the case of Achilles. We need not suppose, and I do not, that the harmonists, believing the revolt of Idomeneus to be true, suppressed it on moral grounds. As historians, which in their way and according to their powers they were, they had reason, upon a balance of authorities, to think it apocryphal. But the belief was probably welcome.

Nevertheless, the episode, as a development of the plot, was well-imagined. It is likely that Achilles would not lack imitators, and the spread of disloyalty was an effective addition to the discomfi-

[1] XII 117.   [2] Book XII and the bulk of XIII, XIV, XV.

ture of Agamemnon and his army.　And the author,
whether Homer or another[1], was a great artist.
The reconciliation[2] is a masterly bit of drama, and
there is more of the same kind, as well as other
merits, in Book x.　The loss of the episode is
among the most regrettable of the sacrifices which
can be traced in the harmony.

We proceed to our third and last question.
Since the mutiny was suppressed, why were the
extant allusions retained?　The answer is again
simple.　Because they were inseparable from other
matter, which the harmonist had neither reason nor
desire to suppress.　The *Doloneia* proper, the night-
adventure of Diomede and Odysseus, is in no way
discredited, as matter of fact, by the rejection of the
mutiny, and it is highly interesting.　But, as an
extract, when and how was the night-adventure to
begin?　A glance over the early part of Book x
will show that to this question there were but two
possible answers.　Either the actual beginning (that
of Book x) must be taken, or a new preface to the
expedition must be composed.　The latter way was
neither warranted by the principles of a harmony,
nor suitable perhaps to the capacity of the harmonists.　So they took the other, and retained so much
of the introductory part as their plan would admit,
excising all mention of the revolt, and trimming the
remainder, as best they might, into a mere preface

---

[1] We have remarked, in the preceding essay, that variant
versions do not necessarily presume difference of hands.

[2] XIII 240–294.

for the expedition. The omissions here must be very large, not less perhaps than the bulk retained. The errand of Diomede is cut off (after *v.* 178), to suppress the refusal of Meges. And at *v.* 180, where the existing story leaps abruptly to the guard-post, a huge cut has swept away the whole errand of Menelaus : his coming to the quarters of Aias and Idomeneus, their reception of him, the arrival of Agamemnon, the quarrel of the kings and mutiny of the Cretan ; the report of this disaster, by the royal brothers and Aias, to Nestor at the guard-post; the behaviour of Meriones at this crisis, and the arrangements leading to the council. This is the least extent of the excisions, which may of course be greater. But of insertion, on the other hand, there is, as in a harmony there should be, the bare minimum, and indeed less. The indispensable requirement for joining the ends was to get Menelaus (and his supposed companions) to the guard-post; he must be ordered to bring them there. This, as we saw, is effected, with discreet audacity, by a couplet in which Agamemnon tells Nestor (what is simply not true) that he has given such an order : " But let us be going ; and them shall we find before the gates, among the sentinels, for that is where I bade them assemble " :

ἀλλ' ἴομεν· κείνους δὲ κιχησόμεθα πρὸ πυλάων
ἐν φυλάκεσσ'· ἵνα γάρ σφιν ἐπέφραδον ἠγερέθεσθαι[1].

[1] X 126–127, where see commentaries. It will be observed that the couplet is not only unnecessary to the context, but interrupts it. Nestor (*v.* 129) replies to what precedes the couplet (*vv.* 120–125), including perhaps a verse or two in the sense of *vv.* 67–71. This would explain οὕτως in *v.* 129.

Even this couplet, we may suspect, is rather a mosaic than an original composition. The extraordinary syntax of the last clause (ἵνα) is just what might be produced by the misapplication of a fragment. Similarly, at the great cut, one verse replaces the errand of Diomede to Aias and Meges, and the next transports all parties, with judicious vagueness of designation, to the guard-post:

"And he (Diomede) went his way, and roused the others from their place, and brought them":

βῆ δ᾿ ἰέναι, τοὺς δ᾿ ἔνθεν ἀναστήσας ἄγεν ἥρως[1].

followed by

"Now when *they* had come among the assembled sentinels..."

οἱ δ᾿ ὅτε δὴ φυλάκεσσιν ἐν ἀγρομένοισιν ἔμιχθεν...[2]

This last (as has been noted by those who certainly had no notion of making evidence for me) is borrowed from III 209,

ἀλλ᾿ ὅτε δὴ Τρώεσσιν ἐν ἀγρομένοισιν ἔμιχθεν,

and the borrowing is not happy, for the description "assembled" is proper in the original place, but here improper and insignificant. *V.* 195 too, Ἀργείων βασιλῆες, ὅσοι κεκλήατο βουλήν, is not from the author. But a few such verses are the sole composition, if such they can be called, inserted in this place by the revisers.

[1] *v.* 179.

[2] *v.* 180, where see Leaf's note. In *v.* 181 note οὐδὲ μέν, which, in the present connexion of the verse, is surely incorrect. It looks as if the reviser really meant *v.* 180 for an independent sentence, using ὅτε δή for *in due course, presently,*—as in *v.* 127 ἵνα is practically made to mean *there*.

It is an interesting point to remark, that the remodeller, not the original composer, is responsible for the strange device, often noted with blame, of summoning a council for consultation outside the camp. In the original story, the assembly there was not planned by any one, but arose from a series of accidents. Agamemnon sends Nestor to visit and stimulate the guards; Nestor insists on being supported by others, whom he summons for the purpose; meanwhile Agamemnon's own business, the consultation of Aias and Idomeneus at their quarters, ends in a quarrel and an ignominious failure. Nothing is left to him then but to join Nestor and his party, bringing with him Menelaus and the obedient Aias. That is a very different thing (far more natural and intelligible) from a deliberate arrangement to hold a council at the guard-post. This the remodeller devised, as the only way to retain this part of the story and yet to suppress all the incidents for the sake of which it was originally contrived.

The result is a narrative in which plainly something is amiss, though the nature of the defect could not have been suspected, had not the other end of the story been preserved in Book XIII. Here the same causes have worked, but in conditions less favourable to the product. It was natural, in the story of the revolt, that the repentant mutineer should redeem his fault by signal exertions. Hence the *Aristeia of Idomeneus*. This indeed, as a battle-piece, may conceivably have existed before the composition of the mutiny-episode, and have been adopted by the author of that episode. We shall so believe, if we think, with some, that the language of Book x marks an authorship distinct from any other part of the *Iliad*. But this question we may leave untouched. The exertions of Idomeneus, the *Aristeia*, might in point of fact have occurred without the mutiny, and, so far, were admissible to the harmonistic collection. There was not indeed in it any proper place for the piece. It is not really possible, as attentive readers have long ago observed, that the *Aristeia of Idomeneus* should take place in the camp. But a harmonist cannot afford to maintain a high standard of possibility. And, to say the truth, the distension of the framework, in this part of the *Iliad*, is so enormous, that the importation of a fight or two is a trifle. If all the fighting at and within the wall was to be intercalated within the errand of Patroclus[1], it made little difference, in respect of harmony, if the *Aristeia* were intercalated in the intercalation, as accordingly it was. But there was this difficulty. The effect of the scene depends wholly upon the entrance of Idomeneus in the midst of the battle. That is the very purpose of it. The result of transferring it to a narrative, which did not recognize Idomeneus as absent, was inevitably what we see,—a cut, deep and conspicuous, at the point where we enter on the business of bringing Idomeneus back[2].

[1] See above p. 200.　　　[2] XIII 206.

Whether the operation might have been performed more artistically, we cannot judge. It has in fact been performed with scarcely a pretence of art, and so that what follows the cut, to the extent of near 100 verses[1], is all more or less unintelligible. How this came about, we may still in part at least discern. The return of Idomeneus contained a scene, in which he was rebuked and exhorted by Poseidon[2]. Now according to the narrative of the fight within the wall, it was Poseidon who, when the wall was lost, reanimated the resistance of the Greeks[3]. Here was a possible link of connexion; which however could not be used, unless in the return of Idomeneus were included his interview with Poseidon. And although the ensuing dialogue with Meriones[4] has, in the present connexion, no point or even meaning, it is yet inseparable both from the sequel and from an earlier passage of the episode[5], so that, if dropped, it must have been replaced by an original composition upon similar lines. In short, the problem here attempted by the harmonist —to retain the *Aristeia* and efface all trace of the mutiny—was insoluble; nor need we suppose him unaware that his product was not flawless. By straining a point, he enriched his collection with the *Aristeia*, expecting doubtless that auditors, at the Panathenaea and elsewhere, would be carried over the rocky places by the volume and force of the stream.

[1] XIII 206–294. [2] XIII 210–238.
[3] XIII 1–135. [4] XIII 239–294. [5] XIII 155–168.

And in this expectation, as the experience of
ages has proved, the harmonist was abundantly
justified. None will deny this, or is in the least
concerned to deny it. Nor on the other hand will
any prudent man deny, what was observed as soon as
there was any one to make such observations,—that
the return of Idomeneus in Book XIII of our *Iliad*
was never composed, as it stands, for the place in
which we find it. But with this observation we
enter at once upon a track which will carry us far.
I have endeavoured to show where it leads.

RHYME AND REASON

IN THE DIALOGUE OF ATTIC TRAGEDY.

"Do you know," says the drunken Heracles of the *Alcestis*, when he lectures on the duty of cheerfulness the poor serving-man who mourns for his mistress, "do you know the conditions of mortality? Doubtless not; how should you? Now listen to me. Death is the debt of all mankind, and never a mortal hath assurance that he will live through the coming morrow. For the term of fate is dark, and the way of it not to be taught or comprehended by skill. Having then listened to this lesson of mine, cheer up, and drink..." etc., etc.

τὰ θνητὰ πράγματ' οἶδας ἣν ἔχει φύσιν;
οἶμαι μὲν οὔ· πόθεν γάρ; ἀλλ' ἄκου' ἐμοῦ.
βροτοῖς ἅπασι κατθανεῖν ὀφείλεται
κοὐκ ἔστι θνητῶν ὅστις ἐξεπίσταται
τὴν αὔριον μέλλουσαν εἰ βιώσεται·
τὸ τῆς τύχης γὰρ ἀφανὲς οἷ προβήσεται,
κἄστ' οὐ διδακτὸν οὐδ' ἁλίσκεται...τέχνῃ.
ταῦτ' οὖν ἀκούσας καὶ μαθὼν ἐμοῦ πάρα,
εὔφραινε σαυτόν, πῖνε[1].

---

[1] *Alc.* 780 ff. Why ἁλίσκεται is marked, will appear when we return to this passage in conclusion.

Listen to me, says the drunken Heracles, and
Having listened to me, says he.   But it is of no use.
Clatter as he may, we do not hear him with our
ears.   The habit of silent reading has made us
slow to catch the sound of what is written.   And
moreover, used to language and poetry constructed
on principles not merely different from the Greek
but diametrically opposed, our attention, even if
given to the sound, brings us no natural and instinctive report.   To logic, rhetoric, pathos, we are alive;
and upon these heads the tragic poets are criticized
minutely; but as to noise, we will not notice it, not
even if we are bidden and bidden again.   Commentaries on the *Alcestis*, scrupulous about other matters,
pass in silence this jabber of Heracles, though it is a
phenomenon more startling, in Euripides, than any
vagary of syntax, and strongly illuminates the character of the personage and the tone of the scene.

The five verses, to which Euripides invites the
attention of our ears, are elaborately rhymed, that
is to say, they are ugly, offensive, and comic.

Of rhyme as we conceive it, and as our language
admits it, rhyme as a harmonious decoration and
pleasing method of emphasis, Greek is by its structure
hardly capable.   Assonance, if used in Greek, must
fall chiefly upon mere formative elements, inflexions,
suffixes, etc. ;   and nothing could be more futile than
to throw a metrical stress upon the fact that an adjective agrees with its noun, or that two adjacent
clauses are both in the same tense.   But indifference
to rhyme, in verse built on the Greek principle of

strict musical measure, is a thing impossible. The repetition of the same sound at regular intervals, if the sound have any considerable volume or the repetition any considerable extent, must be perceptible ; and it must either please or displease. In Greek the effect was necessarily uncouth, and rhyme therefore, generally speaking, was of service only to the artist in grotesque. To him it was invaluable. Aristophanes revels in it, and gets from it many of his broadest effects. Such for example is the description, in the *Acharnians*[1], of the clamour and bustle over the despatch of a naval expedition. This is how the grumbler vents his spleen :

$$\text{ἦν δ' ἂν ἡ πόλις πλέα}$$
θορύβου στρατιωτῶν περὶ τριηράρχου βοῆς,
μισθοῦ διδομένου, Παλλαδίων χρυσουμένων,
στοᾶς στεναχούσης, σιτίων μετρουμένων,
ἀσκῶν, τροπωτήρων, κάδους ὠνουμένων,
σκορόδων, ἐλαῶν, κρομμύων ἐν δικτύοις,
στεφάνων, τριχίδων, αὐλητρίδων, ὑπωπίων,
τὸ νεώριον δ' αὖ κωπέων πλατουμένων,
τύλων ψοφούντων, θαλαμιῶν τροπουμένων,
αὐλῶν κελευστῶν, νιγλάρων, συριγμάτων.
ταῦτ' οἶδ' ὅτι ἂν ἔδρατε.

And to the like tune, with single and double assonance, goes another grumble over the unpunctuality of the Assembly[2]:

$$\text{κᾆτ' ἐπειδὰν ὦ μόνος,}$$
στένω, κέχηνα, σκορδινῶμαι, πέρδομαι,
ἀπορῶ, γράφω, παρατίλλομαι, λογίζομαι,
ἀποβλέπων ἐς τὸν ἀγρόν, εἰρήνης ἐρῶν,
στυγῶν μὲν ἄστυ, τὸν δ' ἐμὸν δῆμον ποθῶν,

[1] *vv.* 545 ff.   [2] *Acharn.* 29.

and so on. This again describes a student, whose
studies are made impossible by the vermin of a dirty
school[1]:

ἀπόλλυμαι δείλαιος· ἐκ τοῦ σκίμποδος
δάκνουσί μ' ἐξέρποντες οἱ Κορίνθιοι[2],
καὶ τὰς πλευρὰς δαρδάπτουσιν
καὶ τὴν ψυχὴν ἐκπίνουσιν
καὶ τοὺς ὄρχεις ἐξέλκουσιν
καὶ τὸν πρωκτὸν διορύττουσιν
καί μ' ἀπολοῦσιν.

It is needless to accumulate examples, for almost
any scene of Aristophanes will supply illustrations[3]
of the ugly effect produced, in a language like
Greek, by metre which hammers upon the termina-
tions, an effect generally reserved, even in comedy,
for situations, emotions, expressions peculiarly disagreeable and unpleasant. For that purpose, an
assonance of more than one syllable is the more
easily made effective; but even the single rhyme is
treated as offensive, whenever it becomes noticeable.
An amusing passage in the *Knights*[4], representing
a contest of loudness between the demagogue Cleon
and his enemies the Chorus, depends chiefly for its
point upon the symmetrical combination of double
and single rhymes. The bawling-match developes
into a sort of hideous stanza, in which the two

---

[1] *Clouds* 709.   [2] κορεῖς, *bugs*.
[3] *Ach.* 30 foll., 180, 199, 356, 547 foll., 595 foll., 878 foll.,
1003 foll.; *Knights* 81, 111, 269–276, 372 foll., 1154 foll.,
1377 foll.; *Clouds* 64, 77, 126 foll., 494 foll., 710 foll., 1428,
1456, 1504.
[4] 266 foll.

parties roar -αι and -ει at one another till the stronger
wins :

ΚΛΕΩΝ.   ξυνεπίκεισθ' ὑμεῖς; ἐγὼ δ', ὦνδρες, δι' ὑμᾶς τύπτομαι
         ὅτι λέγειν γνώμην ἔμελλον ὡς δίκαιον ἐν πόλει
         ἱστάναι μνημεῖον ὑμῶν ἐστιν ἀνδρείας χάριν.

ΧΟΡΟΣ.   ὡς δ' ἀλαζών, ὡς δὲ μάσθλης· εἶδες οἷ' ὑπέρχεται
         ὥσπερεὶ γέροντας ἡμᾶς κἀκκοβαλικεύεται;
         ἀλλ' ἐὰν ταύτῃ γε νικᾷ, ταυτηὶ πεπλήξεται,
         ἢν δ' ὑπεκκλίνῃ γε δευρί, τὸ σκέλος κυρηβάσει.

ΚΛ.   ὦ πόλις καὶ δῆμ', ὑφ' οἵων θηρίων γαστρίζομαι.

ΧΟ.   καὶ κέκραγας, ὥσπερ ἀεὶ τὴν πόλιν καταστρέφει.

ΚΛ.   ἀλλ' ἐγώ σε τῇ βοῇ ταύτῃ γε πρῶτα τρέψομαι.

ΧΟ.   ἀλλ' ἐὰν μὲν τόνδε[1] νικᾷς τῇ βοῇ, τήνελλος εἶ.—
         ἢν δ' ἀναιδείᾳ παρέλθῃ σ', ἡμέτερος ὁ πυραμοῦς.

When comedy and satire used rhyme in such a
spirit and for such a purpose as this, the composers of
dignified drama could have but one rule about it,—to
shun it like a poison.   And such is in fact the general
practice in tragic dialogue, where rhyme, perceptible
rhyme, is rare almost to non-existence.   Between our
three extant poets there is no substantial difference
about this.   Of a single syllable indeed they are habitually not observant.   A single repetition of -ον or -αι,
or even of -τον or -ται, could hardly attract attention,
unless attention were specially called to it[2].   And
though it would not be true to say that such assonance, a final assonance of one syllable, was never
used in tragedy with purpose, yet pairs of this kind
occur not seldom, and sometimes more than a pair,
where evidently the composer is unaware of the fact
or indifferent.   But perceptible rhyme is taboo; and

---

[1] The sausage-seller, as rival demagogue.
[2] As in Soph. *Trach.* 787 ; see below, p. 251.

since the assonance of more than one syllable is
likely to be perceptible, it is avoided.   Aeschylus
and Sophocles give about 2–3 such assonances in
a play, Euripides not much more; and these are
limited to a single repetition, a single pair of verses.
Beyond this, in the way of rhyme, the tragic poets,
so long as they mean to be tragic, will not go.

Now the mere rarity of the thing, proving dislike
and scruple, would suggest that, when it does occur,
it is calculated for some purpose; and inspection
soon makes this certain.   The fact that Medea,
distinguished in this (I think) from all other speakers
in tragedy, *thrice* closes a speech upon a couplet
with double assonance[1], would alone show that Euripides could use such assonance with intention, and
therefore probably does so use it, when he admits it
at all.   But as to the nature of the purpose, an
English reader, who has not examined the facts, is
likely to be mistaken.   It is natural for us to take
such a final couplet, if we observe it, as a sort of
decorative and harmonious close, like those of the
Elizabethan dramatists.   But this conception is the
reverse of the Euripidean; violence, roughness, disharmony are the qualities which Euripides attributed
to such an assonance, and the rhymes of Medea are
not a chord but a scream.

All the double rhymes[2] in the dialogue of tragedy,
if we ignore a few cases possibly negligent, are

---

[1] *Med.* 314, 408, 757.

[2] I do not count as rhyme the repetition of the same word
(e.g. Eur. *Med.* 925). The effect of this is quite different from
mere assonance.

accounted for by the principle, that the sound, to Athenians, was harsh, sharp, and unmusical—a wound to the ear.

We will notice first some places—from the nature of the case not many—where the disagreeable quality of the sound expressly illustrates the context. Thus Odysseus, when he complains that the horrid noise of the agonized Philoctetes made decent life impossible for his comrades in camp, explains himself to the ear by an assonance:

> ὅτ' οὔτε λοιβῆς ἡμίν, οὔτε θυμάτων
> παρῆν ἐκήλοις προσθιγεῖν, ἀλλ' ἀγρίαις
> κατεῖχ' ἀεὶ πᾶν στρατόπεδον δυσφημίαις,
> βοῶν, στενάζων[1].

One can well believe, and the practice of Sophocles tends to show, that the sound of -ιαις was not such as a delicate versifier would care to press upon his auditor's attention. That here it is done with purpose, becomes certain, when we find an approach to the same effect, an assonance of one syllable, in the *Trachiniae*[2]: when the cliffs echo to the screams of the tortured Heracles, the verses echo too:

> ἐσπᾶτο γὰρ πέδονδε καὶ μετάρσιος,
> βοῶν, ἰύζων· ἀμφὶ δ' ἐκτύπουν πέτραι,
> Λοκρῶν ὄρειοι πρῶνες Εὐβοίας τ' ἄκραι.

For the like reason Admetus rhymes[3], when he insists that the repast of his visitor Heracles shall

---

[1] Soph. *Phil.* 8.   [2] *v.* 786.
[3] *Alcest.* 548.

not be disturbed by the lugubrious sounds of a
funeral from another part of the house :

ἐν δὲ κλήσατε
θύρας μεσαύλους· οὐ πρέπει θοινωμένους
κλύειν στεναγμῶν οὐδὲ λυπεῖσθαι ξένους.

So also in the *Phoenissae*[1], when the narrator, who
reports the victory of Thebes and the death of her
princes, breaks out at the close into a reverberating
wail, that "glorious celebration" should thus be
mingled with "grievous lamentation,"—

πόλει δ᾽ ἀγῶνες οἱ μὲν εὐτυχέστατοι
τῇδ᾽ ἐξέβησαν, οἱ δὲ δυστυχέστατοι,—

the hearers, thrilled by the sound and catching sight
at the same moment of the procession which brings
home the slain, exclaim that "the *lamentation* is
now not *audible* only but visible" :

οὐκ εἰς ἀκοὰς ἔτι δυστυχία
δώματος ἥκει· πάρα γὰρ λεύσσειν
πτώματα νεκρῶν.

Similar in principle, but different according to the
character and the occasion, is the rhyme of the
disgusted Polyphemus[2], who finds his enslaved satyrs
dancing, and roars out his commands to stop their
noise and get to work :

τί βακχιάζετ᾽; οὐχὶ Διόνυσος τάδε,
οὐ κρόταλα χαλκοῦ τυμπάνων τ᾽ ἀράγματα.
πῶς μοι κατ᾽ ἄντρα νεόγονα βλαστήματα;...

and so on. And for the like reason probably the
Persian in Aeschylus[3], when he relates how the sea-

---

[1] *v.* 1478. [2] *Cyclops* 204. [3] *Pers.* 309.

washed corpses at Salamis, as they go to and fro,
"butt against the strength of the victorious rocks,"
enhances the horror by a clash which seems to echo
the dunt :

οἱ δ' ἀμφὶ νῆσον τὴν πελειοθρέμμονα
νικώμενοι κύρισσον ἰσχυρὰν χθόνα[1].

Instances of this kind, where a harsh sound is
directly associated with the rhyming verse, are
necessarily few ; but they show the principle, and
account for almost all other applications of it. The
great majority fall into two classes. First, hardness or harshness, as a moral quality, is associated
naturally with hard and unpleasant sound, and therefore in Greek tragedy is repeatedly illustrated by
rhyme. Stubbornness, insult, arrogance, defiance,
so speak and are so described. Secondly, mere
violence of feeling, the extremity of distress or other
emotion, is permitted to produce this disorder of
speech, but only under certain remarkable restrictions :
the application of rhyme, in this looser way, is mainly
confined to the speech of women, and the exceptions
serve only to bring out the principle of the rule.

Of the first class, a simple and compendious
specimen is found in that scene of the *Prometheus*,
in which the stubborn will of the hero meets and
defies that of his persecutor represented by Hermes.
Prometheus strikes the note :

χλιδῶ; χλιδῶντας ὧδε τοὺς ἐμοὺς ἐγώ
ἐχθροὺς ἴδοιμι· καὶ σὲ δ' ἐν τούτοις λέγω.

[1] There is evidence, as we shall see, that a difference of tonic
accent did not save an assonance from objection.

Hermes enforces his warning in the same way:

πρὸς ταῦτα βούλευ'· ὡς ὅδ' οὐ πεπλασμένος
ὁ κόμπος, ἀλλὰ καὶ λίαν εἰρημένος.

And finally the Chorus, who would fain save Prometheus from himself, repeat the counsel of Hermes
with the same minatory emphasis:

ἡμῖν μὲν Ἑρμῆς οὐκ ἄκαιρα φαίνεται
λέγειν· ἄνωγε γάρ σε τὴν αὐθαδίαν
μεθέντ' ἐρευνᾶν τὴν σοφὴν εὐβουλίαν[1].

Sophocles gives the like tone to each of the
arrogant and tyrannical brother-kings of the *Aias*,
both to Menelaus,

καὶ μὴ δοκῶμεν δρῶντες ἂν ἡδώμεθα
οὐκ ἀντιτίσειν αὖθις ἂν λυπώμεθα,

and to Agamemnon,

εἰ τοὺς δίκῃ νικῶντας ἐξωθήσομεν
καὶ τοὺς ὄπισθεν ἐς τὸ πρόσθεν ἄξομεν.

And Teucer, thus provoked, barbs his insulting
defiance of them with the same sharp note:

αὐτὸς δὲ μητρὸς ἐξέφυς Κρήσσης, ἐφ' ᾗ
λαβὼν ἐπακτὸν ἄνδρ' ὁ φιτύσας πατὴρ
ἐφῆκεν ἐλλοῖς ἰχθύσιν διαφθοράν.
τοιοῦτος ὢν τοιῷδ' ὀνειδίζεις σποράν[2];

Euripides gives it twice to Theseus transported by
rage beyond the control of reason and overbearing
the remonstrance of his innocent son[3], and twice to
the Pentheus of the *Bacchae*[4] in his reckless and

---

[1] *P. V.* 972, 1030, 1037 (see 1034-5).
[2] *Aias* 1085, 1248, 1295.
[3] *Hipp.* 917, 937.   [4] *vv.* 459, 642.

obstinate wrath against the preacher of the new
religion.   Peleus comes very near to an assonance,
when he scolds Menelaus in the *Andromache*[1], and
Menelaus, goading him to fury, drives home his
retort with a final couplet[2]:

ἢν δ' ὀξυθυμῇς, σοὶ μὲν ἡ γλωσσαλγία
μείζων, ἐμοὶ δὲ κέρδος ἡ προμηθία.

King Agamemnon in Aeschylus opens with a
couplet the haughty and unfeeling speech which so
fitly precedes his fall[3],

πρῶτον μὲν Ἄργος καὶ θεοὺς ἐγχωρίους
δίκη προσειπεῖν, τοὺς ἐμοὶ μεταιτίους
νόστου,...

offensive alike to sentiment and ear.   In the Euripidean *Orestes*, both the criminal pair, both Electra[4]
and her brother[5], give vent in this way to the
passions by which they are destroyed; and their
fierceness finds an echo in the furious partizan
who relates their condemnation to death[6].   The
Sophoclean Aias means to assume the tone of
softness and submission, when he says,

ἅπανθ' ὁ μακρὸς κἀναρίθμητος χρόνος
φύει τ' ἄδηλα καὶ φανέντα κρύπτεται·
κοὐκ ἔστ' ἄελπτον οὐδέν, ἀλλ' ἁλίσκεται
χὠ δεινὸς ὅρκος χαὶ περισκελεῖς φρένες[7].

But the harsh sounds warn us that the "hard mind"
is there.   And so in the *Oedipus at Colonus*, when

---

[1] *v.* 610.   [2] *v.* 689.   [3] *Agam.* 810.
[4] *v.* 55.   [5] *v.* 567.   [6] *vv.* 928, 945.
[7] *Ai.* 646.

Polynices would propitiate his father by the appearance of humility, his speech bewrays him :

> τί σιγᾷς;
> φώνησον, ὦ πάτερ, τι· μή μ᾽ ἀποστραφῇς.
> οὐδ᾽ ἀνταμείβει μ᾽ οὐδέν; ἀλλ᾽ ἀτιμάσας
> πέμψεις ἄναυδος, οὐδ᾽ ἃ μηνίεις φράσας[1];

Close to the surface here is the temper which belongs to the man by name and nature, and which presently breaks out again when he speaks of his brother's usurpation[2]. We are prepared to see such a speaker repel the pleading of his sister, and rush, self-condemned, to his fate. Harshness, intentional or involuntary, the harshness and hardness of pride, defiance, or anger, is the common note of these speakers and of others[3].

Similar, and indeed scarcely distinguishable, are those cases (we have cited one already[4]), in which extravagance of this kind, though not itself expressed by assonance, is noted and condemned by assonant, and therefore offensive, comment on the part of the observer,—an unpleasant echo. We have a simple case in the *Phoenissae*[5], where Eteocles, the brother and counterpart of Polynices, is vainly admonished not to despise a formidable invader. The headstrong youth replies with contempt, and promises soon to carry the war into the enemies' country. "So I hope," says the monitor, "but I see

---

[1] *O.C.* 1271.   [2] *ib.* 1294.

[3] Aesch. *Suppl.* 946, Eur. *Alc.* 631, 771, *Iph. A.* 954, *Andr.* 435, *Hec.* 326.

[4] Aesch. *P. V.* 1037.   [5] *v.* 718.

many difficulties"; and he clinches the reproof by a rhyme :

ΕΤ. θάρσει· τάχ' αὐτῶν πεδίον ἐμπλήσω φόνου.
ΚΡ. θέλοιμ' ἄν· ἀλλὰ τοῦθ' ὁρῶ πολλοῦ πόνου.

Similarly the Chorus of the *Agamemnon*[1] mark and condemn the fury of Clytaemnestra against Cassandra,

ΚΛ. οὐ μὴν πλέω ῥίψασ' ἀτιμασθήσομαι.
ΧΟ. ἐγὼ δ', ἐποικτείρω γάρ, οὐ θυμώσομαι,—

and so also the prudent worshipper of Aphrodite rebukes the presumption of Hippolytus,

ΙΠ. οὐδείς μ' ἀρέσκει νυκτὶ θαυμαστὸς θεῶν.
ΘΕ. τιμαῖσιν, ὦ παῖ, δαιμόνων χρῆσθαι χρεών[2].

And the old friend of Admetus betrays similar irritation in protesting against the futile attempts of the king to explain and justify his behaviour in the reception of Heracles :

ΑΔ. ...αὐτὸς δ' ἀρίστου τοῦδε τυγχάνω ξένου,
ὅταν περ Ἄργους διψίαν ἔλθω χθόνα.
ΧΟ. πῶς οὖν ἔκρυπτες τὸν παρόντα δαίμονα,
φίλου μολόντος ἀνδρός, ὡς αὐτὸς λέγεις[3];

----

[1] *v.* 1068.

[2] Eur. *Hipp.* 106. This identical rhyme (θεῶν, χρεών) occurs in two other places (Aesch. *Supp.* 502, Eur. *Heraclidae* 587), a strong indication that in all three places it is intentional. The others are noticed below.

[3] *Alcestis* 559. In this class we should include *Bacch.* 951, where the bacchant rhymes in his mocking protest against the mad vaunts of Pentheus. The case is somewhat different, as here both rhymes belong to the speech of the protester; but the reason of the cacophony is essentially the same.

In all these the point lies in the offensive sound of the echo.

This use of rhyme, the offensive use, is the only one which in the dialogue of tragedy is generally admitted, admitted for all speakers without distinction. All kinds of persons speak in verses with final assonance, when their speech is meant to hurt, or plainly has that effect. But a different and special treatment is applied to the emotions of women. In the case of women, but generally speaking in their case only, mere distress, mere agitation, if sufficiently violent, is held by the poets to be appropriately marked by such assonance. The fact is certain, and proved by a list of examples from every part of our collection. They are so simple, that it will suffice to quote a few, and to indicate the remainder by reference.

Queen Atossa, scared by her dream, and flying for advice to her councillors, concludes her appeal with a couplet :—

πρὸς τάδ', ὡς οὕτως ἐχόντων τῶνδε, σύμβουλοι λόγου
τοῦδέ μοι γενέσθε, Πέρσαι, γηραλέα πιστώματα·
πάντα γὰρ τὰ κέδν' ἐν ὑμῖν ἐστί μοι βουλεύματα[1].

Nor does the distressful repetition fail to strike the auditors ; for they answer, " Be assured, O Queen, that, so far as we had the power, thou should'st not *bid us twice.*"

The wail of Atossa for the disaster of Salamis is

[1] *Pers.* 170.

rhymed to an extent hardly known in tragedy proper, rhymed almost on a system[1] :

> ὦ στυγνὲ δαῖμον, ὡς ἄρ' ἔψευσας φρενῶν
> Πέρσας· πικρὰν δὲ παῖς ἐμὸς τιμωρίαν
> κλεινῶν Ἀθηνῶν ηὗρε, κοὐκ ἀπήρκεσεν[2]
> οὓς πρόσθε Μαραθὼν βαρβάρων ἀπώλεσεν·
> ὧν ἀντίποινα παῖς ἐμὸς πράξειν δοκῶν
> τοσόνδε πλῆθος πημάτων ἐπέσπασεν.

In such a sequence as this, even the single rhymes on -ων would not be lost.

So also the horror of the gentle Danaid, divided between duty to father and husband, is reflected in the assonance of

> μίαν δὲ παίδων ἵμερος θέλξει τὸ μὴ
> κτεῖναι ξύνευνον, ἀλλ' ἀπαμβλυνθήσεται
> γνώμην, δυοῖν δὲ θάτερον βουλήσεται
> κλύειν ἄναλκις μᾶλλον ἢ μιαιφόνος[3].

So also speak in extreme distress the women of Sophocles :

> ἔγνωκα γὰρ δὴ φωτὸς ἠπατημένη
> καὶ τῆς παλαιᾶς χάριτος ἐκβεβλημένη.
> οἴμοι, τί δράσω, τέκνον[4];

and the women of Euripides :

> καὶ νῦν φέρουσά σοι νέους ἥκω λόγους,
> φόβῳ μέν, εἴ τις δεσποτῶν αἰσθήσεται,
> οἴκτῳ δὲ τῷ σῷ· δεινὰ γὰρ βουλεύεται
> Μενέλαος ἐς σὲ παῖς τε[5].

---

[1] *Pers.* 472.

[2] ἀπήρκεσε(ν), Cod. Med., is right. The later MSS. change it to ἀπήρκεσαν, to suit the plural οὕς. But the slaughter of Marathon, *regarded as a quantity*, is not a plural idea.

[3] *P. V.* 865.   [4] *Ai.* 807.   [5] *Andr.* 60.

The agony of Eurydice[1],

ὑπτία δὲ κλίνομαι
δείσασα πρὸς δμωαῖσι κἀποπλήσσομαι,

and of Deianira[2], the furious agony of Phaedra[3], the frantic entreaties[4] and loathing insinuations[5] of Hecuba, all raise the same sharp note. Megara so cries in despair[6] to her lost Heracles,

σοὶ τάδ', Ἡράκλεις, λέγω·
θνήσκει πατὴρ σὸς καὶ τέκν', ὄλλυμαι δ' ἐγώ,

and again at the sight of her husband, in a revulsion of such joy as is not distinguishable from pain,

ὅδ' ἐστὶν ὃν γῆς νέρθεν εἰσηκούομεν,
εἰ μή γ' ὄνειρον ἐν φάει τι λεύσσομεν[6].

And the Sophoclean Deianira in similar circumstances does exactly the same[7]. The Euripidean Electra so expresses the horror of expectation with which she watches the approach of her doomed mother[8]. Macaria so expresses the passion of a martyr[9]. The maid in the *Alcestis* so weeps over the sacrifice of her mistress[10]. The assonant verses

---

[1] *Antig.* 1188.

[2] *Trach.* 907—914; note that the narrator is also a woman.

[3] *Hipp.* 727.   [4] *Hec.* 289.   [5] *ib.* 825.

[6] *Heracles* 491, 516.   [7] *Trach.* 232.

[8] Eur. *Electra* 965. The value of the assonance here makes it probable that nothing is lost (as some have supposed) between this verse and the next. There is merely a pause. See Murray's text.

[9] *Heraclidae* 587.

[10] *Alc.* 161. See also *Iph. A.* 1443, *Helena* 786. *Helena* 1387 would *prima facie* be included here, but will be considered separately. None of these (I think) are negligent.

which in the *Bacchae*[1] describe how the possessed women tear live animals to pieces—

> ἄλλαι δὲ δαμάλας διεφόρουν σπαράγμασιν·
> εἶδες δ᾽ ἂν ἢ πλεύρ᾽ ἢ δίχηλον ἔμβασιν
> ῥιπτόμεν᾽ ἄνω τε καὶ κάτω....

reflect perhaps the fierceness of the bacchants rather than the horror of the narrator.

But it is the passions of Medea, fierce, hard, and intensely feminine, which find in this form most conspicuous expression. Not only has she four couplets to her name[2], a list hardly to be matched, but three of these are so placed, at the close of a speech or scene, that they cannot but catch the ear. The purpose manifestly is, little as our habits of language would suggest it, to stamp the temper of Medea as something almost exceeding, in violence and discord, the limits of harmonious representation.

Precisely why the tragic poets of Athens thus habitually assigned this little note of sharpness and disharmony to feminine emotion, is a question which, at this wide interval of time, space, and manners, we can hardly with prudence pretend to answer. But neither do I find the fact surprising. It seems to me consistent with Attic views both of women and of art.

To masculine speakers, assonant verses, as a sign merely of violent emotion, are very rarely permitted, and the exceptions are significant. Assonant verses were, on Attic principles, something harsh, inharmonious, improper. Male speakers rhyme when

---

[1] *v.* 739.   [2] *Med.* 256, 314, 408, 757.

they wilfully transgress harmony, women in all
kinds of painful or violent emotion, apparently
because (in the Attic view) they were, in such
circumstances, always liable to transgress harmony.
And the few males who imitate them are those from
whom, in their state or position, control could not
be expected.   It is not surprising that a man should
so speak, when he has but just recovered from a fit
of homicidal mania, and his half-sane mind is tottering
on the verge of another collapse[1];

> φέρ', ἀλλ' ἐς ἄλλην δή τιν' ὁρμήσω πόλιν·
> κἄπειθ' ὑποβλεπώμεθ' ὡς ἐγνωσμένοι,
> γλώσσης πικροῖς κέντροισι κληδουχούμενοι·
> 'οὐχ οὗτος ὁ Διός, ὃς τέκν' ἔκτεινέν ποτε
> δάμαρτά τε;'—

Nor is it surprising, though instructive, to observe
that this same Heracles utters the like note in an
earlier scene[2],

> ἀλλ' εἶ' ὁμαρτεῖτ', ὦ τέκν', ἐς δόμους πατρί·
> καλλίονές τἄρ' εἴσοδοι τῶν ἐξόδων
> πάρεισιν ὑμῖν· ἀλλὰ θάρσος ἴσχετε
> καὶ νάματ' ὅσσων μηκέτ' ἐξανίετε.—

a scene in which his violent behaviour foreshows
and almost anticipates the approaching outbreak of
his disorder[3].

Two decrepit men, in both of whom the effort
to surpass the strength and capacity of nature is
carried up to, if not over, the verge of the ridiculous[4],
betray by assonance that, in pain, their feelings are

---

[1] *Heracles* 1286, and *ib.* 1362.   [2] *Heracles* 622.

[3] See *Four Plays of Euripides*, pp. 156 ff.

[4] See *Heraclidae* 680—747, *Bacch.* 170—369.

not under masculine control.   In the Cadmus of the
Bacchae this is made especially conspicuous ; for he
enters with a couplet, when he brings from the
mountain the mangled remains of his grandson[1]:

ἔπεσθέ μοι φέροντες ἄθλιον βάρος
Πενθέως, ἔπεσθε, πρόσπολοι, δόμων πάρος.

The effect is much the same as when later, in a
scene of lamentation, an assonant couplet is divided
between the old man and a woman[2].   For the like
reason doubtless the aged Iolaus of the *Heraclidae*
twice rhymes at a critical and agitating moment,
once in his first appeal to the protection of Athens,
and again when the self-devoted Macaria offers to
die for the family[3]:

οὐδ' αἰσχύνομαι
τοῖς σοῖς λόγοισι, τῇ τύχῃ δ' ἀλγύνομαι.

A couplet is divided between Orestes and
Pylades, when, arriving at the Tauric temple, they
first discover, from its bloody decorations, the
hideous peril of their plan to plunder it[4]:

OP.   ...ἀλλὰ πρὶν θανεῖν, νεὼς ἔπι
φεύγωμεν, ᾗπερ δεῦρ' ἐναυστολήσαμεν.
ΠΥ.   φεύγειν μὲν οὐκ ἀνεκτόν, οὐδ' εἰώθαμεν...
ναοῦ δ' ἀπαλλαχθέντε κρύψωμεν δέμας...

If this is not negligent—and it is not likely to be—
it marks the sharpness of a fear that is almost beyond
control.

Slaves and other servants, both male and female,
under great excitement use assonance in several

---

[1] *Bacch.* 1216.   [2] *Bacch.* 1361.   But this may be negligent.
[3] *Heraclidae* 92, 541.   [4] *Iph. T.* 102.

places[1], as we should expect. Control and propriety are not expected of them. We may wonder rather that the Nurse in the *Choephori* does not rhyme; but her part is so short as to give little opportunity.

One speaker, I must say, shows a tendency in this direction, for which I cannot account,—the young temple-minister Ion, who rhymes no less than four times, and upon occasions which, judged by the general practice, are inadequate[2]. The repetition seems to forbid the supposition of negligence, and so does the fact that two of the rhymes are made upon the same word (κεκτημένος), as if the later situation had in some way recalled the former. But I have found no explanation which satisfies me; and negligence is of course conceivable.

Exceptional also, but showing clearly with what consciousness and care these assonances were disposed by the Athenian artists, is the fact that Sophocles twice introduces one at the critical point of a narrative. The breaking out of the fiery poison in the robe sent by Deianira to Heracles (the shirt of Nessus) is related thus :

καὶ πρῶτα μὲν δείλαιος ἵλεῳ φρενὶ
κόσμῳ τε χαίρων καὶ στολῇ κατηύχετο·
ὅπως δὲ σεμνῶν ὀργίων ἐδαίετο
φλὸξ αἱματηρὰ κἀπὸ πιείρας δρυός,
ἱδρὼς ἀνῄει χρωτὶ καὶ προσπτύσσεται
πλευραῖσιν ἀρτίκολλος, ὥστε τέκτονος,
χιτὼν ἅπαν κατ' ἄρθρον[3].

---

[1] *Agam.* 31, 511, *Antig.* 272, *Ion* 1106 (entrance couplet), *Med.* 4, 46, 72. Some of these may be negligent.

[2] *Ion* 322, 430, 590, 641.　　　　　[3] *Trach.* 763.

The rhyme here one would naturally take to be involuntary and negligent; but it certainly is not, for in the relation of the death of Oedipus at Colonus, the mysterious disappearance of the trans-lated hero is heralded by the same artifice of sound[1],—two instances, be it remembered, out of a score in all the plays of Sophocles together. The precise effect intended we can hardly define or appreciate; but it must be some sort of prick to the ear. Euripides too uses the same device in relating how the bride of Jason was devoured by the poisoned robes of Medea[2], a parallel so close to the passage from the *Trachiniae*, that we may count it among the traces of Euripidean influence in that play.

There is one passage of Aeschylus, which, though not exhibiting any perfect assonance, can-not be omitted here, being from our point of view most remarkable, and in tragedy perhaps unique. If there is any feeling, to the expression of which a trick of sound, essentially disagreeable, should seem appropriate, it is perplexity and indecision. The condition is irritating, both to feel and to see; and it is not dignified. The comic stage loves to exhibit it; and, as we might expect, on the comic stage of Athens it had all the advantage, or dis-advantage, of rhyme. Strepsiades in the *Clouds*,

---

[1] *O. C.* 1647.

[2] *Med.* 1184. This point is in favour of the variant reading ἠγείρετο. Note that the assonant syllables (-ετο) are the same as in Soph. *Trach. l.c.*

when, deserted by his son, he debates the question
of submitting himself to the discipline of the sophists,
rhymes almost without pause for seven lines on end,
in six lines out of the seven :

ἀλλ' οὐδ' ἐγὼ μέντοι πεσών γε κείσομαι,
ἀλλ' εὐξάμενος τοῖσιν θεοῖς διδάξομαι
αὐτὸς βαδίζων ἐς τὸ φροντιστήριον.—
πῶς οὖν γέρων ὢν κἀπιλήσμων καὶ βραδὺς
λόγων ἀκριβῶν σχινδαλάμους μαθήσομαι;—
ἰτητέον. τί ταῦτ' ἔχων στραγγεύομαι,
ἀλλ' οὐχὶ κόπτω τὴν θύραν; παῖ, παιδίον[1].

The effect is incompatible with dignity, and in
tragedy I have found no parallel.   But the King of
Argos in the Aeschylean *Suppliants*, in pondering
on a painful choice, comes nearer to the tones of
Strepsiades than might be expected[2] :

καὶ γλῶσσα τοξεύσασα μὴ τὰ καίρια,...
γένοιτο μύθου μῦθος ἂν θελκτήριος[3]...
ἀλγεινὰ θυμοῦ κάρτα κινητήρια...—
ὅπως δ ὅμαιμον αἷμα μὴ γενήσεται
δεῖ κάρτα θύειν καὶ πεσεῖν χρηστήρια
θεοῖσι πολλοῖς πολλά, πημονῆς ἄκη.—
ἦ κάρτα νείκους τοῦδ' ἐγὼ παροίχομαι.

We may observe that, in such a passage, it is
needless to rectify any irregularities of construction.   The syntax is proper to the sound, and
not more surprising.   An Aeschylean speaker, who
thus chimes in his verses, may well break his
sentences too.   There is indeed no perfect and
sequent assonance; but there is something very

---

[1] *Clouds* 126, cf. *ib.* 494 foll., etc.   [2] *v.* 446.
[3] θελκτηρίοις *Cod. Med.*, perhaps rightly.

near a quadruple assonance on three syllables, -αιρια, -ηριος, -ηρια, and again -ηρια. I can find no other such example, and venture to doubt whether Aeschylus, when he composed the *Orestea*, would have cared to tread so close upon the confines of comedy. A touch, but far lighter, of the same quality is given by Sophocles to the hesitation of Philoctetes, whether to go or not go with Neoptolemus to Troy[1]:

> οἴμοι, τί δράσω; πῶς ἀπιστήσω λόγοις
> τοῖς τοῦδ᾽, ὃς εὔνους ὢν ἐμοὶ παρήνεσεν;—
> ἀλλ᾽ εἰκάθω δῆτ᾽; εἶτα πῶς ὁ δύσμορος
> ἐς φῶς τάδ᾽ ἔρξας εἶμι; τῷ προσήγορος;...

The *Oedipus Tyrannus* presents a singular couplet[2]. Creon, reporting the command of the Delphic Apollo to discover the murderer of Laius, and being asked by Oedipus, where and how this can possibly be done, replies thus:

> ἐν τῇδ᾽ ἔφασκε γῇ· τὸ δὲ ζητούμενον
> ἁλωτόν, ἐκφεύγει δὲ τἀμελούμενον.

That this assonance is conscious, one cannot doubt ; but it seems to be quite abnormal. Rudeness is not to be suspected. The speaker, a man, is not even excited, and such emotion as he has is rather pleasurable. The sentence, "What is sought, may be caught, but what is neglected, escapes," has the air of a saw, and possibly in this quarter lies the explanation of the form. Rhyme, whether liked or disliked, aids the memory. It may be observed that Apollo in the *Eumenides*, when he addresses the

[1] *Phil.* 1350.   [2] *v.* 110.

Areopagus in his oracular capacity, more than once
delivers his principles in the form of single-rhymed
couplets, for instance :

> πέδας μὲν ἂν λύσειεν· ἔστι τοῦδ' ἄκος
> καὶ κάρτα πολλὴ μηχανὴ λυτήριος·
> ἀνδρὸς δ' ἐπειδὰν αἷμ' ἀνασπάσῃ κόνις,
> ἅπαξ θανόντος οὐκέτ' ἔστ' ἀνάστασις[1].

It is conceivable that such forms were oracular,
which would explain the rhyme of Creon. But
if this were so, we might expect more evidence of
it ; and we should rather suppose reference to a
popular saying, or citation from some older poet,
who was not in this matter so sensitive as our
three. Some explanation there must be ; for such
an assonance in such a place, however it may sound
to an English ear, is in Sophocles almost portentous.

The *Cyclops*, as a satyric drama, might well
exhibit a comic licence in rhyme, as it does other
such licences of language and metre. And there is
in fact a slight difference, not of quantity but of
quality. The slave-god Silenus, when he sees the
Greek voyagers approaching the home of his can-
nibal master, utters his compassion and dismay in
semi-comic tones[2] :

> ὁρῶ πρὸς ἀκταῖς ναὸς Ἑλλάδος σκάφος,
> κώπης τ' ἄνακτας ξὺν στρατηλάτῃ τινὶ
> στείχοντας ἐς τόδ' ἄντρον, ἀμφὶ δ' αὐχέσι
> τεύχη φέρουσι κενά, βορᾶς κεχρημένοι,
> κρωσσούς θ' ὑδρηλούς. ὦ ταλαίπωροι ξένοι,

---

[1] *Eum.* 645 ; see also *ib.* 658.
[2] *Cycl.* 85.

τίνες ποτ' εἰσίν; οὐκ ἴσασι δεσπότην
Πολύφημον οἷός ἐστιν, ἄξενον στέγην
τήνδ'¹ ἐμβεβῶτες, καὶ Κυκλωπίαν γνάθον
τὴν ἀνδροβρῶτα δυστυχῶς ἀφιγμένοι.

And at the end of the play Odysseus defies the
Cyclops with a strong rhyme :

κακῶς γὰρ ἂν Τροίαν γε διεπυρωσάμην,
εἰ μή σ' ἑταίρων φόνον ἐτιμωρησάμην².

This, as intentionally offensive, would be permitted
even in tragedy, and is clearly proper to a personage
who condescends to such language as κλάειν σ' ἄνωγα,
" Go to the deuce ! "³

To sum up then our review,—final assonance
upon more than one syllable, in the dialogue of
tragedy, is plainly limited in general by principles,
and employed as an artifice. But it may nevertheless be in some places attributable to negligence,
just as in English a composer careful of his rhymes
will, once in a way, give us a weak or a bad one.
In Aeschylus, as a fact, I do not find any clear
negligence⁴. In the *Suppliants* there is indeed an

¹ Or perhaps τὴν (Bothe), an archaic equivalent for the
regular τήνδε. It is not unlikely that a satyr, at such a moment,
might archaize. And it is to be considered, whether we should
change Κυκλωπίαν γνάθον to the archaic γνάθον Κυκλωπίην, which
would keep up the rhyme on -ην.

² *v.* 694. διεπυρώσαμεν Fix, but the middle voice ('brought
to pass the conflagration of Troy') should be kept.

³ *v.* 701.

⁴ *Cho.* 117—118 is scarcely within the general limits, but as
both the speakers are women, and the situation tense, the exception is not striking.

odd instance : the Argive king is about to conduct Danaus to the city, leaving the Chorus (Danaus' daughters) in a place which he supposes to be safe :

στείχοιτ' ἄν, ἄνδρες, says he to his attendants,
εὖ γὰρ ὁ ξένος λέγει,
ἡγεῖσθε βωμοὺς ἀστικούς, θεῶν ἕδρας·
καὶ ξυμβολοῦσιν οὐ πολυστομεῖν χρεὼν
ναύτην ἄγοντας τόνδ' ἐφέστιον θεῶν.

XO.   τούτῳ μὲν εἶπας, καὶ τεταγμένος κίοι.
ἐγὼ δὲ πῶς δρῶ, ποῦ θράσος νέμεις ἐμοί;[1]

Why both King and Chorus should rhyme, is not clear to me ; but, if we have observed the practice of the poet, we shall not easily suppose such a quatrain to be unintentional. That the alarmed women should have a couplet is natural, but that of the king I must leave to the ingenuity of the reader.

Both in Sophocles and in Euripides there are a few assonances which we may well suppose negligent, not merely as having no visible reason, but because they occur in places where negligence might naturally be expected. When Sophocles brings on a *deus ex machina*, one is not surprised to find a certain negligence in the oration :

ἐγὼ δ' Ἀσκληπιὸν
παυστῆρα πέμψω σῆς νόσου πρὸς Ἴλιον[2].

The very nature of such a personage invites to hasty and perfunctory execution, evidence of which, in one way or another, appears in almost every such

[1] *vv.* 500 ff.   [2] *Phil.* 1437.

composition of Euripides. In Euripides the prologue and epilogue to the *Bacchae*[1], and the *Electra*[2]
in both prologue and epilogue, exhibit rhymes without
reason, and for which no reason need be sought. It
is natural in such appendages to be careless[3]. I am
not sure of the purpose, or that there is a purpose,
in *Troades* 1127, and still less in *Electra* 371:

ἤδη γὰρ εἶδον ἄνδρα γενναίου πατρὸς
τὸ μηδὲν ὄντα, χρηστὰ δ᾽ ἐκ κακῶν τέκνα,
λιμόν τ᾽ ἐν ἀνδρὸς πλουσίου φρονήματι,
γνώμην δὲ μεγάλην ἐν πένητι σώματι.

Possibly Orestes here, like Creon in the *Oedipus
Tyrannus*[4], may be repeating a popular saw. But
the assonance is less conspicuous than that in
Sophocles; it may be merely negligent; and other
such there may be, which I have not observed or
have wrongly explained, but not, I will venture to
say, sufficient in number to affect our judgement.

A few cases may be noted, which, for one reason
or another, must be excluded from the reckoning.
In the *Heracles*, v. 1110 rhymes to v. 1111; but it
appears, on considering the action of the scene, that
these verses are separated by a long interval of
silence, and the assonance therefore not noticeable.
Two fragmentary verses, describing locks of hair
offered by Orestes to his native river and to the
grave of his father, have been placed in the prologue

[1] *vv.* 15, 1354. [2] *vv.* 20, 1285.

[3] Compare the anapaests at the end of the *Trachiniae*, in which
not the least fault is the assonance. They are poor, but it is by
no means certain that they are not by Sophocles.

[4] *v.* 110; see above pp. 267, 268.

of the *Choephori*[1]. Each ends in -τήριον, and, if contiguous, they would make a triple assonance; but there is no proof that they were contiguous. The *Suppliants* of Euripides will be found, in almost any investigation of tragic or Euripidean practice, to provide a surprise; and it does so here. In the body of the play I have not noted one double assonance[2]; but the speech of Athena, the goddess *ex machina*, ends with an assonant couplet. She is promising to the Argives vengeance for the defeat of Adrastus by Thebes, and foretelling the success of the Epigoni :

> πικροὶ γὰρ αὐτοῖς ἥξετ' ἐκτεθραμμένοι
> σκύμνοι λεόντων, πόλεος ἐκπορθήτορες.
> [κοὐκ ἔστιν ἄλλως, Ἔκγονοι[3] δ' ἀν' Ἑλλάδα
> κληθέντες ᾠδὰς ὑστέροισι θήσετε·
> τοῖον στράτευμα σὺν θεῷ πορεύσετε.]

The assonance is conspicuous and apparently intentional, but it is unusual; and seeing that the author also gives an unusual title to the *Epigoni*, one may suspect the three last verses to have been added by another hand. An audience fairly acquainted with Greek legend would not need them; but the plays of Euripides came to be performed before audiences not so acquainted. In *Troades* 437—438, dubious rhyme adds a note of suspicion to a passage which is justly suspected,

---

[1] *vv.* 6, 7.

[2] ἐδέξατο—ἤσθετο (393-4) is not perfect, nor πόλιν—πάλιν (1208-9).

[3] So the MSS. (*v.* 1224).

and indeed cannot be correct as it stands[1]. Such
also are the lines which describe how Orestes in
his madness took the voices of animals for cries of
the Furies :

παρῆν δ' ὁρᾶν

οὐ ταῦτα μορφῆς σχήματ', ἀλλ' ἠλλάσσετο

φθογγάς τε μόσχων καὶ κυνῶν ὑλάγματα,

†ᾶς φασ' Ἐρινὺς ἱέναι μιμήματα[2].

Here nothing is certain but that the last verse is
erroneous. The true remedy, I believe, is simply
to omit it : ἠλλάσσετο, *he converted* (*misinterpreted*),
requires no explanation, though some one might
think that it did[3].

I have reserved for separate consideration two
examples of double assonance in the *Helen* of Euripides, not because either is difficult to justify, but
because the passages in which they occur deserve
special attention for the light which they throw on
the character and purpose of that strange play.

The heroine, it will be remembered, is there
pursued by the unwelcome addresses of her host
and protector, Theoclymenus, King of Egypt. Her
husband Menelaus having arrived secretly, she ar-
ranges with him to deceive Theoclymenus, by pretending that she has discovered herself to be now a
widow and is therefore ready to accept his proposal,
so that he shall provide her and her true spouse

---

[1] See commentaries *ad loc.*   [2] *Iph. T.* 291.

[3] *Iph. A.* 809—810 is hardly worth notice. No one will
suppose that Euripides left this speech as we read it.

with a ship, in which they will escape to Greece.
For this plot she requires the connivence and fidelity
of the Chorus, a band of Greek women captured and
enslaved, to whom she holds out hopes, very unsub-
stantial, of their ultimate deliverance from captivity,
and appeals in the following terms[1] :

ἀλλ' ἐκπερᾷ γὰρ δωμάτων ὁ τοὺς ἐμοὺς
γάμους ἑτοίμους ἐν χεροῖν ἔχειν δοκῶν,
σιγητέον μοι· καὶ σὲ προσποιούμεθα
εὔνουν, κρατεῖν τε στόματος, ἢν δυνώμεθα...
σωθέντες αὐτοὶ καὶ σὲ συσσῶσαί ποτε.

The situation and language present, like all this
part of the *Helen*, a close and even verbal resemblance to the *Iphigenia in Taurica*, a resemblance
which must be designed to recall the earlier play
to the minds of the spectators.

I have given elsewhere[2] my reasons for thinking
that the *Helen* is not a serious drama, and that the
relation of the play to the *Iphigenia* in particular is
that of a travesty or parody, in which unreal dangers
and futile expedients are humorously substituted for
the genuine perils and escapes of a tragedy.

Now in the use of assonance by Helen, in her
rhyme upon the syllables -μεθα, there is nothing
remarkable.   If Iphigenia had so spoken in the like
situation, as a woman addressing women in poignant
and painful emotion, the touch would have been perfectly accordant with tragic use.   But the remarkable
thing is this, that in the words of Helen the note of

[1] *v.* 1385.
[2] Essay on the *Helen* in *Four Plays of Euripides*.

pain and distress is put into a sentence so framed that
it must provoke laughter. " I must now be silent,"
she says, " and I would enlist you also as loyal
helpers, and would have us control our lips, if we
can...perhaps effect your escape hereafter as a sequel
to our own." Now surely in no language, native
and familiar to the composer and to the intended
audience, could a playwright frame such a sentence
with the expectation that it would be heard with
gravity. A ruinous misunderstanding is not only
risked, but courted. A pause after the words "if we
can" is not only admissible but suggested by the
versification. Yet if the least pause were made,
even by accident, the audience must laugh. That
women cannot hold their tongues or keep a secret
is a proposition perhaps untrue, but familiar to the
comedy of all ages. No man using his native
language, to say nothing of Euripides, could write
such words, much less recite them, without becoming
aware of their perilous ambiguity. The sentence
is eventually finished so as to save appearances, but
should anyone titter at ἢν δυνώμεθα—and what else
could be expected?—the belated rescue of the meaning would serve only to raise another laugh. In such
a composer as Euripides the thing must in fairness
be regarded as intentionally ridiculous ; and the note
of emotion given by the assonance must be intended,
and would certainly serve, to signalize and sharpen
the jest.

Still more significant is a passage, uncommonly
assonant, which occurs in the subsequent narrative

18—2

of the escape. To appreciate it, we must recall the plot. The pretext upon which Helen and Menelaus obtain the loan of a ship is the alleged necessity of performing at sea, and at some distance from the shore, a funeral rite for Menelaus, who (they say) has been drowned. This fiction succeeds, because, strange to say, not only the enamoured king of Egypt, but all his servants, accept and promote it with enthusiasm. It requires, among other things, that the Greek crew of Menelaus, who have escaped with him from their shipwreck, and are lurking on the shore, shall be admitted to the "funeral-ship." This is effected thus : the king is induced without difficulty to say that his ship and seamen, for the purpose of the funeral, are to be absolutely under the command of the Greek stranger (Menelaus). When the Greek crew, some fifty in number, appear, and are politely invited by Menelaus to take part in the rite, the Egyptians, though dissatisfied, admit them, on the ground (as the reporter maintains) that they could not infringe the royal order to obey the foreigner ! In the same spirit of misapplied subservience they choose for the funeral-ship a new ship in the Egyptian fleet ; and moreover, for no reason whatever, they actually supply it with sails, although, according to the purpose alleged, the vessel is merely to be rowed out a mile or so and rowed back again ! It should, I think, be unnecessary to insist, that such a story, in a respectable and reasonable author, cannot be serious, but is essentially humorous and comical.

Now this aspect of the affair is especially to be remembered when we come to the equipment of the vessel. "On arriving at your enclosed docks," says the narrator to King Theoclymenus, "we launched a ship of Sidon, one new to the sea, having oars and benches to the number of fifty"—the number, as it happened, for which Menelaus could supply Greek hands. "And from this to that the work went on, some planting the mast, some putting in the oars with blade and handle, and white sails too...*for a future day*, or dropping into place the rudder and rudder-bands. In the midst of all this (for which, it appears, they were in watch) a company of Greeks, the sailors who had been with Menelaus, came to the shore, dressed as they had escaped from shipwreck, comely fellows though sordid of mien." These "notwithstanding their suspicious number," upon the invitation of Menelaus are taken on board, and presently seize the ship[1].

ὡς δ' ἤλθομεν σῶν περίβολον νεωρίων
Σιδωνίαν ναῦν πρωτόπλουν καθείλκομεν,
ζυγῶν τε πεντήκοντα κἀρετμῶν μέτρα
ἔχουσαν· ἔργου δ' ἔργον ἐξημείβετο·
ὁ μὲν γὰρ ἱστόν, ὁ δὲ πλάτην καθίσατο[2]
ταρσόν τε χειρί, λευκά θ' ἱστί'...εἰς ἔνην[3],
πηδάλιά τε ζεύγλαισι παρακαθίετο.
κἀν τῷδε μόχθῳ τοῦτ' ἄρα σκοπούμενοι
Ἕλληνες ἄνδρες Μενέλεῳ ξυνέμποροι
προσῆλθον ἀκταῖς, ναυφθόροις ἠσθημένοι
πέπλοισιν, εὐειδεῖς μὲν αὐχμηροὶ δ' ὁρᾶν...

[1] *Helena* 1530 ff.   [2] καθίστατο Barnes, perhaps rightly.
[3] εἰς ἐν ἦν MS., εἰμέν' ἦν Boeckh, *alii alia*.

The prevalent assonance is remarkable, but has here a purpose sufficiently plain. The verse, like the topic, is noisy, and imitates in a mild way the rattle of Aristophanes, when he describes the fitting out of a fleet[1]. Whether Euripides would have admitted such an effect into poetry meant to be dignified, we may question ; but it is proper enough to the *Helen* and to this story. And observing this, we have a larger range for interpreting the words presented to us in the unintelligible form of λευκά θ' ἐστί' εἰς ἓν ἦν. The vocabulary of tragedy does not offer any probable reading, but comedy offers one obvious and exactly suitable. To supply the galley with sails is, as we noted above, an absurd act on the part of the Egyptians. The situation, and the pretended purpose of Menelaus, are such that he could not even ask for sails without betraying his fraud. Yet sails are put in, apparently without the asking, and even " white " sails, that is to say, fresh, new, and fit for the long voyage which the Greeks have really in view. It is the acme of that wilful blindness, that voluntary subservience to deception, which is displayed by the barbarians throughout this business of the escape, and which converts the description into a mere parody of romance, a piece of comic humour. And to make the point clear, the narrator is allowed to drop for a moment into plain jest. He is made actually to say (with a wink, as we might suppose) that the gratuitous sails are " for

---

[1] *Acharn.* 545 ff., cited above p. 247.

a future day "—for the time when they would be wanted, and are presently used ; and he says it in the vulgar tongue, the language not of tragedy, but of comedy.

Such, and so defined, is the use of final assonance in the iambic verse of the three tragic poets. The examples above discussed, including all which I have observed, except that of Heracles in the *Alcestis*, support what we advanced, that *one repetition of a disyllable* (*or, much more rarely, of a trisyllable*) is the limit which the poets will not exceed. Even the recurrence of the assonance in a neighbouring line[1], so that the same disyllable, or nearly the same, appears as a termination thrice in four lines, is of extreme rarity ; and three such, actually contiguous, are, I believe, nowhere to be found. And now let us listen again, as Euripides bids us, to the Heracles of the *Alcestis* (780):

> τὰ θνητὰ πράγματ' οἶδας ἣν ἔχει φύσιν;
> οἶμαι μὲν οὔ· πόθεν γάρ; ἀλλ' ἄκου' ἐμοῦ.
> βροτοῖς ἅπασι κατθανεῖν ὀφείλεται,
> κοὐκ ἔστι θνητῶν ὅστις ἐξεπίσταται,
> τὴν αὔριον μέλλουσαν εἰ βιώσεται·
> τὸ τῆς τύχης γὰρ ἀφανὲς οἷ προβήσεται,
> κἄστ' οὐ διδακτὸν οὐδ' ἁλίσκεται...τέχνῃ.
> ταῦτ' οὖν ἀκούσας καὶ μαθὼν ἐμοῦ πάρα,
> εὔφραινε σαυτόν, πῖνε,...

First, we have here, in effect, four repetitions of assonance. Secondly, this effect is designed ; for

[1] See for example *Persae* 474, *Antig.* 1188, *Medea* 1182, *Helena* 1533.

although the run of the sentence might, if we suppose the writer to be very careless, bring in ὀφείλεται, βιώσεται and προβήσεται, the introduction of ἐπίστα-ται, which completes the sequence, would be perverse, if it had not a purpose.　Thirdly, the bad effect of the rhyme is capped by the equally bad effect of prematurely dropping it.　Ugly as it is, after four repetitions we come to expect that it will continue until we reach some natural close.　And in the fifth line, the last of the five specially commended to our hearing, the expected -εται does appear, but appears too soon, in the fifth foot, so that τέχνη, which follows it and completes the verse, has the air of an afterthought.　It sounds as if the speaker really meant to say

κᾆστ᾽ οὐ τέχνῃ διδακτὸν οὐδ᾽ ἁλίσκεται,

which would bring his favourite termination to the right place.　Having dropped the word τέχνη by accident, he has to put it in at the end.　And there is reason to think that this is so, that Heracles is quoting, or rather misquoting, from poetry, and that his memory fails him.　For if not, what do we make of this?—

"τὰ θνητὰ πράγματ᾽ οἶδας ἣν ἔχει φύσιν;"
οἶμαι μὲν οὔ· πόθεν γάρ;
"Know you the nature of mortality?"
No, I suppose.　How should you?

What is it that the slave cannot be expected to know?　That people die?　The suggestion seems too stupid for drunkenness itself.　What Heracles means is that the ignorant menial is not provided with such apposite and philosophic reflexions, as will occur to an educated person, acquainted with literature, like himself.   The verse

τὰ θνητὰ πράγματ' οἶδας ἣν ἔχει φύσιν;

shows by its language (οἶδας, for the normal οἶσθα), that either (as is more probable) it is actually cited from an Ionic poet, or (which is practically the same thing) it is meant by Euripides to sound as if it were.   We may suspect then that the common-places which follow—

βροτοῖς ἅπασι κατθανεῖν ὀφείλεται,

οὐκ ἔστι θνητῶν ὅστις ἐξεπίσταται
τὴν αὔριον μέλλουσαν εἰ βιώσεται,

τὸ τῆς τύχης γὰρ ἀφανὲς οἷ προβήσεται
κἄστ' οὐ τέχνῃ διδακτὸν οὐδ' ἁλίσκεται,

were also familiar maxims of the copy-book.   To popular saws the form of rhyme seems appropriate, and we have noted examples elsewhere[1].   But combined like this, they make a torture to the ear, especially since Heracles, who, we are told, has been cheering his solitary repast with " howls unmusical[2]," is doubtless careful to enforce his wisdom by bawling the verses, and particularly the rhymes, at the top of his voice.   Even comedy will hardly supply a more extravagant example of this kind.   It would be received, by an audience trained upon Euripides or Sophocles, with laughter and disgust, and is enough

---

[1] See above pp. 267, 271.   [2] *v.* 760.

in itself to deprive the scene and the personage of all pretence to dignity.

Euripides, says a Greek commentator, "errs in making the demi-god moralize when he is drunk and would be apt rather to ridicule such reflexions in another": οὐκ εὐλόγως τὸν ἥρωα εἰσήγαγε φιλοσο-φοῦντα ἐν μέθῃ, ὃν ἔδει καὶ ἄλλου φιλοσοφοῦντος διαπαίζειν. Unfortunate Euripides!

Most readers, however, will not find it surprising that a drunken man should try to be impressive and succeed only in being ridiculous. But I must leave it to those who think that the Heracles of the *Alcestis* is meant for a hero, a personage above the common level, to account for the fact that he is here made guilty of an offence in tone which apes, if it does not rival, the Aristophanic performances of Di-caeopolis and Strepsiades. And those again who believe that, according to the conception and purpose of Euripides, the demi-god, after this exhibition of his quality, goes forth to an encounter with Death, from whom he victoriously rescues the soul and body of a self-devoted heroine,—these also have here something to consider. It is for them to say how, in that case, we should estimate the taste of the poet, or of the Attic audiences, who, seeing, as they must have seen, this trait and many other such in the story, nevertheless continued to suppose that Euri-pides meant to depict in it the circumstances of a resurrection.

REMAINS OF PHRYNICHUS IN
THE PERSIANS OF AESCHYLUS.

"ACCORDING to Glaucus *On the Plots of Aeschylus*,"
says the Greek prefatory note to the *Persians*, "this
play was composed upon the model of the *Phoenissae*
of Phrynichus. He alleges, *inter alia*, the beginning
of the *Phoenissae*,

> Of those who long ago from Persia marched,
> These are...

Only in Phrynichus it is a eunuch who begins by
announcing the defeat of Xerxes, and prepares
certain thrones for the assessors of the sovereignty,
whereas here the opening is spoken by a Chorus of
Elders. The scene of the play is at the tomb of
Darius, and the theme is as follows: Xerxes made
an expedition against Hellas [with a great power,
bringing with him cavalry without number and ships
one thousand two hundred and seven, or fourteen][1],
and after being defeated by land at Plataea and by
sea at Salamis, fled through Thessaly and passed
over into Asia."

This statement is in both parts remarkable
among the notes of this kind which are preserved to

---

[1] These clauses are not in the principal MS.

us : the first part for interest and precision, the latter
part, the summary of the *Persians*, for a degree of
falsity which, with every allowance for ignorance
and inattention, cannot easily be explained.

The *Persians* was exhibited in 472 B.C., seven
years after Plataea and eight after Salamis.   It
followed therefore close upon the exhibition of the
Phoenissae of Phrynichus, which is assigned to the
year 476.   The relation between the two plays was
evidently close and peculiar, going far beyond a mere
similarity of subject.   What sort of resemblance is
meant by the expression "composed on the model of
the *Phoenissae*" (ἐκ τῶν Φοινισσῶν παραπεποιῆσθαι),
appears from the example cited.   The commencement of Phrynichus,

$$\text{Τάδ᾽ ἐστὶ Περσῶν τῶν πάλαι βεβηκότων...,}$$

is verbally paraphrased by that of Aeschylus,

$$\text{Τάδε μὲν Περσῶν τῶν οἰχομένων....,}$$

and the general resemblance of the openings was so
close that a difference of speakers is marked as a noticeable exception.   It is further implied, that this was
but one among other such parallels[1].   Aeschylus
then, it is plain, not only followed Phrynichus on
this occasion in the choice of a theme, but used his
play by way of pattern and material, and, far from
disguising this debt (which indeed in the circumstances would be impossible), was at pains to make
it conspicuous.

---

[1] ἐκτίθησι δὲ καὶ τὴν ἀρχήν...Note καὶ, "inter alia."

Now the *Persians*, as I propose to show, exhibits certain phenomena which, without this information, would be puzzling, but in the light of it are intelligible and instructive. It contains some passages which, as appears from internal evidence, cannot be the pure and original work of Aeschylus, but must come, in the main, from some other hand. Further there is, in the structure of the play and the relation of the story to historical fact, a certain difficulty and inconsistency, such as would arise from the adaptation of material not perfectly suitable to the plan ; and this difficulty, upon examination, is found to inhere precisely in those passages which are marked by internal evidence as of foreign origin. The prefatory note illuminates and accounts for this state of things, and indicates, as a near and natural source for the foreign elements, the work of Phrynichus which was used as a basis. Considering that we have elsewhere scarcely a verse of tragedy from any predecessor or contemporary of Aeschylus, the specimens of Phrynichus, which may thus be disengaged, are of some interest.

Conversely, the extant play throws light upon the latter part of the prefatory note, and invests it with an interest which otherwise it would not merit. As a summary of the *Persians*, it is strangely and perversely erroneous. The writer states, clearly and explicitly, that, in "the play," by which evidently he means the play of Aeschylus, the battles of Salamis and Plataea are combined together as constituting the defeat of Xerxes, who, after this event or these events, retreats and repasses into Asia. But according to fact, and also according to the *Persians*, the return of Xerxes intervened between the battle of Salamis and that of Plataea, which was fought, after his return, by the army which he left in Greece. In the Aeschylean play, which represents the arrival of Xerxes at his palace, the event of Salamis is narrated, but that of Plataea is still future, and is the subject only of forecast and prophecy[1]. In these circumstances we are moved to wonder how the framer of the prefatory note in its present form, who may have been ignorant or inattentive but had no motive for falsehood, was led to make a statement which is false not only to history but to Aeschylus. The explanation I believe to be this. In the play of Phrynichus, as appears from portions of it embodied by Aeschylus, the historical facts really were thrown into such a perspective as the note suggests. The campaign under Mardonius, and the battle of Plataea, were slurred over, sunk and embraced in one defeat and retreat of Xerxes. This is not the plan of the *Persians*, but it was the plan of the *Phoenissae*; and to the *Phoenissae* we should refer the statement in the note respecting "the theme of the play," although, in the course of transference from the original authority to our extant writer, this truth has been mistaken and misrepresented.

First then, we are to show that the *Persians* comprises passages which were not originally composed by Aeschylus.

[1] *vv.* 780—820. (The numbers are those of Dindorf's *Poetae Scenici*, but I do not adopt his changes of the text.)

The principal of these passages is the narrative of the Persian retreat.   It is in two portions.   The first (*Persians* 465—471) is attached without pause to the story of the defeat at Salamis and its conclusion in the massacre of Psyttaleia :

"And Xerxes cried aloud to see the depth of the woe ; for he had a seat commanding view of all the host, upon a lofty hill near the main sea.   He tore his robes and shrilly wailed, and sending an order quick to the armament on land, sped[1] them in disordered flight.   Such is the lamentable misfortune which thou must add to what went before."

Here the narrative is interrupted by a lament from Queen Atossa, after which, and in reply to a question on her part, it continues thus (*v.* 480) :

"And the remnant of the ships, under their captains, took hasty flight, in no order, as the wind might carry them.   The rest of the host meanwhile was perishing, partly in Boeotia, where some were lost in struggling for the spring water in their thirst, while we others, our breath all gasped away, passed on into Phocis, and into the land of Doris, and the bay of Malis, where Spercheus waters the plain with kindly draught ; and next the Achaean soil received us, and the towns of Thessaly, scanted as we were of food.   There most died of thirst and of hunger, for there were both together.   So we came into Magnesia and the country of the Macedonians, to the stream of Axius, the marshes

---

[1] Or "rushed away" (ἵησι).   The ambiguity is perhaps not insignificant.   See hereafter.

and reeds of Bolbe, and the mountain of Pangaeus in the land of Edonis.　Here in a night God made cold beyond the season, and froze all the river of holy Strymon.　He that never believed in gods before, then offered supplication, with reverence to earth and sky.　Then, after many an invocation done, the host passed over the ice-bound stream. But only those of us, who set forth before the rays of the Power in heaven were cast abroad, had the hap to escape.　For the sun's bright orb, blazing with light, loosed asunder the stream in the midst with heat of flame ; and they fell one upon another ; and happy was the man who soonest cut off the breath of his life.　Those that were left and found deliverance, having traversed Thrace with pain and sore labour, came safely, some few, to the land of their homes.　Wherefore the Persian state may bewail the loss of our country's dearest manhood. These things are true, though my tale has omitted much of the woe which high Heaven hath hurled upon Persia."

465　Ξέρξης δ᾽ ἀνῴμωξεν κακῶν ὁρῶν βάθος·
　　　ἕδραν γὰρ εἶχε παντὸς εὐαγῆ στρατοῦ,
　　　ὑψηλὸν ὄχθον ἄγχι πελαγίας ἁλός·
　　　ῥήξας δὲ πέπλους κἀνακωκύσας λιγύ,
　　　πεζῷ παραγγείλας ἄφαρ στρατεύματι,
470　ἵησ᾽ ἀκόσμῳ ξὺν φυγῇ.　τοιάνδε σοι
　　　πρὸς τῇ πάροιθε συμφορὰν πάρα στένειν.

480　ναῶν δὲ ταγοὶ τῶν λελειμμένων σύδην
　　　κατ᾽ οὖρον οὐκ εὔκοσμον αἴρονται φυγήν·
　　　στρατὸς δ᾽ ὁ λοιπὸς ἔν τε Βοιωτῶν χθονὶ
　　　διώλλυθ᾽, οἱ μὲν ἀμφὶ κρηναῖον γάνος

δίψῃ πονοῦντες, οἱ δ᾽ ὑπ᾽ ἄσθματος κενοὶ
485 διεκπερῶμεν ἔς τε Φωκέων χθόνα
καὶ Δωρίδ᾽ αἶαν, Μηλιᾶ τε κόλπον, οὗ
Σπερχειὸς ἄρδει πεδίον εὐμενεῖ ποτῷ·
κἀντεῦθεν ἡμᾶς γῆς Ἀχαιῖδος πέδον
καὶ Θεσσαλῶν πόλεις ὑπεσπανισμένους
490 βορᾶς ἐδέξαντ᾽· ἔνθα δὴ πλεῖστοι θάνον
δίψῃ τε λιμῷ τ᾽· ἀμφότερα γὰρ ἦν τάδε.
Μαγνητικὴν δὲ γαῖαν ἔς τε Μακεδόνων
χώραν ἀφικόμεσθ᾽, ἐπ᾽ Ἀξιοῦ πόρον,
Βόλβης θ᾽ ἕλειον δόνακα, Πάγγαιόν τ᾽ ὄρος,
495 Ἠδωνίδ᾽ αἶαν· νυκτὶ δ᾽ ἐν ταύτῃ θεὸς
χειμῶν᾽ ἄωρον ὦρσε, πήγνυσιν δὲ πᾶν
ῥέεθρον ἁγνοῦ Στρυμόνος. θεοὺς δέ τις
τὸ πρὶν νομίζων οὐδαμοῦ τότ᾽ ηὔχετο
λιταῖσι, γαῖαν οὐρανόν τε προσκυνῶν.
500 ἐπεὶ δὲ πολλὰ θεοκλυτῶν ἐπαύσατο
στρατός, περᾷ κρυσταλλοπῆγα διὰ πόρον·
χὥστις μὲν ἡμῶν, πρὶν σκεδασθῆναι θεοῦ
ἀκτῖνας, ὡρμήθη, σεσωσμένος κυρεῖ.
φλέγων γὰρ αὐγαῖς λαμπρὸς ἡλίου κύκλος
505 μέσον πόρον διῆκε, θερμαίνων φλογί·
πῖπτον δ᾽ ἐπ᾽ ἀλλήλοισιν· ηὐτύχει δέ τοι
ὅστις τάχιστα πνεῦμ᾽ ἀπέρρηξεν βίου.
ὅσοι δὲ λοιποὶ κἄτυχον σωτηρίας,
Θρῄκην περάσαντες μόγις πολλῷ πόνῳ,
510 ἥκουσιν ἐκφυγόντες, οὐ πολλοί τινες,
ἐφ᾽ ἑστιοῦχον γαῖαν· ὡς στένειν πόλιν
Περσῶν, ποθοῦσαν φιλτάτην ἥβην χθονός.
ταῦτ᾽ ἔστ᾽ ἀληθῆ· πολλὰ δ᾽ ἐκλείπω λέγων
κακῶν ἃ Πέρσαις ἐγκατέσκηψεν θεός.

That these passages have been touched by
Aeschylus is possible, and certainly cannot be disproved; but that they are his pure and original
composition, we are not free to suppose.

The principal, or most patent, ground for suspicion is that of metre, respecting which we may
say, not less truly than briefly, that these passages
violate every fundamental rule and practice of
Aeschylean versification.   The prosody, the rules of
quantity, are those of Aeschylus, but in everything
else upon which the effect of verse depends, this
writer exemplifies what the way of Aeschylus is not.

First, as to word-division.   The familiar rule, in
all the three tragic poets, is that every verse, with
exceptions so rare as to be negligible in the general
effect, must have word-division in one at least of two
places :

> ἦρξεν μέν, ὦ δέσποινα, | τοῦ πάντος κακοῦ
> φανεὶς ἀλάστωρ | ἢ κακὸς δαίμων ποθέν.

The exceptions are not only extremely rare, but
subject to various reservations, of which we will
here notice only two.   Firstly, some of the irregular
lines (and this is a point specially interesting to us
here) have the appearance of quotation from older
poetry, for instance :

> εἶπον δὲ καὶ πρίν, οὐκ ἄνευ δήμου τάδε
> πράξαιμ᾽ ἄν, οὐδέ περ κρατῶν, μὴ καί ποτε
> εἴπῃ λεώς, εἴ πού τι μὴ τοῖον τύχοι,
> ‘ ἐπήλυδας τιμῶν ἀπώλεσας πόλιν[1].’

It is obvious to suspect that the last verse may be
proverbial, a quotation[2].   Secondly, in the majority

---

[1] Aesch. *Supp.* 398.   The reading μὴ τοῖον is doubtful, but
possibly correct, "something other (than was calculated)."

[2] See also Aesch. *Eum.* 26, and Eur. *Suppl.* 303, the first
a professed reminiscence (see the context), the second likely
to be a popular locution.

of such lines the missing word-division is actually
marked in some way, however slightly, as it is in
that just cited by the separation of the preposition in
ἀπ-ώλεσας. All this, though the statistics are slightly
different for the three poets respectively, is true for
Aeschylus as well as his successors, including as
Aeschylean (for the moment) all instances in the
Persians not comprised in the story of the flight.

But this story, in both the component passages,
obeys an opposite rule, proper enough in itself, but
incompatible with that established by Aeschylus,—
that divisionless lines (as we will call them) are a
normal and desirable variation of the rhythm. In
forty-two verses there are six without division[1]; and
if in some a particular design may be supposed, in
others[2] it cannot. In four of the six[3] the regular
divisions have not the slightest mark, and in three
of them[4] (a thing equally remarkable in Aeschylus)
not any foot is divided between two words. There
is also a line of that rare type in which normal
division is represented only by an elision,

χώραν ἀφικόμεσθα, | ἐπ᾽ Ἀξιοῦ πόρον[5].

In short, the neglect, or rather avoidance, of
division is treated by this writer as a thing habitual
and commonplace, a regular variation. This point
is justly pressed by Paley, who assigns to "another
hand" the first of our two passages and a portion

---

[1] *vv.* 465, 469, 489, 501, 503, 509.
[2] *vv.* 489, 501.   [3] *vv.* 465, 469, 503, 509.
[4] *vv.* 465, 469, 509.   [5] *v.* 493.

(*vv.* 488 ff.) of the second, but calls them "interpolations," and leaves us to suppose that they were
substituted for some different passage or passages,
which (*ex hypothesi*) must have originally occupied
the same place and function. The difficulty, or
rather impossibility, of saying by whom and with
what motive the work, as left by Aeschylus, can
have been so handled, is, I suppose, the reason why
the criticism of Paley has not been much regarded.
All his remarks here deserve careful attention.

Equally unlike Aeschylus is the method of
punctuation. In Aeschylus the stops, especially
the stronger stops, are found (1) regularly at the
verse-end or at one of the normal word-divisions,
(2) not unfrequently, as a variation, after the first
foot or in the middle of the second[1], (3) rarely anywhere else. But these forty-two lines have two
strong stops after the fourth foot[2], a liberal in-
fusion of minor varieties, and above all, one stop
which Aeschylus, so far as I can discover, never
exhibits, and which is indeed inconsistent with the
regular movement of his verse :

καὶ Δωρίδ' αἶαν, Μηλιᾶ τε κόλπον, | οὗ
Σπερχειὸς ἄρδει πεδίον εὐμενεῖ ποτῷ.

Irregular also is the resolution of long syllables
(∪∪ for –), types of which, rare in Aeschylus, are
here not rare[3]. The effect of all this is to give the

---

[1] *Persae* 391, 409.

[2] *vv.* 470, 497. In all the rest of the play I find but two
other such, *vv.* 180, 454.

[3] *vv.* 491, 492, 501.

verse a movement widely different from any other
part of the play, or any passage of Aeschylus elsewhere.

Now if this peculiarity of rhythm stood alone, we
might perhaps suppose it an artifice, designed to
represent by the disorder of the sound the confusion
of the disorderly flight.   Whether this, as an artistic
motive, would be adequate, and whether a composer
could if he would, or would if he could, thus change
in a moment his principles of metre, are questions
which we may set aside.   For the peculiarity of
rhythm does not stand alone.   We have to ask why
the composer, at the same moment, should adopt a
different notion of poetry, an imagination different
in species and order.   And why another language ?
And why, above all, should he assume for these
few minutes a conception of the story discrepant
from the rest of his work, and likely, as he elsewhere admits, to give a false impression of his
meaning ?

First then, the style, the quality of imagination,
is not that of Aeschylus.   I do not say that it is
inferior ; it is in its own way powerful and impressive ;
but Aeschylean it is not.

The style of Aeschylus, especially in descriptive
passages, is signally bold and picturesque in imagery,
full of decoration, richly adorned with phrases and
points not copied from the object or the fact, but
superadded to it for the sake of dignity.   Let us
take specimens only from the narrative of the battle,
the narrative which immediately precedes this story

of the flight.   The straits of Salamis are "sea-
sounding,"

ἔκπλους φυλάσσειν καὶ πόρους ἁλιρρόθους,

not for the sake of fact, but because to call them
so heightens the tone.   The sunlight "dies" (φέγγος
ἡλίου κατέφθιτο) ; the Persian officers are "masters
of arms" (ὅπλων ἐπιστάτης) ; day comes "with white
steeds" (λευκόπωλος ἡμέρα), and "fair-bright to the
eye" (εὐφεγγὴς ἰδεῖν); the trumpet "blazes over" the
Greek quarters (πάντ᾽ ἐκεῖν᾽ ἐπέφλεγεν) ; the Persian
cheer is like the talk of the waves (Περσίδος. γλώσσης
ῥόθος); the massacre of the drowning is "like the
spearing of tunny-fish" (ὥστε θύννους); night has a
"darkened eye" (κελαινῆς νυκτὸς ὄμμα); the island of
Psyttaleia is "the haunt of dancing Pan"(ἣν ὁ φιλόχο-
ρος Πὰν ἐμβατεύει).   These are but specimens of a
habit which every reader of Aeschylus will recognize
as characteristic, and which any Aeschylean narrative,
such as that of the beacons in the *Agamemnon*, or
the wanderings of Io in the *Prometheus*, will illustrate
copiously.   But where does this habit appear in our
forty-two lines ?   The vocabulary of the writer is
doubtless decorative : he uses many words (such as
κρυσταλλοπήξ) which could not appear in prose,—and
some, as we shall see, which are scarcely natural to
the dialogue of Aeschylus.   But in thought he is not
decorative ; he is precise, realistic, a man who writes
with his eye on the object.   In all the forty-two lines
there is not, so far as I can perceive, a single touch
which is not literal matter of fact, or at least so

intended, unless we class as such the title of *Power*
(θεός) bestowed on the sun[1], but this too, as the
context shows, is meant literally.   By merely alter-
ing words, by changing γάνος to ὕδωρ, θεοκλυτῶν to
εὐχόμενος, and so on, sentence after sentence might
be turned into prose.   But try this experiment on the
beacons or the storm in the *Agamemnon,* or on the
battle of Salamis in this play.   And again, the style
of Aeschylus is full of metaphors, τέμενος αἰθέρος,
ῥεῦμα στρατοῦ, κακῶν πέλαγος, συμφορὰ ἀντιση-
κοῦσα, φράξαντες ὅπλοις δέμας[2]; of adjectives purely
ornamental, εὐήρετμος, εὐφεγγὴς (ἡμέρα), εὔψυχον
(θράσος), χαλκόστομα (ἔμβολα), εὔχαλκος[3], of figures
purely imaginative, such as οἰμωγὴ κατεῖχεν ἅλα,
"wailing took possession of the sea[4]."   But our writer
has nothing of the kind ; for a poet, a forcible poet,
a descriptive poet, he is remarkably bare and plain.
In the whole piece there is scarcely a superfluous
word, and absolutely nothing in the way of decorative imagination, unless it be imaginative to speak
of woe as *deep* or drink as *kindly*[5].   The freezing of
the Strymon, as a natural or miraculous phenomenon,
may be incredible ; but for the writer evidently it
is a fact, and he describes it simply as fact, giving
in plain terms exactly what he supposes to have
happened, without any excursion of thought or
fancy whatsoever.   His conceptions and colouring
are those of a historian, and with Aeschylus he has

[1] *v.* 502.   [2] *Persae* 365, 412, 433, 436, 456.
[3] *ib.* 376, 387, 394, 415, 457.   [4] *ib.* 426.
[5] *vv.* 465, 487.

nothing in common except the vocabulary common
to verse.

In the mere vocabulary and grammar there
is little or nothing which might not come from
Aeschylus. But this we should expect if the piece
were by a contemporary. Average pieces of Euripides and Sophocles will show no decisive discrepancy
of this kind. A little divergence there is, not in itself
noticeable, but significant in the whole estimate. On
the one hand, the diction of our writer is all drawn
from the common fund of poetry. There are no
words of original stamp, such as one might suppose
never to have been so used before or again, words like
διάπλοος (in the sense *sailing to and fro*) or τοσουτ-
άριθμος (*so many in number*)[1], a species of which
Aeschylus is prolific. But on the other hand, the
common stock of poetry is employed in our passage
with less discrimination of quality than we generally
find in Aeschylus. The eighty lines describing the first
part of the battle[2], while they do present the highly
characteristic compounds just cited, do not present any
word which we might not naturally expect in the dialogue of tragedy, any word which one would naturally
rank as lyrical[3]. But ἄφαρ, *quickly*, is such a word;
ἄγχι, σύδην, and μόγις[4], though warranted or warrant-
able, are on the border-line; so is ῥέεθρον, instead of
ῥεῖθρον. Not one of them, nor all together, would
deserve remark in a passage otherwise normal; but

---

[1] *vv.* 382, 432.   [2] *vv.* 353—432.

[3] κνέφας is perhaps an exception, but it has authority.

[4] *v.* 509, if we can trust the MS.

if it is thought that the proportion is not more than might be expected, let an experiment be made on any equal piece of Aeschylean dialogue taken at random. My own conclusion, after experiments, is that our writer, in respect of vocabulary, is less inventive than Aeschylus, and a little less punctilious in choice. He seeks variety by the use of rare material, Aeschylus rather by original combination of common material[1].

But about all such points, and about the range of variation which may be expected in the same author, individual judgements will differ. Metrical and linguistic evidence alone, though it may favour an opinion upon authorship, can seldom constitute a proof. What clinches the argument here, and does, in my judgement, complete a proof against the authorship of Aeschylus, is the discrepancy of substance and statement between this passage and the play as a whole.

This story of the flight is in some things reticent and ambiguous, notably so as to the personal movements of Xerxes, but in one thing it is perfectly clear. It purports, beyond possibility of question, to account for the whole Persian armament, both naval and military. The narrator professes indeed to be summary, and to have "omitted many disasters[2]"; but this remark only strengthens the impression that his relation covers the whole of what is foreshown

[1] See further Paley, who notes several peculiarities not remarkable singly, but collectively significant.

[2] *v.* 513.

in the first announcement—"The host of Asia is utterly destroyed," στρατὸς πᾶς ὄλωλε βαρβάρων[1]— the final loss and annihilation, as a belligerent force, of the entire expedition. The disastrous retreat which he describes is expressly attributed to the whole armament with the exception only of the ships[2]; nor is there anywhere the least suggestion that the generality of this term is subject to any further abridgement. No one could suppose, and the composer certainly does not conceive, that the stronger, if not larger, portion of the Persian army may still be left in Greece, to expect a second campaign in the following year. Yet this was the situation at the time supposed, both in fact and according to the play of Aeschylus.

Nor has this inconsistency escaped the notice of Aeschylus himself. The subsequent dialogue between the ghost of Darius and the Persian councillors has been curiously framed so as to diminish the objection as far as possible[3]. The councillors look forward to revenge. "We shall send," they say, "a picked force, light and easily moved." "Nay," says the prophetic spirit, "not even that army, which now remains in Greece, shall find safe return." "What mean you?" exclaims the respondent in natural surprise. *"Does not the whole armament of Asia pass* from Europe over the Strait of Helle?" "Few out of the many, if we may trust

---

[1] *v.* 255.

[2] *vv.* 480 ff. ναῶν ταγοί,...στρατὸς ὁ λοιπός.

[3] *vv.* 795 ff.

prophecy," answers Darius, and proceeds to reveal
the future disaster of Plataea :

> ΧΟ. πῶς εἶπας; οὐ γὰρ πᾶν στράτευμα βαρβάρων
>   περᾷ τὸν Ἕλλης πορθμὸν Εὐρώπης ἄπο;
> ΔΑ. παῦροί γε πολλῶν, εἴ τι πιστεῦσαι θεῶν
>   χρὴ θεσφάτοισι.

The question, it will be observed, is ambiguous,
and more distinctly so in Greek than in English.
The tense—*Do they not pass?* οὐ περᾷ ;—may
refer either to present time or future—*Are they not
passing?* or *Are they not destined to pass?*—and
according as it is construed will imply or not imply
that the speaker now hears for the first time of an
army left in Greece. *Prima facie*, it would bear
the present sense, but Darius takes and answers
the question as referring to the future. Clearly
this ambiguity is deliberate : the composer is steer-
ing with some care round a difficulty created by the
original narrative of the flight.

But why was the difficulty created, or permitted
to exist? Doubtless it is dramatically proper and
necessary that the episode of Plataea should be
reserved entire for the revelation of the ghost ; and
for mere omission this would sufficiently account.
We should not expect, according to the plan of the
Persians, that the narrative of Salamis would lay any
stress upon possible developments of the enterprise,
or perhaps even point to them at all. But neither
could we expect that the author, having in mind
the event of the year 479, and intending to make
use of it, should; of his own motion and without

prompting, compose a narrative which, upon the face of it, excludes the possibility of such an event,—and this although his audience knew the facts. For what conceivable purpose should he thus mislead them as to the scope of his work and its relation to history? That the story is not reconcilable with history is indeed in itself a thing of little or no significance. A poet, even in matter of history, may suppose almost anything that he pleases. What is significant is the inconsistency with the *Persians*, that is to say, with Aeschylus. Paley has perhaps impaired the force of his striking observations by combining or confounding these different objections. If the narrative agreed with the *Persians*, we might dismiss with small concern difficulties based upon the actual practice of the Empire in the transmission of despatches. These things Athenian poets and audiences could ignore. But it is another thing to find Aeschylus cutting away the foundation of his own scenes.

In my opinion, this discrepancy of substance, taken with the suspicious details of workmanship, compels the inference that the narrative of the flight is imported into the play of Aeschylus from some other source; and the adoption of it must be due to Aeschylus himself, since for subsequent interpolation of this kind there could be no motive or opportunity. The source, and the motive for adoption, we could not guess, were it not for the evidence of the preface, that the play was a confessed imitation of the *Phoenissae*. This being so, it was natural that

some of the original work, if any adaptable piece
could be found, should be actually embodied and
retained, as an acknowledgment and compliment
to the originator. Of plagiarism, we should remark,
there could be no question. The fact that Aeschylus
followed the lead of Phrynichus was palpable, and,
considering the close proximity of time, one might
even suppose that he did so with consent. At all
events he did it without disguise; and therefore,
the nearer he could keep to the track, and the more
he could adopt of the model, the better and the less
invidious would be his relation to the predecessor.
The *Phoenissae*, we must remember, was not a
failure, but a success. Fifty years later, the lyrics
in it were still remembered and repeated with
affection[1]. The design of Aeschylus, as appears
by the conspicuous borrowing noted in the preface,
was not to obliterate the preceding work, but to
put beside it a parallel though dependent work, in
his own different and probably much more dramatic
manner. To avoid the appearance of hostility was
the part of prudence, to say nothing of taste; and
for this purpose nothing could be more effective than
to include some considerable adaptations.

Now there is no difficulty in conceiving a play,
to which the narrative of the flight, as given in the
Persians, would be strictly appropriate, a play in
which the naval victory at Salamis, the Athenian
victory, was treated as practically final, and the sequel,
Plataea and all, was dismissed summarily in a vague

---

[1] Aristoph. *Wasps* 219 f.

outline of rout.   Such a plan might well be adopted
by an Athenian composer—provided that he kept
to it—even when the sequel and whole event were
actually known.   And moreover it is possible that
Phrynichus, when he planned the *Phoenissae*, was
without this knowledge.   It may have been written,
or shaped, as early as the autumn of 480 B.C., before
it was known or could be known that the Persians
had resolved to try their fortunes again, and when
the Greeks doubtless hoped, and perhaps believed,
that the whole land-force would forthwith retreat,
as it does in our story of the flight.

At all events there are indications that the
Phoenissae, whenever written, presented the story
in this light.   First the title, proving that the
Chorus were "Women of Phoenicia," shows that
the destruction of the navy, in which their country-
men served, was the principal subject of the piece.
The Phoenicians had nothing to do with Plataea.
And secondly, as we noted above, the preface to
the *Persians* describes such a play, a play showing
how Xerxes, defeated by land and sea, fled by way
of Thessaly and the Hellespont into Asia.   The
compiler of the preface appears to think that the
play so described is the *Persians*.   I should be the
last to insist on the virtues of these prefaces, in
which valuable information is mixed with all sorts
of error.   But so prodigious and gratuitous a falsehood seems to demand explanation, and will obtain
it, if we attribute the description to the play of
Phrynichus, and suppose it to be derived, but with

misapplication, from the book *On the Plots of Aeschylus*, in which the two plays were compared.

Why Aeschylus, if desirous to adopt some conspicuous passage from his predecessor, chose this one, is easily guessed. It is precisely at this point that the rough style of the insertion (for the style is rough) is most effective in contrast with his own stateliness. The juncture, though it is not perfectly artistic, and though it involves some disturbance of the Aeschylean plan, is telling at the moment, and would readily be accepted under the circumstances of the composition.

The seam, in the MS. text, is a little more distinctly visible than in some modern editions. The narrator of the flight pauses after mentioning the order of Xerxes for the retreat of the land-force, and resumes his story in answer to a question from Atossa as to the fate of the fleet. But he begins his reply irregularly with an *And* :

νεῶν δὲ ταγοὶ τῶν λελειμμένων σύδην....

This δέ was of course long ago[1] changed to γε, but the correction cannot be allowed as certain, in view of the fact that another δέ, not normal and not thus corrigible, appears in another place, where the very words of Aeschylus suggest that he is arranging material not quite obedient to his purpose. " Now *go back*," says Atossa to the narrator, when he has given the roll of the captains slain at Salamis, " Go

[1] Robortello, but see on the contrary Hermann, Paley and others. A γε, though intelligible, is not pleasing.

back, and tell me this.   *And* what was the number
of the Greek ships, that they dared to contend with
the Persian armament ? "

> ἀτὰρ φράσον μοι τοῦτ᾽ ἀναστρέψας πάλιν·
> πόσον δὲ πλῆθος ἦν νεῶν Ἑλληνίδων[1];

The conjunction here is admissible, but it is not
usual[2].   After τοῦτο, *this*, one would expect simply
πόσον πλῆθος;   Nor is it hypercritical to ask why
Atossa should speak of "going back," as if the
present question came out of its place.   There is
no earlier point in the dialogue at which it should
or might more naturally have been asked.   But all
is accounted for if the composer is following and
remodelling a known text, the track of which he
has quitted and here re-enters.   Just such slight
irregularities, as are these two conjunctions, might
be looked for in a work produced, however skilfully,
by such a method.   If the verse

> πόσον δὲ πλῆθος ἦν νεῶν Ἑλληνίδων;

comes from Phrynichus, it presumably required, in
its original context, the copula which, in the present
context, is only possible.

It is noticeable, and has been often noticed[3], that,
in the answer to this question about the numbers
of the contending fleets, Aeschylus insists on his
accuracy in regard to the Persians, and appears
to be correcting somebody[4].   The mere existence
of discrepant statements would hardly account for

---

[1] *vv.* 333 ff.

[2] See examples cited by Paley after Peile.

[3] Paley, *ad loc.*   [4] *v.* 341 καὶ γὰρ οἶδα.

this not very graceful attitude in a poet. But it
is excusable, perhaps necessary, if Aeschylus here
varies, upon an important point, from a poet whose
work he uses and professes to follow. Among all
competitors for the honour of the observation
Phrynichus should certainly be preferred.

The next question of Atossa, which calls for and
produces the narrative of Salamis, suggests by its
language one of several doubts which we cannot
settle. "How did the clash of the ships begin?
Tell me. Was it the Greeks who attacked first,
or was it my son, contemptuously confident in
numbers?"

τίνες κατῆρξαν, πότερον Ἕλληνες, μάχης,
ἢ παῖς ἐμός, πλήθει καταυχήσας νεῶν;

In the last verse the normal word-division (in καταυχήσας) is not regularly, but only slightly, marked.
Of course this may signify nothing. The licence,
as a licence and rarity, is Aeschylean, and may or
may not be here due to adaptation or imitation of
Phrynichus. But the *Phoenissae* must have contained
a story of Salamis—very different in style, we may
be sure, from that of the *Persians*—and a similar
question leading up to it. If the παῖς ἐμός, *my son*,
were attributable to the predecessor, we should have
to suppose that he too had an Atossa. There is
no evidence (so far as I can perceive) either for or
against the supposition. And generally, the extent
and limits of borrowing or imitation are beyond our
discovery. There is however one passage where

such influence is probable, because it exhibits that discrepant view of the story and situation, which belonged to the work of Phrynichus. It is the first general announcement of the disaster:

> ὦ γῆς ἁπάσης Ἀσιάδος πολίσματα,
> ὦ Περσὶς αἶα καὶ πολὺς πλούτου λιμήν,
> ὡς ἐν μιᾷ πληγῇ κατέφθαρται πολὺς
> ὄλβος, τὸ Περσῶν δ' ἄνθος οἴχεται πεσόν.
> ὤμοι, κακὸν μὲν πρῶτον ἀγγέλλειν κακά·
> ὅμως δ' ἀνάγκη πᾶν ἀναπτύξαι πάθος,
> Πέρσαι· στρατὸς γὰρ πᾶς ὄλωλε βαρβάρων[1].

The last words, "Our whole armament is lost," though inconsistent with the situation in the *Persians*, placed in time between the campaign of Xerxes and that of Mardonius, would of course not in themselves afford ground for suspecting an alien influence. They would pass for the exaggeration of grief. But in the actual circumstances of the composition, they are more probably due to adaptation; and to the same source therefore, to adaptation or imitation of Phrynichus, we should probably assign the irregular, though expressive, phrase:

> ὡς ἐν μιᾷ πληγῇ κατ-έφθαρται πολὺς
> ὄλβος.

But neither is the passage pure Phrynichus, if we estimate that poet from the story of the flight. The phrases *wide haven of wealth* and *Persia's fallen flower* exhibit precisely that note of Aeschylus in which the "Flight" is signally deficient. Thus, as a

---

[1] *vv.* 249 ff.

whole, the passage confirms that impression of the relation between the two poets, which is suggested by the specimen cited in the preface :—the *Persians* was in part and to some extent a *rifacimento* of the *Phoenissae*, following it actually in words and phrases; but even in these parts the material was worked over, and converted into something essentially different. Large portions of the play, and the most important, such as the dream of Atossa, the narrative of Salamis and Psyttaleia, and the whole part of Darius, are doubtless Aeschylus pure and simple.

And, in general, the relics of the predecessor are probably confined to words, phrases, and other *tessellae*,—everywhere but in the story of the flight. Here, I think, we have certainly more, some forty lines of Phrynichus, which Aeschylus may have touched indeed, but cannot have altered much, or they would not be so bare, as they are, of all that is characteristic of his hand. Small as it is, the specimen serves to illustrate what Aristophanes means when he speaks of the "solemn phrase" of tragedy as the original product of Aeschylus[1]; it serves to show how very much, which extant tragedy makes us conceive as fundamental, was so established by Aeschylus first and singly. Phrynichus, a contemporary, had a widely different notion of the way to write iambic verse ; and, if these fragments are near his average, he was far indeed from pomp and from majesty. The work is fine in its own way, very

---

[1] *Frogs* 1005 f.

fine, as we should expect it to be, if it comes from Phrynichus.   The author of

$$\Xi\acute{\epsilon}\rho\xi\eta\varsigma\ \delta'\ \mathring{a}v\acute{\omega}\mu\omega\xi\epsilon v\ \kappa\alpha\kappa\mathring{\omega}v\ \mathring{o}\rho\mathring{\omega}v\ \beta\acute{a}\theta o\varsigma,$$

and of

$$\pi\hat{\iota}\pi\tau ov\ \delta'\ \mathring{\epsilon}\pi'\ \mathring{a}\lambda\lambda\acute{\eta}\lambda o\iota\sigma\iota v\cdot\ \mathring{\eta}\mathring{v}\tau\acute{v}\chi\epsilon\iota\ \delta\acute{\epsilon}\ \tau o\iota$$
$$\mathring{o}\sigma\tau\iota\varsigma\ \tau\acute{a}\chi\iota\sigma\tau\alpha\ \pi v\epsilon\hat{v}\mu'\ \mathring{a}\pi\acute{\epsilon}\rho\rho\eta\xi\epsilon v\ \beta\acute{\iota}ov,$$

had great gifts, both of thought and speech.   But they were different from those of Aeschylus; nor did he comply with some of the technical rules, which Aeschylus imposed both on himself and his successors.

THE LADY OF COS.

A STUDY IN THE SOURCES OF HERODOTUS[1].

THE purpose of this essay is to prove, in two cases of special interest, the truth of a proposition which, taken generally, is not likely to be disputed : that Herodotus depended, for some part of his many statements and anecdotes of which the source is not obvious, upon the evidence of public monuments. That he was a diligent visitor of the places where such monuments were collected is as plain, in all parts of his work, as that he was not an explorer of archives, not even of such modest repositories as certainly existed and were accessible in his time. Explicit reference to the monuments, and professed quotation, we should not expect from him ; it would be inconsistent with the tone and manner of his narrative. But for all that, it may be possible in some instances to trace his proceedings and even to recover his texts, as we may see from the parallel case of the treatment which he applies to literature.

[1] Reprinted (by permission) from the *Classical Review*, Vol. XVII (1903).

To quote poetry for decorative purposes formally and openly, after the fashion of Cicero and Plutarch and generally of all writers accustomed to libraries, is not the practice of Herodotus nor suitable to his colouring.   Yet not only is it visible that, in the treatment of topics which are akin to popular poetry, he is profoundly influenced by it both in thought and style; but not unfrequently it will be seen, upon closer inspection, that his imitations are, in all but form, quotations, the poetical material being reproduced so exactly that we can with ease reverse the composer's process and restore the metre which he has turned into prose.   For example, when he writes (8. 3),

ἀντιβάντων δὲ τῶν συμμάχων, εἶκον οἱ Ἀθηναῖοι, μέγα πεποιημένοι
περιεῖναι τὴν Ἑλλάδα, καὶ γνόντες, εἰ στασιάσουσι περὶ τῆς ἡγεμονίης,
ὡς ἀπολέεται ἡ Ἑλλάς, ὀρθὰ νοεῦντες· στάσις γὰρ ἔμφυλος πολέμου
ὁμοφρονέοντος τοσούτῳ κάκιόν ἐστι, ὅσῳ πόλεμος εἰρήνης,

the change of style and vocabulary in the final sentence does not escape the ear, and the conjecture is obvious that this change is due to the imitation of a proverb in verse.   But the truth is, that the very words of the gnomic poet are before us :

. . . . ὀρθὰ νοεῦντες·
εἰρήνης γὰρ ὅσῳ πόλεμος, [τοσσῷδε] κάκιον
ἔμφυλος πολέμου στάσις ἐστὶν ὁμοφρονέοντος.

Two entire hexameters has the historian consciously or unconsciously reproduced without the change of a syllable, except the necessary translation of τοσσῷδε into the corresponding prose-form τοσούτῳ.

Nor is it only gnomic poetry proper which furnishes material for such treatment. The maxims of Attic tragedy are also susceptible of it. Thus in that banquet at Thebes (9. 16), which is perhaps the most tragic in feeling of all incidents in the history, the Persian guest is made to express his useless foreknowledge of disaster in these terms :

ξεῖνε, ὅ τι δεῖ γενέσθαι ἐκ τοῦ θεοῦ, ἀμήχανον ἀποτρέψαι ἀνθρώπῳ·
οὐδὲ γὰρ πιστὰ λέγουσι ἐθέλει πείθεσθαι οὐδείς. ταῦτα δὲ Περσέων
συχνοὶ ἐπιστάμενοι ἑπόμεθα ἀναγκαίῃ ἐνδεδεμένοι. ἐχθίστη δὲ ὀδύνη
ἐστὶ τῶν ἐν ἀνθρώποισι αὕτη, πολλὰ φρονέοντα μηδενὸς κρατέειν.

Here those words which belong only to the special occasion, the sentence ταῦτα δὲ...ἐνδεδεμένοι, are genuine prose, original prose, which, like other such composition, cannot be converted into metre of any sort without changing the substance. But the general maxims, with which the speech begins and ends, are not such prose, as the very sound and feeling of them betrays. The second is a transcript of two verses from tragedy :

ὀδύνη δ᾽ ἐν ἀνθρώποισιν ἐχθίστη [πέλει]
αὕτη, φρονοῦντα πολλὰ μηδενὸς κρατεῖν.

The πέλει, characteristic of the proverbial style in tragedy, Herodotus could not borrow, but must translate ; nor could he dispense, like the poet, with the article τῶν. But so far as he possibly could, he borrows the very words, not shunning even the palpably poetical turn of the phrase φρονοῦντα πολλά. Having seen this, we may fairly suspect that the preceding maxim also imitates poetry not only in tone (this is plain) but in words; and the suspicion is confirmed, as the reader may ascertain, by the facility with which the sentence will run into hexameters.

Now such remarks, in themselves merely curious, point the way to possible observations of higher interest. Literature in whatever shape, dramas, tales, moralities, was not the only kind of metrical composition with which our historiographer was familiar, nor the most nearly related to his purpose. The sacred places of Hellas were already full of monuments, interesting to the enquirer and explained not unfrequently by inscriptions in metre. What we now see is this: that where Herodotus made use of such, as we may presume that he occasionally did, there is a likelihood, from his habits of composition, that we may learn from his work more than he designed to tell us. We may expect that a narrator, whose taste and memory prompted him to verbal fidelity in the adapting of mere decorations, will deal sometimes not less faithfully with verses which furnished the very foundation of his story. If so, he will supply us with an instrument of no small importance, especially in our dearth of such instruments, for criticising and estimating his method.

In his account of the battle of Plataea there is one incident, which, both in the character of the facts and in the manner of telling, presents a remarkable contrast to the rest of the narrative. For the most part, indeed everywhere else, that account is

merely such as from the means open to Herodotus
we might expect it to be : it includes nothing, and
pretends to no exactness, which may not fairly be
accounted for by popular tradition. For example,
while Herodotus claims to have, as he well might
have, a clear and tolerably complete knowledge of
the military movements on the Greek side, those on
the Persian side are left vague and obscure. The
story is made less intelligible, but more authentic,
by a defect corresponding to the natural limits of
his information. In few places is there any minute-
ness of detail, and in these, for the most part, only
with regard to incidents which, like the parading
of the corpse of Masistius or the mutiny of
Amompharetus, must or might be widely known,
and might therefore naturally be learnt by that sort
of enquiry which, in reference to transactions within
memory, Herodotus seems to profess. One incident,
and one only, is otherwise related, related with a
fulness of detail such as could be really warranted only
in an eye-witness ; and this is the more remarkable,
inasmuch as the particular fact is of such a nature,
that at first sight we cannot easily imagine any
probable way in which the details could be preserved.

When the Barbarians had been laid low by the Hellenes at
Plataea, there approached to them a woman, the concubine of
Pharandates the son of Teaspis a Persian, coming of her own will
from the enemy, who, when she perceived that the Persians had
been destroyed and that the Hellenes were the victors, descended
from her carriage and came up to the Lacedemonians while they
were yet among the slaughter. She had adorned herself with
many ornaments of gold, and her attendants likewise, and had

put on the fairest robe she had.   And when she perceived that
the director of all things there was "Pausanias," being before well
acquainted with his name and birth, which she had heard often,
she knew him for who he was, and taking hold of his knees she
said thus : "O king of Sparta, deliver me thy suppliant from the
slavery of the captive: for thou hast also done me service hitherto
in destroying these, who have regard neither for demigod nor yet
for god.   I am a native of Cos, the daughter of Hegetorides son
of Antagoras ; and the Persian took me by force in Cos and kept
me a prisoner."   He made answer thus : "Woman, be of good
courage, both for that thou art a suppliant, and for that perchance
thou speakest true, and art the daughter of Hegetorides the Coan,
who is happily my best friend of all that dwell in those parts."
Having thus spoken, for the time he gave her in charge to those
Ephors who were present, and afterwards sent her away to Aegina,
whither she herself desired to go[1].

If we compare this story with the context, we
must be sensible of the contrast above indicated,
and shall see reason for asking why, of this particular scene, concerning people of no importance
and not elsewhere mentioned, Herodotus claims
to be far more exactly informed than of anything
else which passed upon the Plataean field.   No
other scene is presented with anything like this
completeness of persons and properties : chariot,
jewels, dress, attendants, ephors.   That Herodotus
thought himself at liberty to invent all this, no one,
who will study at length his account of the battle
and sequel, will easily suppose.   From what witness
then did he derive it ?   Not from any witness, but
from a document, a document of which part, but a
part only, was in writing and is reproduced by the

[1] 9. 76 ; translation of G. C. Macaulay, slightly modified.

historian with the utmost exactness compatible with
his manner of using it. The speech of the rescued
lady to Pausanias has been copied closely and carefully, word after word, from a version in five hexameters. Here is the original[1] :

Ὦ βασιλεῦ Σπάρτης, λῦσαί μ' ἱκέτιν [δοριλήπτου]
δουλοσύνης. σὺ γὰρ ἐς τόδ' ὄνησας τούσδ' ἀπολέσσας,
τοὺς οὐχ [ἡρώων?] οὐ θεῶν ὄπιν [οὔτιν'] ἔχοντας.
Κώῃ δ' εἰμὶ γένος, θυγάτηρ Ἡγητορίδαο
Ἀνταγόραο· βίῃ δὲ λαβὼν Κῷ μ' εἶχεν ὁ Πέρσης.

And here is the transcript of Herodotus :

Ὦ βασιλεῦ Σπάρτης, λῦσαί με τὴν ἱκέτιν αἰχμαλώτου δουλοσύνης·
σὺ γὰρ καὶ ἐς τόδε ὤνησας τούσδε ἀπολέσας, τοὺς οὔτε δαιμόνων οὔτε
θεῶν ὄπιν ἔχοντας. εἰμὶ δὲ γένος μὲν Κώῃ, θυγάτηρ δὲ Ἡγητορίδεω
τοῦ Ἀνταγόρεω. βίῃ δέ με λαβὼν ἐν Κῷ εἶχε ὁ Πέρσης.

It appears that δοριλήπτου, the only word not
admissible in prose, has been translated (as πέλει to
ἐστί in the before-cited fragment of tragedy) into
the precisely equivalent αἰχμ-αλώτου, a translation
which also has the desirable effect of obliterating
the close of a hexameter. With the same purpose
οὔτινα is dropped ; in the other three verses the
effect is accomplished, or rather accomplishes itself,
by the mere substitution of the Herodotean forms
for the epic. The epic locative Κῷ in the last verse

---

[1] The words in brackets are inferred from the text of Herodotus, but not found in it. In *v.* 3 τοὺς οὔτε δαιμόνων (Herodotus)
points *prima facie* to τοὺς οὐ δαιμονίων. But it is doubtful whether,
even for metrical convenience, δαιμόνιον could be used at this date
(*circ.* 475 B.C.): ἡρώων was suggested to me by Sir R. C. Jebb.
Possible also are ἀντιθέων and ἡμιθέων: see L. and Sc. s. vv.

becomes of course ἐν Κῷ; some less common term
(ἥρως ?) is replaced by the normal δαίμων; the article
(τήν v. 1, τοῦ v. 5) is inserted where prose requires
it and verse rejects; and a few additional conjunctions (καί, τε, τε, μέν, δέ), natural to common speech,
complete the disguise sufficiently.   We notice however that the disguise is not quite perfect; for, as in
the tragic proverb the poetical phrase φρονῶν πολλά,
so here the poetical combination αἰχμάλωτος δου-
λοσύνη remains to a careful ear perceptible, though
the narrator doubtless felt, and with reason, that in
a scene of so much passion and pathos it would not
offend.   We may notice also, as a justification, if
any were needed, for the historian's fidelity, that
even this change of a word, necessary though it is,
slightly obscures the connexion of the whole as
framed by the original composer; for δορι-λήπτου
points forward to λαβών in the final verse, which
the substituted αἰχμάλωτου does not.

Now upon observing this, we might at first
suspect that the whole story is taken from an
original in verse, a thing in itself by no means
inconceivable or even improbable.   But such is not
the fact; for this speech is the only portion susceptible of such re-translation, a thing not otherwise
to be naturally explained but by supposing that this,
and this only, is a translation.   We may try the
experiment upon the preceding sentence—

ὁρῶσα δὲ πάντα ἐκεῖνα διέποντα Παυσανίην, πρότερόν τε τὸ οὔνομα
ἐξεπισταμένη καὶ τὴν πάτρην, ὥστε πολλάκις ἀκούσασα, ἔγνω τε τὸν
Παυσανίην καὶ λαβομένη τῶν γουνάτων ἔλεγε τάδε—

where a very brief inspection will prove that restoration of metre is impracticable. Even the reply of Pausanias, which might well be expected to follow the model, if model there were, exhibits such hopeless material as this—ὃς ἐμοὶ ξεῖνος μάλιστα τυγχάνει ἐὼν τῶν περὶ κείνους τοὺς χώρους οἰκημένων. The speech of the lady therefore, and nothing more, Herodotus had before him in hexameter verse; but this he derived from a source so authentic that he thought fit to preserve it textually.

Now the problem so presented, at first sight puzzling, becomes, I think, not difficult of solution, when we note that the narrative, full as it is, contains nothing which would not be given by a picture of the principal situation, a picture in the Greek style: the lady upon her knees before the "king," Persian corpses upon the ground (one of them named, Φαρανδάτης Τεάσπιος), two maids on the one side balancing two ephors on the other (these also identified by their costume or by lettering), and the chariot for a background. Such a representation, drawn or in bas-relief, with an inscription explaining its purport, the heroine of the story seems to have dedicated, in gratitude for her escape, at some temple in Aegina. Hence the historian is able to say that to Aegina she was sent; and we see that this is just all that he can tell of her subsequent adventures,—except indeed that Aegina was "whither she wanted to go," not an extravagant inference from the fact that thither she went. That the declarations of her speech, as inscribed, were the

cause of Pausanias' clemency is also a fair inference
from the mention of them; and Herodotus accordingly expresses this in his usual manner, by a speech
assigned to the king, which acknowledges the name of
Hegetorides as one which especially appeals to him.

As to this name, however, the historian has
followed a construction of the document which,
were it not for his authority, would be disputable.
He assumes that, in the verse, Ἡγητορίδαο Ἀνταγόραο is the genitive of Ἡγητορίδης Ἀνταγόραο
"Hegetorides, son of Antagoras," as of course it
might be; and perhaps he knew of such a "Hegetorides" otherwise. But he gives no sign of such
knowledge; and, as an interpretation of the document, I should certainly have otherwise preferred
"Antagoras, son of Hegetor," taking "Hegetorides"
as a patronymic. Nor, as it is, should I absolutely
discard this interpretation, although, or perhaps
because, it would curiously illuminate the king's
acquaintance with the name of his "best of friends."
That he commended the lady to the ephors is more
certain; it would appear in the picture from his
attitude. That Pharandates was the Persian captor
Herodotus deduced, and properly, from the otherwise irrelevant assignment of that name to one of
the corpses; and the place, Plataea, was indicated
sufficiently by the name of the king. The rich
attire of the suppliants was visible upon them, the
"gold" no doubt actually gilded; and we may go
with Herodotus in supposing, all things considered,
that it was their best. Nor need we object to his

prudent and highly characteristic intimation, through
the mouth of Pausanias, that the lady's account of
herself *may* have been more pathetic than true;
Pausanias preferred the charitable assumption,—εἰ
δὴ πρὸς τούτῳ τυγχάνεις ἀληθέα λέγουσα.

At this same Aeginetan sanctuary, we may
observe, Herodotus probably also learnt, from some
pious *cicerone* commenting on a monument, the
edifying story of the noble Aeginetan Lampon,
which almost immediately follows (9. 78). It
savours strongly of the preacher, and recalls the
manner of Delphi.

The other example, which I would allege as
exhibiting the use of a verse-inscription, is closely
similar. The description of the events which immediately followed the battle of Salamis, otherwise
natural and probable, is interrupted (8. 114) by an
astounding statement. The Spartans (we are told),
receiving at this moment a command from Delphi
"to demand of Xerxes satisfaction for the slaying of
Leonidas, and to accept whatever the king should
offer," actually despatched a herald with the commis-
sion, who, taking "the quickest way," overtook the
retreating monarch "in Thessaly" before he had
parted from Mardonius, and delivered his message
in the presence of both; whereupon Xerxes, pointing to Mardonius, said that "here was the man who
should give such satisfaction on the part of the
Persians as the Lacedaemonians ought to receive"
—which in due course and to the glory of Apollo
Mardonius did at Plataea.

The historical value of this anecdote is scarcely
worth discussion. It has every mark of the apocryphal, improbabilities moral and physical, amounting
almost to the impossible, vagueness and uncertainty
in all the circumstances. Assuredly if any Greek
had at this time bearded the Great King, and returned to report the interview, it would not have
been forgotten who was the hero and where was the
scene of this transcendent experience. What may
be worth enquiry is the nature of the evidence upon
which Herodotus, who about oracles in particular
expressly claims to be reasonably though not
obstinately critical, accepted a statement, the objections to which he did not overlook[1].

We have some light upon this question when we
observe, that, while the rest of the anecdote was
composed freely, so far as appears, by Herodotus,
the speech of the herald, like that of the lady
from Cos, was not so composed, but translated
from verse:

> ὦ βασιλεῦ Μήδων, Λακεδαιμόνιοί τε φόνοιο
> αἰτοῦσίν σε δίκας Σπάρτης ἄπο θ' Ἡρακλεῖδαι,
> Ἑλλάδα ῥυόμενόν σφιν ὅτι κτεῖνας βασιλῆα.

The prose of Herodotus runs thus :—

> ὦ βασιλεῦ Μήδων, Λακεδαιμόνιοί τέ σε καὶ Ἡρακλεῖδαι οἱ ἀπὸ
> Σπάρτης αἰτέουσι φόνου δίκας, ὅτι σφέων τὸν βασιλέα ἀπέκτεινας
> ῥυόμενον τὴν Ἑλλάδα.

[1] Note the simple but significant suggestion that the herald
took "the quickest way." One might wonder what way, at the
moment, this was. It is uncertain whether Xerxes was then in
Thessaly at all.

As in the former example, so also here, the document is followed word for word. The possessive-dative (σφιν, in *v.* 3) might perhaps have been retained without offence; but with the prosaic arrangement and emphasis, the genitive σφέων, answering to Μήδων, is more natural. The other changes are merely those inevitable for prose.

Here again therefore we have to do, not with a narrative in verse, but with a fragment of a narrative, such a fragment as could hardly exist except as an inscription, as an explanatory appendage to a reciprocally illustrative work of art. From this work itself, the painted or sculptured group, comes the principal scene, Xerxes answering the herald by "pointing to Mardonius"; and the story comes from the religious custodians of the monument, the Delphians or whoever they were. But we may now divine how and by what stages this story grew and came to be accepted. It is open and natural to be supposed, that the authors of the work neither asserted nor intended it to represent an actual event. It was a symbol, legitimate and appropriate, of the truth that Plataea was the Spartan's revenge for Thermopylae. But when the exhibitors, for obvious reasons, preferred to regard and explain it as historical, it seemed, to a mind perfectly honest but not sufficiently versed in the sifting of such testimony, to be an independent witness of the truth. It produced upon Herodotus the sort of effect which, upon persons not accustomed to analysis, is now produced when something, which they are not unwilling to believe, is actually shown to them in print.

THE DEATH OF CYRSILUS, *ALIAS* LYCIDES.

A PROBLEM IN AUTHORITIES.

Few events so remote as the year 479 B.C., and perhaps none relating to the fate of an ordinary person, are so well known to us and so fully attested, as the vengeance taken by the Athenians on the unfortunate councillor, who ventured to recommend for consideration the proposal of Mardonius,—that Athens, upon favourable terms for herself, should make peace with the King of Persia and abandon the common cause of the Greek nation. We possess three notices of the story, two summary and one more full, which have, all of them, high pretensions to authenticity. Of the two summaries, one at least is derived directly from an official document almost contemporary with the event itself. The fuller account is not indeed thus warranted, and may be supposed rather to depend on oral relation ; but our narrator must have had and used the opportunity of consulting eye-witnesses. All three accounts may be combined without difficulty, and, except in one unimportant detail, they exhibit no discrepancy.

The outline of the story is this. The Persian proposal was laid before the Athenian Council by an envoy sent from Athens, which was then in the hands of the enemy, to the island of Salamis. Here the Athenians, or so many of them as had ventured to return to their homes upon the retreat of Xerxes in the year before, had again taken refuge, when Mardonius, after wintering in Boeotia, had re-occupied the desolate city. One councillor, apparently alone, moved that the terms offered should be referred to the Assembly. By the exasperated patriotism of his colleagues this advice was regarded as treacherous and corrupt; and such was their indignation, that, upon the rising of the Council, they and others joined in stoning him to death. The Athenian women, upon hearing what had occurred, were seized with a like fury, rushed to the man's house, and killed in the same manner his wife and his children. These proceedings became the subject of a decree (*psephisma*). The text of this document is not preserved, nor its purpose specified; but since it is cited as approving what was done, we can hardly be wrong in supposing that it was designed to put a legal face upon the matter, and to prevent the perilous consequences likely to arise out of acts which, however popular, were in law nothing better than murders.

In all these facts our three authorities, Herodotus (9. 4), Lycurgus (*contra Leocratem* 122), and Demosthenes (*de corona* 204), so far as they go, concur,— Demosthenes not less than the others, as shall

presently be shown. The decree is mentioned by
Lycurgus only, who cites it, though the quotation,
as usual, is omitted in our copies of his speech. He
describes the decree as "concerning" or "relating
to the man who came to his end in Salamis" (περὶ
τοῦ ἐν Σαλαμῖνι τελευτήσαντος),—a phrase which
could not naturally be used of a sentence to death,
but only of an enactment "concerning" the death,
that is to say, relating to it *ex post facto*. With this
agree the allusion of Demosthenes, which implies[1],
and the story of Herodotus, which asserts, that the
man and his family were not regularly executed, but
lynched. Doubtless therefore this is the meaning
of Lycurgus also, though in saying that "the
Council" stoned the man, and that before doing
so they "took off their wreaths," he colours the act
with certain touches of solemnity. The participation of persons from the Council, as individuals, is
affirmed by Herodotus; the colours of Lycurgus
come probably from the decree, which, if designed,
as we must suppose, to give a retrospective sanction,
naturally put upon what had been done the most
plausible construction which it would bear. The
act of the women, the killing of the wife and the
children, cannot possibly have been legalized
a priori; and it is plain, upon all three accounts,
that the killing of the man, however the decree may
have coloured it, was also a mere act of popular
vengeance and equally without formal justification.

[1] By including the action of the women, which cannot have
been legal.

We may doubt indeed, though we need not here discuss, whether at this date any Athenian court would have deliberately awarded, for a lawful expression of opinion, a species of punishment which an Athenian poet, only twenty years later, classes with impalement and other tortures, as a barbarity fit only for fiends[1]. However that may be, our authorities agree in showing that upon this occasion there was no legal award.

It is extremely important to note, for reasons which will presently appear, that Demosthenes, though he does not mention the decree and has no need to do so, cannot reasonably or fairly be supposed ignorant of it. The allusions of both orators are so introduced as to convey the impression that in their time the case, and the public pronouncement on it, as examples of the fervency of Athenian patriotism, were notorious and celebrated. And when we consider what were the character, vocation and pursuits of Demosthenes, it is beyond belief that he was not acquainted, and perfectly familiar, with a document so remarkable and in all respects so interesting to him as this. We may presume then, and must necessarily presume, that the account of the affair, which he gives in the most famous and finished of his compositions, is consistent, so far as it goes, with the authoritative record. In the case of Herodotus there is of course no such presumption. He was neither lawyer nor consulter of archives;

---

[1] Aesch. *Eum.* 189. It seems, however, to have been a possible punishment; see Macan on Herod. *l.c.*

and although the decree, being no part of the story as a story, would not perhaps have interested him much if he had heard of it, we may suppose more probably that he never did. Nevertheless, as to the main and material facts, his graphic narrative agrees with those of his more learned successors. His conception of the event is just that which we might have formed by combining the data of Lycurgus and Demosthenes, and discarding their flourishes. One addition he makes, though it cannot be called a discrepancy. He tells us, at the close of the terrible tale, what neither of the orators chooses to comprise in his encomiastic allusion,—that the crowd of enraged women pelted to death not only the wife of the delinquent, but also his children: κατὰ μὲν ἔλευσαν αὐτοῦ τὴν γυναῖκα, κατὰ δὲ τὰ τέκνα. Lycurgus refers to the man only, Demosthenes only to the adults. Their motives for such limitation are obvious; and their reticences afford no reason to doubt, that the recital of the decree, if we had it, would be found to confirm the completeness and candour of the historian.

In one detail only, and that not affecting the substance of the narrative, Herodotus disagrees with those who had access to the official document; and here he must have been misinformed. The name of the offender, according to Demosthenes, who had for it the testimony of the *psephisma*, was Cyrsilus (Κύρσιλος). Herodotus gives it as Lycides (Λυκίδης). Whether his variation may be accounted for, we will consider presently. But if it cannot, if it is a mere error, there is nothing in it to raise difficulty or suspicion. In things of no significance, the best oral tradition will be inaccurate; and in this case the personality of the victim was apparently of no significance. It is not alleged that, apart from his fate, he had any importance, nor does the story imply it. In Lycurgus he is actually anonymous— ὁ ἐν Σαλαμῖνι τελευτήσας. That Herodotus should have picked up a wrong name is not surprising and hardly worth notice.

Let us repeat then, and firmly remember, that this instructive incident, in its substance and essential features, is absolutely certain. It must have happened when, where, and as these authorities assert. Evidence so authentic and concordant would outweigh much improbability. But there is no improbability. The Athenians of Salamis and Plataea were incomparably the most civilised people of the time. But they were not more civilised, or more safe from excesses of passion, than the Hollanders of the seventeenth century, who, in a crisis not dissimilar, tore in pieces the innocent and illustrious De Witt.

Where then, it will be asked, is the problem? Why, in editions of Herodotus or the *de corona*, is the story treated as a puzzle? Why are there histories in which it is canvassed as dubious, or even altogether omitted? The cause is typical, and, as such, worthy of attention.

In the *de officiis* of Cicero (3. 11, § 48) the anecdote is cited as follows: "The Athenians, being unable to withstand the Persian invader, determined to abandon their city, *putting their wives and children in Troezen, and themselves on board the fleet, which was to defend at sea the liberties of Greece*; and they stoned to death one Cyrsilus, who advised that they *should remain in Athens and should admit Xerxes.*" Now between this version and that of the Greek authors no conciliation is possible. Cicero has changed almost every circumstance,—the date, the place, the position of the Athenians at the time. Above all, he changes the essential matter, the proposal of Cyrsilus and the connexion of his conduct with his fate. According to Cicero, the proposal was, that in the year 480, and before the battle of Salamis, the Athenians should submit wholly and unconditionally to the King of Persia. Nothing is said of any offer to them from Xerxes, nor indeed would it be credible that, before Salamis, any offer was made. Athens and Attica, with their population, were to be surrendered to the King and the army then under his command,—a surrender which would have extinguished the Athenian state as a factor in resistance, so that the naval force of Hellas would have been practically annihilated, and, as Cicero plainly and necessarily supposes, no sea-defence whatever could have been made. How such a submission could have been "advantageous (*utile*)" for Athens, is not apparent; but certainly it would have been, in the highest degree, "dishonourable." Moreover (a point more vital yet) we are told that by Cyrsilus this submission was positively approved and recommended. But in Herodotus the Athenian councillor is not so committed. Mardonius offers, in consideration of a separate peace, to respect the independence of Athens, and to give her what territory she chooses to ask (Herod. 8. 140, 9. 4). The offer is made to "the Council," and the proposal of the councillor is simply that it should be referred to the Assembly. To treat this as a proof of treason was a mere extravagance, a frenzy of popular enthusiasm; and Herodotus expressly allows that the conduct of the councillor may have been honest. But the Ciceronian proposal, that Athens should, accept slavery without striking a blow, without reward, and with every reason to expect the severest treatment, would have gone near to prove treason (if not rather insanity), and the execution of the proposer might well have followed in course of law, as Cicero would let us think that it did.

But the disagreement of Cicero with the Greek authorities would of course not suffice to impeach them, or to throw upon them any shadow of doubt. It would be enough to say that his statement, improbable upon the face of it, is proved by history to be altogether erroneous. We need not even ask how he came by his mistake. He is mistaken, and there we might leave him. Why then, we have still to ask, have the Greek authorities been treated as dubious?

Because it is said, and repeated in book after book, that, on the essential point of date, Cicero is

supported by Demosthenes : that Demosthenes also
puts the affair of Cyrsilus before the battle of
Salamis, and represents the offers, which Cyrsilus
wished to accept or to consider, as having been
made by Xerxes during his march upon Athens
in the year 480.

Now if this were so, we should have a problem
indeed, and a problem hopeless of any satisfactory
solution.   Both Herodotus and Demosthenes, for
different reasons, are in this matter authorities of
the greatest weight.   Yet to accept both, if in substance they differ, and to suppose that an incident
so remarkable was repeated, with no other variation
than the name of the principal victim, in two successive years, is an escape not worth discussion.
The logical and practical conclusion would be that,
for the most interesting part of Greek history, we
have no trustworthy witnesses at all.

But we are in no such position.   It is not true
that the blunders of Cicero are supported by
Demosthenes.   It is true that they can be read
into Demosthenes.   But that is an injury to the
orator, who says nothing which is not consistent
with the truth as it appears in the other Greek
testimonies.

Demosthenes says (*de corona* 204) that the
Athenians had the endurance (ὑπέμειναν) to abandon
their country and city, and take to their ships, rather
than do what the Persians required of them ; and he
adds, in proof of their resolution and stubbornness,
that "they elected Themistocles, the adviser of this

course, for their *strategos*, and stoned to death
Cyrsilus, who suggested compliance." Now if this
were our only account of the matter, and if we knew
nothing about the history of the time, we might
doubtless suppose that these two facts, the advice of
Themistocles and the suggestion of Cyrsilus, were
contemporaneous, and therefore that the act of
Cyrsilus as well as that of Themistocles took place
in the year 480, when Themistocles was elected
strategos.

But why should we so suppose, since it was not
the truth, and since not only Demosthenes, but
many or most of his audience and readers, must
have known that it was not the truth? Demosthenes does not say so. The abandonment of
Attica and Athens extended (in effect) from the
summer of 480 to the autumn of 479, from before
the battle of Salamis until after the battle of Plataea.
Demosthenes here speaks of it, quite correctly, as
one single course or action, disregarding, as in such
a retrospect is natural, whatever precarious and
temporary re-occupation may have occurred in the
winter between. The facts which he subjoins are
given as illustrations of the resolution with which
this painful policy was adopted and pursued. The
election of Themistocles marks the deliberate adoption of it; the treatment of Cyrsilus displays the
passionate adhesion to it in spite of bitter experience.
To suppose the two facts contemporaneous is not
only unnecessary to the purpose of the orator, but
unsuitable; since the two together would then only

show the high spirit of the Athenians before the trial, and not their perseverance in enduring it.

Nor is Demosthenes incorrect or inaccurate when, in a passage preceding (§ 202), he says that the offers, by which Athens was tempted to abandon the cause of Hellas, came "from the King of Persia" (παρὰ τοῦ Περσῶν βασιλέως). He does not thereby say or suggest that they were made by Xerxes during his personal campaign in the year 480. The offers of Mardonius in the following winter and spring, the offers recommended for consideration by Cyrsilus, were made on behalf of the King, by his express sanction and command (Herod. 8. 140, and by reference 9. 4), and indeed would not otherwise have been worth attention. The terms offered are described by Demosthenes as they are by Herodotus; he translates Herodotus, we may say, into language of his own[1]. There is no reason therefore to doubt, that it is to the offers made by Xerxes through Mardonius, the only offers ever made, that Demosthenes refers; and he speaks truly when he says that, rather than accept them, the Athenians (for the second time) abandoned their country.

But though the statements of Demosthenes are true, they are ambiguous, and would easily be misunderstood by a reader having no external information. Probably they misled Cicero, or the intermediary person, if there was one, by whom

---

[1] Herod. 8. 140 τοῦτο μὲν τὴν γῆν σφι ἀπόδος, τοῦτο δὲ ἄλλην πρὸς ταύτῃ ἑλέσθων αὐτοί, ἥντινα ἂν ἐθέλωσι. Demosth. *de cor.* 202 ὅτι βούλεται λαβούσῃ (τῇ πόλει) καὶ τὰ ἑαυτῆς ἐχούσῃ.

Cicero was misled. For this ambiguity, as for any, two different causes may be suggested. It might be thought intentional. Demosthenes, we might suppose, was willing to hint what he dares not assert, namely, that Athens, though she received no offers from Persia before the battle of Salamis, might then or at any time have obtained advantages at the expense of Hellas, if she had chosen to ask for them. But there is an alternative supposition, more candid and more reasonable,—that the ambiguity, unperceived by Demosthenes, was possible to him just because the facts were notorious, and because the false construction, the construction of Cicero, was not thinkable. It never occurred to Demosthenes as imaginable (and why should it have occurred?), that Xerxes, before receiving any check, would have consented to favour, or even to spare, the state which was the chief object of his vengeance. Unfortunately Cicero was capable of this conception; and Cicero, by a natural consequence, has misled others, who, but for him, would have done Demosthenes the justice of taking his words, as they may be taken, consistently with the facts of history.

But when we have made this observation, the historical problem disappears. The date given by Cicero for the stoning of Cyrsilus is a blunder, a misreading of the *de corona*. Demosthenes, Lycurgus, and Herodotus all give, or admit, the true date, after Salamis and in the year of Plataea; and they agree in all other respects, except that Herodotus

gives the name of the victim not as Cyrsilus (which
it was) but as Lycides.

It remains only to consider, whether the name
Lycides is, as it well may be, a mere error, or
whether it admits of explanation. Is it not possibly
a patronymic? There was such a name as Lycus
(Λύκος). May not Λυκίδης represent ὁ Λύκου? We
cannot, of course, suppose that Herodotus so understood it, since he does not use patronymics, and in
any case would not prefer such a description to
the true name. But if it were, in this sense,
applicable to Cyrsilus, it may well have been used
for its significance (*wolfling*) by those who stoned
him for treachery. It is even possible, in that age of
omens, that this ill-sounding appellation contributed
to his horrible fate. Herodotus himself (7. 180)
makes a like conjecture about one Leon (*lion*), who
was killed by the Persians as a sacrificial victim,
possibly, as the historian supposes, because of the
name. His conjecture, whatever it may prove about
the Persians, is significant as to the feelings of a
Greek. If thus explained, the use of the appellation
by Herodotus would be not so much an error as
a misapprehension. But upon this we need not
speculate. In any case the misnomer, corrected
(from the documentary evidence) by Demosthenes,
is no reason for questioning the narrative of
Herodotus, or for raising any doubts respecting an
incident unimpeachably certified.

CHRIST BEFORE HEROD[1].

LUKE XXIII 1—16.

THE part played in the proceedings of the Passion by Herod Antipas, tetrarch of Galilee, is one of those incidents which are peculiar to the third Gospel of the canonical four. The narrative has been vigorously assailed by modern criticism. Some have declared it destitute of any foundation. And even in the more conservative historians we find assumptions and concessions, respecting the purport of the story as intended by the Evangelist, which, if valid, create difficulties and doubts. The purpose of this essay is to suggest, with the submission due from one having no special competence in the subject, that the case against the narrative is itself entirely mistaken, and rests, so far as it has any basis at all, upon a traditional misapprehension and misinterpretation of the statement impeached.

The present position of the question, as it appears from the sceptical side, will be seen in a full quotation translated from the commentary of Loisy. My

---

[1] Reprinted (by permission) from the *Journal of Theological Studies*, Vol. X p. 321.

investigation of the matter, as a case in some ways typical and important, was conceived in the course of studying his two elaborate and interesting volumes on the Synoptic Gospels. Criticism, he says[1], has seen in this episode

a legendary fiction accepted, or even invented, by Luke. The latter hypothesis must be rejected as improbable, since everywhere else the evangelist depends upon written documents. He found the mention of Herod in one of the gospels which he knew and used. But did this document deserve complete confidence? May not its *data* have been somewhat modified by Luke for the purpose of inclusion in his narrative? It has been remarked that, not having mentioned the silence of Jesus before Pilate, he has put this touch into the appearance before Herod; that the accusation of the priests seems to be imported from the same source; and that the soldiers of Herod and the "splendid robe[2]" similarly take the place and part of the Roman soldiers, who, in the first two Gospels, and in the fourth, array the Saviour in a robe of purple. The "splendid robe" of Luke need not be white[3], and if it be, the purple may have been discarded by the evangelist as an object not possible for the mockery of a king.

On the other hand, the story of Luke has long prepared us for the intervention of Herod. We are informed first that the tetrarch desired to see Jesus[4], and again later[5], that he designed to put him to death, and that upon this occasion the Pharisees who gave warning of the design were requested by Jesus to tell Herod that, for the death of a prophet, the only possible place was Jerusalem. All this, in the conception of the evangelist, is connected with the incident now before us. But the train of events he probably did not make; he found it ready-made in a document or documents, containing notes of the relation between Jesus and Antipas. A passage in the *Acts*[6], a prayer of the disciples in

---

[1] *Les Évangiles Synoptiques* II 638. [2] *robe brillante.*

[3] Some Latin versions render the adjective by *albus.*

[4] ix 7. [5] xiii 31. [6] iv 27.

which Herod is expressly noted as a participant in the condemnation of the Saviour, is inspired by the same source or derived
from the same tradition. In that passage is mentioned a
prophecy, which was in the mind of the author when he describes
in his Gospel the parts taken, in the story of the Passion, by the
Jewish priests and people, by Pilate, and by Herod: "Why did
the nations rage and the peoples imagine vain things? The
kings of the earth assembled, and the rulers were gathered
together, against the Lord and against his Christ[1]." This text
from the *Psalms* may have had some influence in shaping the
Gospel-narrative, but has not affected it very much, and certainly
cannot have created it.

It was supposed by Renan, that Luke was acquainted with
a document, "in which the death of Jesus was by mistake
attributed to Herod," and that, "in order not to lose this *datum*
totally," he "pieced the two traditions together." A pure mistake
it could not be, but there is room for mistake with design. The
apocryphal *Gospel of Peter* gives a glimpse of the way in which
legend enlarged the part of Herod in the Passion, and thus
improved upon the lead of the Synoptic Gospels in shifting the
responsibility from Pilate; but the part of the procurator could
not conceivably be suppressed. The document, upon which
Luke has drawn for information about the attitude of Herod
towards Jesus, cannot, so far as concerns Herod's part in the
Passion, be that which was used by Mark. It was a source
resembling the *Gospel of Peter*, possibly a former edition of this
Gospel, and parallel to Mark and to Matthew. In it, all the
main points of the trial by Pilate were transferred to Herod, so as
to let it appear that the tetrarch gave the sentence and directed
the execution. So free a treatment of history the framer of our
third Gospel could not admit; but he has summarized that
version in a scene, which, so far as it goes, serves to exhibit the
innocence of Jesus and the goodwill of Pilate, and to throw upon
the Jewish king and his soldiers the odium of the mockery really
enacted at the residence of the Roman governor....The purpose
of clearing Pilate explains why, in the original document, his

[1] Ps. ii 1, 2.

place was in a manner filled by Herod, and the substitution may be, to some extent, an echo of the original *data* respecting the measures which Antipas was disposed to take against the preaching of Jesus in Galilee.

Now it will be seen at once that the key-stone of this criticism, the base, hinge, handle, sum of it, is the resemblance, between the trial by Pilate and the trial (so called) by Herod, in the remarkable particular of the mockery. Were it not for this, the suggestion that the two scenes are suspiciously parallel, and the inference that one may be an invention which imitates the other, would never have occurred to any reasonable mind. Except in this, the resemblance, so far as it exists, is the natural and even necessary result of the circumstances. The accused, who made but little answer to the examination of Pilate, made none to the questions of Herod. We may well suppose so. The accusers were in both places the same persons or some of them. Of course they would be. But the repetition of the mockery is a different matter. The derisive play or performance of the Roman soldiers after the condemnation, whatever its nature or occasion, is an exceptional and irregular incident, a thing which, though in no way improbable, could by no means be presumed from the circumstances. And if, as all seem to understand, and as we must understand from the description of the interview with Herod as now interpreted,—if it is alleged by the author of the third Gospel that the tragic farce of the legionaries was previously re-

hearsed, as it were, by the Jewish prince; that at
an earlier and totally different stage in the proceedings Herod anticipated the Roman performance
both in idea and in detail; that he also fixed upon
the title "King of the Jews" as a topic for
sport, and expressed his parody by a symbolic
investiture, and above all, as if to eke out the lack
of resemblance in his own person, actually incited or
encouraged his soldiers to assist in the exhibition;—
if that is the allegation of Luke, it is certainly surprising. And when it is added, that of the four
canonical narratives, that of Luke, the only one
which notices the act of Herod, is also the only one
which does not notice the act of the legionaries, the
suspicion of a transference, repetition, or mistake of
some kind cannot with prudence be rejected, and,
if admitted, may, or even must, extend to the whole
source, in the use of which the third Gospel is here
peculiar. It would be easy to show that such doubts
have had their legitimate effect upon minds as
remote as possible from prejudice against the
canonical witnesses.

It is therefore of some interest to enquire, what
precisely is the extent of resemblance between the
behaviour of Herod Antipas, as described by
St Luke, and that of the Roman soldiers as
described by the rest. We may, perhaps, find that
in fact there is no resemblance, and that the
contrary assumption, though ancient, wide-spread,
and readily explained, is none the less certainly
wrong.

To approach the subject properly, we must first review what is said or suggested by the first three Gospels, and especially by the third—the fourth has nothing relevant—respecting the attitude or sentiments of the tetrarch towards the movement in his little dominion, which has given him such an unenviable celebrity. In this respect already, there is a noticeable difference between the original documents and the common colouring of accounts which are intended to reflect them. The "hostility of Antipas," "the designs of Antipas," "the danger from Antipas," are phrases easily found, as one may say, anywhere except in the Evangelists. Nor is this surprising. The tetrarch of Galilee, by all accounts, was a bad, weak man, whose poor appearance in history would be unnoticed, were it not that, during certain obscure occurrences, soldiers, who swore by his head, must have stared in the streets of Chorazin and Capernaum, of Nazareth and of Nain. He shares the horror of a name, which, wherever the Bible stories are told, has perhaps of all names the most detestable sound to the ears of the simple and tender. The "Herod" of infantile imagination, the legendary "Herod," compiled from the criminal record of the whole family, is a creature scarcely human. It is rather a sort of ogre, who massacres the babes of Bethlehem, to whose table the head of John Baptist is brought in a charger, who stretches forth his hands to vex certain of the Church, who kills James, the brother of John, with the sword, who, "because he saw it pleased the

Jews," proceeds further to take Peter also, and
whose proper and exquisitely hideous end is to be
eaten of worms and give up the ghost.   It may not
be altogether easy, even for the learned and critical,
to disengage from this genial confusion, and to
weigh strictly upon evidence, the question whether,
in a particular case and relation, the wickedness of
an individual Herod was of a specified quality,—
whether the sentiments of Antipas, respecting the
Preacher of the Kingdom, are, or should be, defined
as hostile sentiments.   They are not so described in
the Gospels.   The first two can scarcely be said to
throw any light on his feelings; the third is explicit about them, and excludes the supposition of
hostility.

If we depended only on St Mark and St Matthew,
we should hardly regard the tetrarch as having any
connexion, except indirectly and remotely, with the
figure and story of Christ.   In those narratives he
is connected rather with the Baptist, and upon the
death of the Baptist disappears from the scene.
We are told indeed with some emphasis, that when,
by the preaching and works of the Twelve, the
name of their Master was brought to the ears of
"the king," then, among various popular opinions
about him, the one which commended itself to
Herod was this,—that the new prophet must be in
some sense a resuscitation of the former: "it is
John, whom I beheaded; he is risen from the
dead[1]."   The notice seems to promise a sequel, but

[1] Mark vi 16 (cf. Matt. xiv 1).

there is none. This silence however is significant and expressive. It forbids us to attribute to the ruler of Galilee or his government any overt act of hostility to the movement; of which surely, had it occurred, the tradition must have preserved some trace. It forbids even the supposition of anything properly called a design; for to imagine this would be to raise gratuitously the question why the design was not executed, and who or what it was that protected from the sovereign the humble objects of his machination. It is clear that, so far as Christian tradition remembered, Antipas, during the activity of the Founder, neither did nor devised against him anything at all. Of the prince's mere disposition and feelings, so long as this was the case, people in the rank of the disciples could scarcely know anything; nor do they pretend to know. If we were to admit, as literally and precisely correct, the statement about Herod's opinion which is quoted above, what sentiments should we properly infer from it? How would a king esteem, and how would he be likely to treat, the resuscitated embodiment of a person whom he had reluctantly put to death? It seems impossible to say, and the Evangelists give us no guidance. Only, inasmuch as they here take occasion to relate the story of Herodias and her daughter, of which the plain purport is, that in persecuting the Baptist Herod acted against his own feelings and will; that it was the women of his family who forced him to imprison, and tricked him into beheading, a man whom he personally regarded with interest and a certain awe; we should perhaps suppose, if anything, that upon this view he would be rather disinclined than inclined to molest another John who gave no provocation.

For by the successor no provocation was given; and this again is a point in which the silence of the Gospels is significant for our purpose. On one occasion only, and that private, are any words, referring to the tetrarch personally, attributed to the Saviour. The passage is from Luke[1], and will be considered presently. On another occasion[2], also private, the habitual warning against the religious leaders of the time, against the "leaven" or spirit of the Pharisees, is coupled with a warning against "the leaven of Herod," the mixture of Jewish practices and foreign culture, of which the family were representative. And elsewhere in private discourses an oblique reference may be discovered or suspected. But in the preaching not a word is reported reflecting even remotely upon the ruler of Galilee or his administration. On political topics the Preacher, so far as appears, was invariably silent; and indeed it is obvious that, apart from any consideration of danger, no other course would have been consistent with the essential novelty of the teaching, the non-political colour which was put by the Teacher upon the announcement of "the Kingdom of God." At the very end of his career, his enemies are still trying, and trying in vain, to

[1] xiii 31.   [2] Mark viii 15.

extract from him a condemnation or repudiation of the secular authorities[1].

This last affair, concerning the test-question of the tribute-money, is one of the few places in which the Gospels bring upon the scene the persons or class who are described as "the Herodians." The impulse of the attack comes from the religious adversaries, "the Pharisees," but "Herodians" are for this occasion joined with them. And similarly in Galilee, when the religious leaders become definitely hostile to the new teaching, and design to get rid of the Teacher, they endeavour, apparently with some success, to draw in supporters of the tetrarch: they take counsel on the subject with "the Herodians[2]." It is manifest that, for persons destitute of official protectors or patrons, this situation, however small the number, and however limited the powers, of those moving or disposed to move against them, was in itself dangerous. There was from this time danger in Galilee; and we may legitimately use the fact to explain whatever it will explain—the interval of privacy in the teaching, the journey in the direction of Tyre, and the like. But when we come to the question with which we are here concerned, how nearly these "Herodians" were connected with Herod, and whether what is said about them implies anything about him, the answer must be purely negative. In a recent book by a specialist in this history, the

[1] Mark xii 13, Matt. xxii 15, Luke xx 20.
[2] Mark iii 6.

Pharisees who take counsel with the Herodians are described in modern terms as "complaining to the police[1]." The expression is probably adequate. For the less high in rank we place the persons concerned, the more natural is the apparent fact, that their acts, if they acted, and their measures, if they took any, had no visible result, and that, during all the months, or perhaps years, of the Galilean ministry, neither Master nor disciples were on any recorded occasion arrested, molested, or even prohibited, by command or in the name of the public authority. When the most is made that can be made of "the Herodians," it remains possible and not unlikely that, from Herod and those about him, from the government, the Christian movement, as a matter of politics, had received no consideration at all. And we shall see that this, or something like it, is assumed and implied by St Luke, when he describes the action and behaviour of the tetrarch on the day of the Passion.

If, going beyond the record, we ask what is presumable, we shall be as far as ever from the conclusion, that Antipas, from the necessity of his position as ruler of Jewish subjects, must have regarded the Messiah with hostility. The assumption is not uncommon, but it seems to overlook an important and essential part of the facts. If the expectation of a Messiah and of a theocratic state had been now first created, if the announcement of

[1] Burkitt, *The Gospel History and its Transmission*, p. 91. See the whole context and chapter.

"the Kingdom" had been, as such, new, then indeed it would of course have been dangerous and
detestable to a ruler in possession. But since the
expectation and the political danger of it already
existed, why should such a ruler be alarmed or
displeased by the doctrine that "the Kingdom" was
not to be realized by force? Surely nothing is
more certain than that such was the doctrine of
Christ, and that, so far as the new teaching bore
upon politics, precisely here lay its novelty, and the
distinction, for example, between Christ and the
Baptist. The effect of this doctrine, if accepted,
was surely to eliminate the existing danger ; and if
all the Jewish subjects of the tetrarch could have
been instantly converted to the principles of the
Sermon on the Mount, his position would have
been, so far, not less but much more secure.
Undoubtedly the new Messiah proclaimed, like the
predecessor, that "the kingdom of heaven was *at
hand*," and that in some way, but without rebellion,
without violence, without ordinary means, it was in
some form to appear and be established forthwith.
But, without entering into subtleties of interpretation, which were certainly not in the view of
Antipas, we may surely think that, in a statesman
of Greek education and Roman experience, this
prophecy, merely as such, would excite feelings
quite different from alarm. When we add that,
according to the Gospels, the Messianic claim, during
the Galilean ministry, had been, so far as possible,
concealed, and that in Galilee, so far as we are told,

no demonstration had occurred, upon which it was even possible to put a political colour, it will appear that, if we are to speculate, the indifference of the Galilean government and sovereign, as politicians, should be supposed rather an indifferent goodwill.

And now let us consider precisely the statements of the third Gospel. These are, after all, our only authority for the expectations which the author means us to bring to the interview which he only describes. When we have noted, but without pressing, the indications that the source or sources special to him, as compared with Mark and Matthew, were connected in some way with the person or household of Herod[1], let us next observe that, when he uses the same sources as the other two, he omits, if he had before him, even the slight traces, which they exhibit, of collision between the Christian movement and the party or principles of the prince. The "leaven of Herod" and "the Herodians" disappear, when passages, which in the other versions contain such mention, are almost identically reproduced[2]. We may perhaps, without affirming anything upon this evidence, infer safely that it was not in the design of the author to prepare us for enmity on the part of Herod against Christ, since he has neglected what, for this purpose, lay to his hand.

Over the relations between Antipas and the Baptist he passes summarily, but without changing materially the *data* of Mark. In the description of

[1] Luke viii 3 (cf. xxiii 49).
[2] Luke xii 1 (Mark viii 15), Luke xx 20 (Mark xii 13).

the Baptist's ministry, his imprisonment is mentioned
by a brief anticipatory note[1], with the addition that
the rebukes, by which it was provoked, referred not
only to the connexion with Herodias, but to the
"many other evil things which Herod had done.'
His immorality is common ground and unquestion-
able. The death of John is not related at all, but
is assumed in describing how Herod regarded the
successor[2]. Here St Luke modifies the common
tradition significantly. Upon the variety of popular
opinions—that in the new preacher and worker of
miracles " John was resuscitated," or " Elijah had
appeared," or "one of the ancient prophets had
arisen "—Herod remained in doubt : " 'John,' he
said, ' I myself beheaded ; but who is this, of whom
such things are reported to *me* ?' And he was
desirous to see him." The correction, by which the
supposed resuscitation of the Baptist is no longer
represented as credible to the tetrarch, points to
better knowledge of him, or at least a more likely
conception. What the narrator asserts positively,
and all that he asserts, is that the report of the new
performances, and especially of the remarkable
cures[3], excited the prince's curiosity, so that he
wished to see the Physician, to whom, and to whose
pupils, such things were attributed. To this carefully limited proposition the Evangelist recurs in the
final scene. To keep in his track, we must ignore
what he ignores, and hold by the statement, as the

[1] Luke iii 18.   [2] Luke ix 7.
[3] See the context.

whole of what we are to assume about Herod, that he was curious about Jesus, especially as a performer of miracles, and therefore desirous to see him.

Between this and the interview, St Luke has but one reference to Herod. The passage is peculiar to his Gospel, and must be read in the author's own light. It occurs among the mass of anecdotes, remarks, and discourses which the Evangelist puts together, without pretence to definite sequence or chronology, in connexion with the last journey to Jerusalem[1].

Just at this time[2] came some Pharisees, saying to him, "Depart and go hence, for Herod desires to kill thee." And he said to them, "Go and tell this[3] fox: Behold, I cast out devils and accomplish healings to-day and to-morrow, and the third day I am perfected. Only I must journey on to-day and to-morrow and the day after, for it cannot be that a prophet should perish out of Jerusalem. O Jerusalem, Jerusalem, thou that killest the prophets, and stonest them that are sent to thee, how often did I desire to gather thy children, even as a hen gathers her brood under her wings, and ye would not. Behold, your house is to be left unto you desolate. Verily, I say to you, ye shall not see me till the time be when ye shall say, 'Blessed is he that cometh in the name of the Lord.'"

The reader will consider, whether there is here anything relevant to our enquiry. The main point

---

[1] Luke xiii 31 ff. For a full discussion see Loisy, *Évangiles Synoptiques*, ii 125.

[2] ἐν αὐτῇ τῇ ἡμέρᾳ (or ὥρᾳ). But the context (see *ib.* 22) does not give any place or time, and we must take the phrase loosely.

[3] ταύτῃ, not (as in A. V.) "*that* fox." See further the note at the end of this essay.

is plainly the imminence of the end, the foreseen imminence of the only possible end. The warning of the Pharisees, mentioned for the sake of the answer, implies what the author has told us before, that Herod was a bad man, to whom an evil purpose might be attributed. And so much the answer confirms. But that more is meant, that we are to infer anything positively about the tetrarch, seems impossible, since everything material to such an inference is undetermined. With what purpose and in what spirit the warning is given, whether it is true, whether authorized, whether believed,—all is uncertain. We have still therefore, as the sum of what the narrator has told us of Herod's mind, the statement, that he was curious about the reported performances, and desirous to see the performer.

Coming then, with this preparation, to the final scenes at Jerusalem, we read in Luke that, after the night-arrest, the prisoner is detained at the house of the high priest till morning, when a meeting of the Sanhedrin is held there. From his replies to questions touching his Messianic and superhuman claims, they conclude that, from their point of view and on grounds of religion, "no further testimony" is needed to justify their next proceeding[1], which is to go in a body to Pilate, the Roman governor or procurator of Judaea, and prefer at a public audience an accusation of political treason. "We found this man perverting the nation, and forbidding to give tribute to Caesar, saying that he himself is Christ

[1] Luke xxiii.

a King." Pilate, after an examination, declares that
no crime is made out. The report of the interrogatory is extremely concise, and does not signify the
topics or the ground of conclusion ; but from the
reference in the accusation to the payment of tribute,
a point upon which, as we have been expressly told[1],
the enemies of the defendant had recently tried,
and failed, to obtain from him a declaration suitable
to their purpose, we must understand that, so far,
the case has rested upon what has happened in
Jerusalem since the triumphal entry. The procurator decides, as he well might, that these
proceedings, as described in the Gospel, do not
support the charge of rebellion against the Empire.

The accusers however persist, and try to
strengthen their case by a new statement[2]: "He
stirreth up the people, teaching throughout all
Judaea[3], beginning from Galilee unto this place."
The emergence of Galilee, as the place where the
alleged agitation had commenced, draws from Pilate
the question, whether the man is a Galilean. "And
on learning that he was from the dominion of Herod,
he sent him up to Herod[4], who was himself also at
Jerusalem in these days." The last words probably

[1] Luke xx 20.

[2] ἐπίσχυον λέγοντες in *v.* 5 seems to be so meant.

[3] Used, as the context shows, loosely for the Jewish parts of
Palestine.

[4] ἐπιγνοὺς ὅτι ἐκ τῆς ἐξουσίας Ἡρώδου ἐστίν, ἀνέπεμψεν αὐτὸν
πρὸς Ἡρώδην. The preposition in ἀνέπεμψεν, for which we have
no exact equivalent, seems to signify merely that the sending to
the tetrarch was a means of "referring" the question to him.

mean what we should at all events suppose, that the occasion of the tetrarch's visit was the Passover.

Now it is of the first importance, for conceiving and interpreting rightly the scene which follows, to fix precisely the motive and legal nature of the procurator's reference, and the part which, by this reference, the tetrarch is invited to take. It is common to assume, expressly or tacitly, that Herod is invoked as a judge. The Authorized Version itself betrays this tendency, by putting upon the clause "he was from the dominion[1] of Herod," that is to say, from the territory of which Herod was ruler, the narrower and more limited sense "he belonged unto Herod's *jurisdiction*," which suggests the personal relation of ruler and subject, and a judicial competence in Herod, grounded upon this relation. Similar language pervades modern descriptions generally. M. Loisy, to take the nearest instance, speaks of the tetrarch's "office as a judge." The "trial before Herod," the "judgement of Herod," and the like, are phrases in common use. And the same conception underlies the view, too familiar and too often repeated to need illustration, that the reference to Herod is an exhibition of Pilate's weakness, and that Pilate's purpose in it is to diminish or shift his own responsibility for a judgement. But how can this possibly be? How should the procurator be able, or imagine himself able, to give the tetrarch of Galilee jurisdiction in Jerusalem? And why should so unreasonable an

---

[1] Literally, *power*, ἐξουσία.

explanation be sought for a step which, upon the
facts as presented by the Evangelist, was surely
not only justifiable but necessary? The accusation,
when it assumes that form, which the narrative
represents, quite naturally, as a second form, an
expansion and reinforcement of the original charge,
becomes this: that the occurrences in Jerusalem,
which Pilate had already declared to be no proof
of sedition, were only part of a course of seditious
preaching, an insurrectionary movement originated
in Galilee. Moreover, according to the story presented by St Luke, which, whether it be complete
or defective, we must here take for granted, the
procurator would learn upon enquiry, that of the
teaching and career, which were alleged to be
seditious, not only the beginning, but almost the
whole, had taken place in the territory of the
tetrarch.

But this charge, the charge in this amended
form, was such that, in justice to the parties and
the public interest, no judgement could be given
upon it without consulting the government of
Galilee, whose knowledge or whose ignorance must
be material and almost decisive. We may well
suppose indeed that precisely for this reason the
Sanhedrin or their representatives did not at first
take this line of attack, but tried to make out their
case upon what had passed within or about Jerusalem. Upon the second charge, the charge as
amended, they could hardly expect to procure a
conviction without the assistance of the tetrarch;

and on this, as the sequel shows, they could not count. But whatever their motives, when they did take this line, the course for the procurator was obvious,—to obtain a report or information from Galilee, to ascertain whether or not the Galilean authorities concurred in the accusation. And if no Galilean authority had been immediately accessible, the case, it would seem, must necessarily have stood over for enquiry. In the actual circumstances, the tetrarch himself, being in the city and lodged perhaps in the very building, was the obvious and indispensable informant. And since a person of his rank and independence could not be summoned, the proper and only way was that which the procurator took, to address an enquiry to the prince, sending of course with it the prisoner and some supporters of the accusation, so that Herod, before answering, might examine them if he thought fit.

Therefore, in figuring the scene at Herod's residence, we have to remember that it is no public or prepared audience. Nor is it a trial. Representations in art, which show the prince in robes, and surrounded by the pomp of a tribunal, guards, apparitors, and so forth, betray an error which, though mainly arising from a misinterpretation presently to be considered, owes something probably to mistake at the point now before us. The tetrarch at Jerusalem was a private person, and the visit which he receives, as related in the Gospel, implies nothing inconsistent with this fact. What sort of state he kept in the city as a visitor, is, I suppose, not ascertainable; but in whatever condition he habitually spent a private morning, in that he would be found. The party sent from the procurator's court would be small and inconspicuous, and would most probably go by private communications,— circumstances, we may note in passing, which explain why the incident was unknown to the tradition represented by Mark : we may well suppose that, of the spectators at Pilate's tribunal, few were aware for what purpose the hearing was suspended and the prisoner withdrawn. Of those who went, fewer still, and the fewest possible, would be admitted to the prince's presence—the prisoner, one of his guards, the messenger of Pilate, two or three of the Sanhedrin[1], some six persons, let us say, altogether. Of Herod's attendants the story, as we shall see, says nothing. We may assume perhaps that he would not choose to receive the party alone; and indeed the servants in waiting are the most probable source of the information which Luke has reproduced. But they would be few—two perhaps, a secretary and a page—and naturally not military, or at all events not in arms. The apartments and access, whether or not connected internally with the *praetorium* itself, would doubtless, in such a city

---

[1] The words of Luke, in describing the accusers before Herod (οἱ ἀρχιερεῖς καὶ οἱ γραμματεῖς, "the chief priests and the scribes"), would imply, if pressed, that two of the three classes of the Sanhedrin were represented, and each by more than one person. But to press the words thus would be unsuitable to the style. Nothing is meant but that some of the Sanhedrin were there, that the accusers were represented.

and time, be well guarded; but a prince does not sit with his guards. The whole scene, including in all something under a dozen persons, must be figured as purely domestic; and it is in this atmosphere only that the interview described in the Gospel finds a fit and natural setting.

Since we propose now to show, *first*, that this narrative is simple, harmonious, and adapted to the context, so long as we do not import the supposed mockery of the prisoner; *and further* that, with this importation, it becomes absurd, inconsistent, and inexplicable either as a reality or as an invention; *and finally* that for the mockery, as now supposed, or indeed for any mockery at all, the author offers no warrant; it will be convenient first to consider the passage as it would run, if the words, in which the mockery is now discovered, were omitted[1].

---

[1] Ὁ δὲ Ἡρώδης ἰδὼν τὸν Ἰησοῦν ἐχάρη λίαν· ἦν γὰρ ἐξ ἱκανῶν χρόνων θέλων ἰδεῖν αὐτὸν διὰ τὸ ἀκούειν περὶ αὐτοῦ· καὶ ἤλπιζέ τι σημεῖον ἰδεῖν ὑπ᾽ αὐτοῦ γινόμενον. ἐπηρώτα δὲ αὐτὸν ἐν λόγοις ἱκανοῖς· αὐτὸς δὲ οὐδὲν ἀπεκρίνατο αὐτῷ. εἱστήκεισαν δὲ οἱ ἀρχιερεῖς καὶ οἱ γραμματεῖς εὐτόνως κατηγοροῦντες αὐτοῦ. ἐξουθενήσας δὲ αὐτὸν ὁ Ἡρώδης...ἀνέπεμψεν αὐτὸν τῷ Πιλάτῳ. ἐγένοντο δὲ φίλοι ὅ τε Ἡρώδης καὶ ὁ Πιλᾶτος ἐν αὐτῇ τῇ ἡμέρᾳ μετ᾽ ἀλλήλων· προϋπῆρχον γὰρ ἐν ἔχθρᾳ ὄντες πρὸς ἑαυτούς.

Πιλᾶτος δέ, συγκαλεσάμενος τοὺς ἀρχιερεῖς καὶ τοὺς ἄρχοντας καὶ τὸν λαόν, εἶπε πρὸς αὐτούς, Προσηνέγκατέ μοι τὸν ἄνθρωπον τοῦτον ὡς ἀποστρέφοντα τὸν λαόν· καὶ ἰδού, ἐγώ, ἐνώπιον ὑμῶν ἀνακρίνας, οὐδὲν εὗρον ἐν τῷ ἀνθρώπῳ τούτῳ αἴτιον, ὧν κατηγορεῖτε κατ᾽ αὐτοῦ· ἀλλ᾽ οὐδὲ Ἡρώδης· ἀνέπεμψα γὰρ ὑμᾶς πρὸς αὐτόν· καὶ ἰδού, οὐδὲν ἄξιον θανάτου ἐστὶ πεπραγμένον αὐτῷ· παιδεύσας οὖν αὐτὸν ἀπολύσω. Luke xxiii 8—16.

And when Herod saw Jesus, he was exceeding glad: for he was desirous to see him of a long season, because he had heard many things of him: and he hoped to have seen some miracle done by him. And he questioned him at much length, but he gave him no answer. And there stood the chief priests and the scribes, accusing him with all their might. But Herod thought him of no importance,...and sent him back to Pilate. And at this time Pilate and Herod were made friends, for before they had been at enmity with one another. And Pilate, when he had called together the chief priests and the rulers and the people, said to them, You have brought this man to me, as one that perverts the people[1], with the result that[2] I, having examined him before you, have found in this man no ground for the accusation which you make against him. No, nor yet Herod; for I sent you to him[3]; and it appears that nothing deserving of death has been done by him. I will therefore give him a lesson, and let him go.

In brief, Herod, by his reply to the enquiry, disowned the capital charge altogether. The narrative, which here as everywhere follows the external aspect of the proceedings and not the technical machinery, notes the tenor of the reply only when it becomes public by the declaration of the procurator. The documents, script and rescript, are not mentioned, any more than presently the sentence of Pilate will be recorded in technical form[4]: we are to suppose the necessary correspondence. Respect-

---

[1] τὸν λαόν, the Jewish subjects.

[2] Such is the effect of ἰδού in both places. The Biblical style ("behold") hardly gives, in this passage, a true reflexion of the original.

[3] On the doubtful reading here, which does not affect the present question, see note at the end of this essay.

[4] v. 25 τὸν δὲ Ἰησοῦν παρέδωκε τῷ θελήματι αὐτῶν.

ing the precise limits assigned to Herod's disclaimer,
there is room for doubt. If it were exactly reflected
by the words "nothing *deserving of death* has been
done by him," it would admit or suggest that the
prisoner might deserve the "lesson" which Pilate
next proposes to inflict. But upon the whole story,
and in consideration of what we shall observe hereafter, we should not construe the words in this way.
The limitation "deserving of death" comes from
Pilate, and refers only to the question arising, for
him, upon the rejection of the capital charge. The
contribution of the tetrarch is concluded in the
"No, nor yet Herod." In Galilee, as in Jerusalem,
the defendant, so far as was known, had committed
no act of sedition. With this negative the legitimate
function of the tetrarch was exhausted ; and that
he exceeded his function, to the prejudice of the
accused, is most improbable, when we see how the
accusers were received.

For in the foregoing scene, nothing is more
apparent than the absence of all co-operation, sympathy, or touch, between the tetrarch and the
Sanhedrin. The mere fact that he gives them no
assistance is remarkable, and should be found
strange by those who assume "the hostility of
Antipas," and suppose the Christian movement to
have been regarded with fear, malevolence, or
suspicion by the government of Galilee. What
then prevented the unscrupulous Herod from using
the weapon put into his hand, and crushing the
agitator by simply informing Pilate that he was

a dangerous person? But the Evangelist is in no such difficulty, having alleged nothing contrary to what he alleges here,—that Herod contemned the defendant, "thinking him unimportant," insignificant, or more exactly, "a cipher," "nothing," that is to say, politically nothing, of no account for the purpose of the accusation, not appreciable as a disturber of the peace. This supposed, the capital charge was ridiculous. Herod so opined, and reported accordingly to the procurator.

But further we see, and it is a chief trait in the scene, that the prince, notwithstanding his nominal religion, behaved on this occasion to the reverend and learned councillors, who waited on him, with a negligence and nonchalance which cannot have been without malice. His delight in the appearance of the Galilean, whom, as a celebrated wonder-worker, he had long been desirous to meet, and his hopes of a performance, pre-occupied him, it appears, completely. Upon this topic (so the connexion implies) he pressed the famous Magician with an interrogatory not at all abridged by an absolute lack of response, or by the invectives of the impatient delators. "And the chief priests and the scribes stood there, accusing him with all their might[1]." Eventually, when their turn comes, they are dismissed with a contempt which, though pointed at

---

[1] Literally "at full strain," or "full pitch," εὐτόνως combining both suggestions. English does not seem to afford any compact equivalent. *Vehemently, energetically,* etc., are near, but miss the note of sarcasm.

the prisoner, glances inevitably upon those who
would represent him as formidable. Anything more
offensive to clerical magistrates than the whole
performance one cannot conceive. And to the
original observer and reporter—who, though in the
service of Herod, may be supposed, since his report
reached the disciples, not partial either to the prince
or to the visitors—to him at least it seemed, that
the mortification was designed. For it is added,
without relevance to the story of the defendant,
that there ensued a truce and alliance between
Herod and Pilate; Herod, for some reason, such
as in the political tangle of Judaea is easily conceivable, was at this moment well pleased to
disoblige and snub the Sanhedrin, and to range
himself with their adversary, the Roman governor.
So at all events he did, both by his behaviour and
by his report. In all this, his part is perfectly
consequent.

But now let us try the effect of inserting, with
the current interpretation, the words of "the
mockery":

And the chief priests and the scribes stood and vehemently
accused him. *And Herod with his men of war set him at nought
and mocked him, and arrayed him in a gorgeous robe, and sent him
again to Pilate*[1].

Herod, that is to say, before dismissing the
defendant, indulged himself and his military suite

[1] ἐξουθενήσας δὲ αὐτὸν ὁ Ἡρώδης σὺν τοῖς στρατεύμασιν αὐτοῦ
καὶ ἐμπαίξας, περιβαλὼν αὐτὸν ἐσθῆτα λαμπράν, ἀνέπεμψεν αὐτὸν
τῷ Πιλάτῳ.

with the amusement of flouting such a "King of the Jews," and improved the jest by robing him suitably—and disrobing him, doubtless, like the Roman soldiers afterwards, when the farce was done.

Now as to the mere probability of such a performance by a prince, we will not say much. It may be differently estimated. There have been princes capable of behaving so, royal bullies and players of pranks, reckless alike of the victim and of their own dignity,—Caligula, for instance, and Henry III of France, and perhaps, in certain moods, our own Richard II. We are to suppose that Antipas was a specimen of this peculiar class, a tyrannical buffoon. The fact wants proof; but let us suppose it. Even then, even in a Caligula, we should expect a method in madness, the pursuit, however extravagant and indecent, of some idea, the choice and hold of an object. But Herod, according to the representation, was incapable even of this. He was discharging "the King of the Jews," dismissing him as innocent. He was about to inform the procurator that he found no fault in the man. Whatever his motive, honesty, pride, or malice against the prosecutors, that was the line which he took. And then, as part of this proceeding, as an incident in the acquittal, he gets up a charade—for the robe at least must be fetched— which means, if anything, that the charge is true, and that the defendant is guilty of the pretensions for which he is mocked. Herod discharges the accused, but treats him first as the executioners did after sentence. The thing seems senseless and, on the face of it, incredible.

But if the mockery makes difficulty for those who would conceive the scene as a reality, still greater, and every way desperate, is the embarrassment of those who would explain the whole story, including this incident, as an invention. The theory of sceptical criticism, upon the evangelical narratives of the Trial and the Passion, is in general, as we saw at the beginning, this : that Christian tradition tended to exculpate the officials of the Roman Empire by transferring the odium of their acts to the detested Jews. Thus the tetrarch, a Jew, was made to take, or to share, the responsibility of the procurator as judge. A Jewish trial was devised to replace the Roman. And the third Gospel, which inserts the trial and mockery by Herod, betrays, it is said, this purpose, by omitting the Roman mockery, which was recorded in the source common to Luke and Mark.

This last point however (let us note in passing) depends plainly upon the assumption that, according to Luke, the Roman mockery *did not happen*, was not a fact. If he had a motive for omitting the incident, though it was a fact, the argument from the omission collapses. And such a motive he exhibits. It is he who, at the moment of the crucifixion, records the prayer, so sacred and so pathetic that it will hardly bear quotation in debate, for the executioners who "know not what they do."

It is surely conceivable that such a narrator should pass over in silence the brutal sport of the legionaries, as he passes in silence the scourging which they inflicted, not because these things did not happen or because he wishes so to suggest—for the scourging was an incident of the sentence, and, if not denied, would be supposed as of course,—but because he thought, with some reason, that there was no moral interest in actors hardly more responsible for their parts than the reeds, rods, nails, and the cross.

But however this may be, and though we were to grant that the Herodean mockery, according to Luke, replaces the Roman, suppressed as *non factum*, it is still impossible, as the critics have perceived and acknowledged, to account on these lines for his version of the Herodean episode as a whole[1].

For it is obvious that, to relieve Pilate, Herod must condemn, whereas, according to St Luke, he acquits, thus increasing and not diminishing the culpability of the procurator, in giving sentence contrary not only to his own opinion but also to that of his referee. Accordingly we discover a new motive for the fiction: the episode was imported in order that the innocence of the accused might be certified by two judges instead of one. But here again we stumble upon the mockery, which, as we

[1] See here the citation from M. Loisy, *supra* p. 336, noting the successive stages of the theory, for which the author gives full references.

saw and as all see, clashes with the acquittal, and goes far to annul its effect. So in fine we have, from M. Loisy, a third and composite theory. First some one, not Luke, is to invent a Herodean trial, condemnation, and mockery, parallel to the Roman, by way of counterpoise to Roman responsibility. The evangelist accepts the trial, but, to get the advantage of Herod's testimony, changes the condemnation to an acquittal, but yet again retains the mockery, because this compensates for that of the legionaries, which, out of tenderness for Romans, he will suppress. To shun the opposing rocks we run (so it seems) upon both. The method and performance of Luke are surely on this showing utterly incomprehensible. The truth is that the procedure of Herod as now supposed, by which the defendant is first flouted as a usurper of royalty and then absolved of rebellion, is incoherent. Take it as fact or as fiction, and turn it however we will, we shall not explain what does not agree with itself.

To eliminate the acquittal is impossible: the " No, nor yet Herod " is as clear as words can be. Error of interpretation must be found, if anywhere, in the verse :

And Herod with his men of war set him at nought, and mocked him, and arrayed him in a gorgeous robe, and sent him again to Pilate[1].

---

[1] ἐξουθενήσας δὲ αὐτὸν ὁ Ἡρώδης σὺν τοῖς στρατεύμασιν αὐτοῦ καὶ ἐμπαίξας περιβαλὼν αὐτὸν ἐσθῆτα λαμπρὰν ἀνέπεμψεν αὐτὸν τῷ Πιλάτῳ : Trans. A. V.

Here there is at any rate one term which, as a translation, is artificial and unsatisfactory. Herod's "men of war," that is to say, the soldiers present (as this version assumes) at the interview, and partners in the mockery, appear in the original as his *strateumata*, his "troops," or rather "forces." But if such is the author's meaning, his choice of a word is amazing. The irony of M. Loisy, "We must not ask how the tetrarch should have *armies* in Jerusalem," touches the objection truly, but ignores the chief part. It is quite true that a corps of guards, such as might accompany the prince on such a journey, should not be described as a *strateuma*, and still less by the plural *strateumata*. We are not, of course, to demand precision from the author in military matters any more than in judicial. We are not surprised when, in his *Acts of the Apostles*, the garrison of Jerusalem appears as the *strateuma* or "force" of its commander Claudius Lysias, both in the narrative and in the commander's report to his superior[1]. The term, whether technically correct or not, is intelligible and natural. And we will go so far as to suppose, though it does not follow, that a body of guards, if assembled and acting under the prince's command, might, by the same author, be called his *strateuma*, or conceivably, by a stretch of magnificence, his *strateumata*. But here the author is speaking, as the interpretation assumes, of soldiers in waiting,

---

[1] Acts xxiii 10 ἐκέλευσε τὸ στράτευμα καταβὰν ἁρπάσαι αὐτὸν ἐκ μέσου αὐτῶν, and *ib.* 27.

companions or personal servants, who are found with their master in the room or place where he receives unexpectedly a civil deputation. Such persons, if such there were, would be indicated as *stratiotai*, "soldiers." To call them *strateumata*, "forces," is a mere abuse of language, unnatural, and not easily to be imagined.

Nor, even if properly described, would they fit their place in the narrative. "Herod, with his soldiers, *contemned*" the prisoner. But what sort of co-operation is this? The word marked[1] describes a feeling or judgement of the mind; it means literally "to make nothing of," to regard as a cipher, and so to despise or contemn. And the tense used signifies that Herod came to, took, this contemptuous view or opinion. The impropriety of saying, that he formed his opinion with the help of his guards, is veiled in the Authorized Version, which, to suit the prevalent idea, adopts the dexterous modification "*set* him at nought," thus suggesting and preparing us to expect some action or performance. Of this in the original word there is no trace.

But if, dismissing all preconceptions, we take the phrase as it is, and write "Herod, with his forces, contemned him," or, more exactly, "Herod, with his forces, thought nothing of him," there is surely, so far, no difficulty. The English means that to a sovereign supported by military power the prisoner seemed an insignificant adversary; having troops at his back, he contemned such a person in

ἐξουθενήσας.

the character, imputed by the accusers, of a dangerous rebel and claimant to the throne. And the Greek may and should mean the same. It may perhaps be implied, that the strength of the prince was in some way represented by the state or attendance with which he, or his apartment, was surrounded. But the words do not say so, and at all events it is not the point.

To this it is next added that "he jested upon him" or "thereupon[1]." Here again we must carefully observe, that the original word, though it would admit the explanation supposed to be given by the sequel, and might signify a mockery by performance, a mockery in action, neither contains any such notion in itself, nor even can be so understood, if interpreted, as is natural, by what precedes. "Herod, *with his forces*, thought nothing of (the prisoner), and jested thereupon[2]." The jest is explained by the words "with his forces,"—a connexion more apparent in the original, from the order of the words[3], than it can be made in the order of English. The suggestion that the prisoner was a rebel, with pretensions to Herod's throne, was received with a sneer: "I and my forces are not afraid of him," or the like,—a form of speech, let us note, in which

[1] καὶ ἐμπαίξας.

[2] ἐμπαίξας (αὐτῷ). Though the pronoun supplied is doubtless masculine, the translation "thereupon" is more correct than "upon him," because the context marks that it is as *an adversary of Herod and his forces* that the person is derided.

[3] Because σὺν τοῖς στρατεύμασιν αὐτοῦ is brought close to ἐμπαίξας.

the rhetorical amplification *strateumata* (plural) is natural. And the jest, let us note also, might be so delivered that the sting of it would be all for the accusers; and so, from the drift of the whole anecdote, we should understand. The "priests and scribes," who would signalize a danger to the military establishment of Galilee, are told in effect to mind their own affairs.

So far, then, there is no hint of personal affront to the defendant. It remains to consider the act of robing. Here, from the structure of Greek and its habit of accumulating participles, there is a doubt as to the grouping and connexion of words. Part for part, the passage runs thus:

> But Herod with his forces contemning him and jesting (there-) upon putting on him fine apparel sent him back to Pilate.

Grammar admits equally the connexion of *putting* either with *jesting* or with *sent*. Which is meant? With the current conception of the scene, presupposing the hostility of Herod to the prisoner and the co-operation of the "men of war," we should decide for the connexion with *jesting*, as apparently all interpreters, more or less definitely, now do. And it would then be possible, and preferable, to hold that, in spite of the order of words, the robing, or rather *having robed*, precedes the mockery, or is included within it. The translation of M. Loisy, for example[1]—

> Et Hérode, l'ayant traité avec mépris et tourné en dérision avec ses soldats, *après* lui avoir fait mettre une robe brillante, le renvoya à Pilate—

[1] *Les Évang. Syn.* II 636.

inclines this way; and our Authorized Version, though likewise ambiguous, is so understood and doubtless so intended. But the contrary, a disjunction of the robing from the jest, and a connexion only with the dismissal, is indicated not only by the order but by the balance of the period[1]. If then the robing is derisive, this colour must be found wholly in the act and the description of it.

Now that the words do not necessarily convey this is certain. They are not even the obvious words for such a purpose. The derision must turn upon the "royalty" of the prisoner, upon his claiming the title of "king." And since in this scene, in the interview with Herod, that title has not been mentioned at all, and it has been mentioned but once before, we should expect here, for the supposed purpose, some reminder of it, some such phrase as "*royal* apparel[2]." But that is not said. What *is* said, the exact shade of the words, is not quite easy to fix. The term *apparel* (not necessarily a single robe) suggests certainly something not common. Indeed that is just all that it does suggest. The original (*esthes*) is a word for clothing which, by a certain poetical colour, escapes the note of commonness, but which must be defined according to the occasion. The robes of Herod Agrippa at

---

[1] ἐξουθενήσας δὲ αὐτὸν ὁ Ἡρώδης σὺν τοῖς στρατεύμασιν αὐτοῦ καὶ ἐμπαίξας, περιβαλὼν αὐτὸν ἐσθῆτα λαμπρὰν ἀνέπεμψεν αὐτὸν τῷ Πιλάτῳ. There is nothing in the rhythm to suggest a comma after λαμπράν.

[2] ἐσθῆτα βασιλικήν, Acts xii 21.

his last audience are called *esthes*, with the addition
of the epithet *royal*[1]. At the sepulchre it is in
raiment (plural), which "shines like lightning," that
the "two men" appear to the seekers of the body[2].
Clothing merely as such is not *esthes*, and there is
perhaps a shade of dignity in the word used for
"putting on[3]." But "arrayed him in a gorgeous robe"
(A.V.) is not exact either in the substantive or the
epithet, and shows, like the whole verse, the deflect-
ing influence of the prevalent assumption. "Fine
apparel," "splendid apparel," seems about right;
the epithet[4] here adds little, if anything, to the
denotation of *esthes*. However, the clothing is rich;
and apparently, though it would be brought by a
servant, the prince himself puts it on. That is what
is said, and there is no reason to gloss it[5]. On the
whole then clearly the act is a mark of honour.

But why should we suppose it ironical? It is
now so supposed, because we take for granted that
Herod is hostile to the defendant, and because
otherwise there is no part for the "men of war."
But since there are no such performers, and since
Herod declares in favour of the defendant, why
should he not dismiss him with honour?

There is every reason, from Herod's point of
view, why he should. It is the proper outcome of

---

[1] ἐσθῆτα βασιλικήν, Acts xii 21.
[2] Luke xxiv 4 ἐσθήσεσιν ἀστραπτούσαις.
[3] περιβαλών. See Luke xii 27.
[4] λαμπράν, a common metaphor in such connexion.
[5] As in "après lui avoir *fait* mettre," Loisy.

the situation and the proceedings. Herod, from the first and throughout, according to the story, exhibits an eager interest in the Galilean thus brought into his presence, because of the reports about his extraordinary powers and performances. That he overacts this sentiment, for the discomfiture of the accusing magistrates, seems to be suggested, but not at all that the feeling is feigned. The reports, as they appear in the Gospel, must have excited interest, and a certain respect, in any one not prepossessed on the other side ; and Herod was no fanatic either of religion or (as far as we know) of philosophy. The opinions and feelings, which he brings to the interview, he retains to the end. The refusal of the magician to respond to his advances, though it could not please, must stimulate his curiosity, and might naturally increase his respect. He "was hoping to see some miracle done by him," and, on parting with him, he hopes so still. Backed by his opinion, Pilate will dismiss the ridiculous charge of sedition. The wizard will then be at liberty, and able, if willing, to satisfy the royal desire. In this expectation, Herod, before parting with him, bestows on him a royal gift and mark of favour. The form of it, a rich and valuable costume, is familiar in oriental practice, and such as the garb of the prisoner, after the outrages of the night, might suggest as acceptable. The act of investiture is conceived in the spirit, however different in the circumstances, of that commanded by Ahasuerus for Mordecai. If it is a little extravagant (and this seems to be meant), that is in keeping with Herod's attitude throughout. He overacts his respect at the departure, as he does his interest at the arrival, with an eye to the prosecutors and a certain pleasure in disagreeing with them. And he does his best to publish his disagreement, by the changed appearance which the defendant will present on his return to the *praetorium*. But the compliment, after all, is royal, and itself signifies the prince's political "contempt." Only a conscious superior could take such a liberty. That he accompanied the gift with a jest, and a jest upon the "royalty" of the recipient, is conceivable, but would be hardly congruous; and at all events it is neither said nor suggested.

The whole passage will run somewhat thus:

Herod, when he saw the celebrated[1] Jesus, was delighted above measure. For he had been wishing to see him a long while, because he had been hearing much about him. He was hoping too to see some feat performed by him. And he persisted in questioning him at some length, though the Master[2] made him no answer. And there stood the chief priests and the scribes, accusing him with all their might. But Herod "with his forces" thought him not important and jested thereupon, and, having clothed him with fine apparel, sent him back to Pilate. And that very day Pilate and Herod were made friends, having before been at enmity with one another.

[1] τὸν Ἰησοῦν. In Greek such as that of the Gospels, this shade of expression is often not significant; but the phrasing of this anecdote, for some reason, is more delicate than that even of Luke is usually. The article therefore should, I think, be pressed.

[2] Or perhaps merely "the other," but I think αὐτός has the more specific sense. It indicates partly Herod's conception, partly that, quite different but analogous, of the reporter.

But if this interpretation be correct, evidently the alleged resemblance and parallelism between this scene and the mockery by the Roman soldiers, as related in the other Gospels, is nothing. In language the only noticeable points of contact are that the verb *to jest* or *mock*[1] appears, but with a different connexion and meaning, in *Mark* and *Matthew*, and that, in *John*, the soldiers *clothe*[2] their prisoner. There is a robing here and a robing there. But in substance and spirit there is neither likeness nor opposition. There is simply no analogy at all. Circumstances, actors, things said and done, the meaning of them,—all are different; and it is not even conceivable that the story of Luke should be an equivalent or compensation for the other.

To complete the consideration of the subject as presented by M. Loisy, a word must be said about the allusion to Herod's part in the Passion, which we read in the *Acts of the Apostles*, and also about that part as it appears in the *Gospel of Peter*. In the *Acts*[3] "Herod and Pontius Pilate with nations and peoples of Israel" are conjoined as acting against the Messiah. The passage, part of a prayer, may possibly not have been composed by the author of the *Acts*; but since he gives it without remark, it should be, in his view, not inconsistent with what he has related of Herod in his Gospel. Nor is it inconsistent, even if the action of Herod, mainly favourable to the defendant upon any interpretation, was, as it is here interpreted, in purpose favourable

---

[1] ἐμπαίζειν.   [2] περιέβαλον.   [3] iv 27.

altogether. Herod stands in the Gospel, as he is
joined in the allusion, with Pilate, favourable too,
and is also contributory to the result. His behaviour,
though not ill-meant, is inconsiderate and unworthy
of his position. His innocent subject is threatened
by formidable enemies. He declares indeed in
favour of the accused, but does it, from personal
and irrelevant motives, in such a way as to exasperate
the accusers, and then leaves the affair to its course.
He may well be placed, without discrimination,
among those who accomplished what was "determined before to be done[1]."

On the other hand, it does not appear that his
part, as described in the third Gospel, resembles at
all, in fact, colour, or tendency, what is alleged in
the recently discovered fragment of the *Gospel of
Peter*. It may be true (the enquiry does not here
concern us) that this document contains some peculiar
and authentic traditions. But in the political and
judicial aspects of the matter, where our third Gospel
is solid, the other seems to ignore the very elements
of the situation. A writer who apparently conceives
"the Jews," the tetrarch of Galilee, and the procurator of Judaea, as acting together in a joint council
or tribunal, where, when Pilate has retired, " Herod
the King" takes the lead and awards execution[2],

---

[1] Acts iv 28. See further remarks at p. 386.

[2] The fragment begins just here, but such is the representation:
τῶν δὲ Ἰουδαίων οὐδεὶς ἐνίψατο τὰς χεῖρας, οὐδὲ Ἡρώδης οὐδ᾽ εἷς τῶν
κριτῶν αὐτοῦ· καὶ μὴ βουληθέντων νίψασθαι ἀνέστη Πειλᾶτος. καὶ
τότε κελεύει Ἡρώδης ὁ βασιλεὺς παραλημφθῆναι τὸν κύριον κ.τ.λ.

whatever were his motives and his sources of information, in these affairs is neither guided by our third Gospel nor admissible for the interpretation of it. If his object was "to minimize the sin of the Procurator by laying the chief guilt at the door of Herod, the representative of the Jews[1]," it was one which, as we have seen, cannot possibly have affected St Luke, whose story has the contrary effect.

It is possible, that is to say, not irrational or illogical, to suppose the story, as given by St Luke, to have been invented for the sake of the acquittal, and in order to confirm the favourable opinion of Pilate by that of Herod. The interpretation here given removes an obstacle to this supposition, by showing that Herod's acquittal is not qualified, according to St Luke, by any such performance as the mockery. But of course in any history, any allegation not irrelevant must have a conceivable motive, and must be, so far, explicable as an invention. That, in itself, is no ground for suspicion, and in the present case we do not find any other.

The gift of Herod, the "fine apparel," has a consequence in the story, not indeed important, but worth attention, because the fact, though stated in the third Gospel only, illustrates an incident common to all. The clothes of a person executed were the perquisite of the executioners. Now upon this occasion, the partition of the clothes among the soldiers, who carried out the sentence, was made with more

---

[1] Swete, note to the *Gospel of Peter*, *l.c.*—Is it not however possible, that these absurdities are due to mere ignorance?

care and attracted more attention from the spectators than we should naturally expect, if it were not for the special circumstance of Herod's donation. The narrative of Mark in particular throws this detail into picturesque relief : the dividers cast lots " what every man should take." To suggest, as some do, that this may be supposed an invention, because others[1], but not the original narrator, regard it as the fulfilment of a prophecy, is surely not legitimate. But if the pitiable booty, which the soldiers divide, had been such as from the general circumstances of the case we should have imagined,—common clothes, not costly, which had sustained the soil and violence of all that passes between the "small upper room" and "the place of a Skull"; we might wonder, while accepting the fact, that "what every man should take" was a matter worth arbitrament, and that, in such a scene, so rapid and colourless a transaction was perceived and remembered. If the pieces could differ in value, then, being such as are commonly worn in the East, they might, as one narrator reminds us[2], be parted by tearing them up. But the gift of the tetrarch, though unknown to the tradition of St Mark, accounts for what his informants observed. The additions or substitutions of Herod were things of price, such as the gazers at an execution would seldom see, and which would fetch a sum important to a legionary ; and they were moreover, it is likely enough, such that to tear

[1] Matt. xxvii 35 ; John xix 24.
[2] John xix 23—24.

them would ruin their value. The "seamless tunic"
of the fourth Gospel, whatever be the purpose of the
author in dwelling upon it, is a property compre-
hensible with, but not easily without, the investiture by Herod, regarded not as a disguise for the
moment, but as a gift. For men on military wages,
the clothes, so augmented, would be an exciting wind-
fall; and only the lot could settle the momentous
issue, who should take the pieces which came from
the wardrobe of a prince.

By St Luke the incident of the partition is
touched slightly, as are most acts of the soldiers
which do not disappear[1]. But the use of the lot he
notes, nor does he forget the cause of it, and whence
came the spoil which made an allotment necessary.
"And in parting his clothes," he says, "they cast
the lot; and *there stood* the people, gazing." The
word, and the turn of phrase, are identical with those
which he has used in describing the attitude of the
councillors during the proceedings of Herod: "*There
stood* the chief priests and the scribes, accusing him
with all their might[2]." The touch refers us back,
with a note of irony, from the fate of the gift to the
intent of the donor; and "the people[3]," spectators
of the despoiling, follow their leaders, who railed

[1] See above, p. 338, and compare Luke xxiii 34 with Mark
xv 24 and Matt. xxvii 35.

[2] Compare Luke xxiii 34—35 διαμεριζόμενοι δὲ τὰ ἱμάτια αὐτοῦ,
ἔβαλον κλῆρον· καὶ εἰστήκει ὁ λαὸς θεωρῶν (to be joined and
punctuated so), with Luke xxiii 10.

[3] The term ὁ λαός marks the crowd not as such (ὄχλος), but
as representative, in some sort, of Judaism. See Loisy *ad loc.*

at the putting on. To these, in fact, the narrator immediately returns, adding that "the magistrates too," that is to say, such persons as composed the Sanhedrin, "sneered along with them, saying, *He saved others, let him save himself, if this is the anointed one, the chosen one of God*[1]."

In this mockery, the text of Luke exhibits a divergence not insignificant, upon which perhaps some light may be thrown from our point of view. By writing "*the anointed one of God, the chosen one*[2]," and by omitting "along with them" from the introductory words, one class of copies gives to the sneer a purely religious bearing, pointed solely at the claim of *the* Christ, the Messiah or Anointed, and attributes it consistently not to the populace, but to the hierarchy, by whom this "blasphemy" had been resented and avenged. But there is reason for thinking that, in the mouths of the mob, the sarcasm "He saved others; let him save himself" was associated with the proverb "Physician, heal thyself," and was aimed not so much at the claimant of the Kingdom as at the performer of miraculous cures. A link between the two aspects may be found in the fact that the particular method of healing, which, as practised by the disciples of the new Doctor, would be commonly supposed typical of his "school," was that of chrisms or anointing[3]. Now it was

---

[1] ἐξεμυκτήριζον δὲ καὶ οἱ ἄρχοντες σὺν αὐτοῖς, λέγοντες, Ἄλλους ἔσωσε, σωσάτω ἑαυτόν, εἰ οὗτός ἐστιν ὁ Χριστὸς ὁ τοῦ Θεοῦ ἐκλεκτός.

[2] ὁ Χριστὸς τοῦ Θεοῦ, ὁ ἐκλεκτός.

[3] Mark vi 15.

through these performances of the disciples that the
attention of Herod was first called to the Master[1];
and we have seen, that a curious interest in the
worker of wonders, the supposed adept in medicine
and magic, is the sole idea which Luke assigns to
Herod as the cause of his favour and largess. Thus
between the partition of the apparel and the sneer
at the impotent "saver," so far as this related to the
miraculous cures, there is for the Evangelist a connexion of thought; and this fortifies the case for the
readings which maintain the connexion, as against
those which would obliterate it[2].

[1] Mark vi 15, where see the following context, and compare
Luke ix 6—9.

[2] In what sense precisely the jest, according to Luke, is taken
up by the soldiers (xxiii 36—37), is not clear. They offer ὄξος
(*vinegar*), i.e. probably *posca*, and say, εἰ σὺ εἶ ὁ βασιλεὺς τῶν
Ἰουδαίων, σῶσον σεαυτόν. In Greek this seems to have no point,
nor reference to the action accompanying. Latin is open (and
for the soldiers perhaps more likely), for we are immediately told
that the inscription, giving the title "King of the Jews," was in
Latin as well as in Greek and in "Hebrew." And in Latin, low
Latin, a poor but pertinent jest can be made: "Si tu es *regulus*
Iudaeorum, *regula* te ipsum," meaning "prescribe for yourself,"
"diet yourself." This would combine the "king" and the
"doctor," and would explain more or less the offer of drink.
But the point, whatever it was, seems to have been lost in
transmission, perhaps through more than one language; nor do
the parallel accounts give any light. That Roman soldiers should
allude to the religious connexion, in Jewish thought, between the
ideas of *king* and *saviour*, seems, as M. Loisy remarks, not probable. But his suggestion that the narrator thought of Jewish
soldiers, "soldiers of Herod," depends upon the current misunderstanding of στρατεύματα in Luke xxiii 11, and upon those

The Double Text of Luke XXIII 15.

I have deferred to this place, as a detail not important to our purpose, though relevant, the variations of text which make Pilate, after declaring that Herod, like himself, found nothing in the accused to justify the charge of the priests, continue either thus :

"No, nor did Herod : *for he sent him back to us*[1],"

or thus :

"No, nor did Herod : *for I sent (referred) you to him*[2]."

The question is not important ; for even if we take the first, we cannot suppose the author to mean that Pilate had no other evidence for Herod's opinion than the bare fact of the return of the prisoner, and that Herod made no communication of his view. We could hardly believe this, even if it were alleged or implied ; but the words may quite fairly be understood, on the contrary, to include and imply the communication. The facts of the story are therefore the same either way.

But the choice offers a problem, and perhaps, after careful consideration, it will be not merely a

deductions therefrom which this essay is designed to prevent. After all, it is perhaps not necessary that the mockery of the soldiers should have any definite point ; they might be supposed to repeat, loosely and ignorantly, what was said around them by others.

[1] ἀνέπεμψε γὰρ αὐτὸν πρὸς ἡμᾶς, Alexandrine text.

[2] ἀνέπεμψα γὰρ ὑμᾶς πρὸς αὐτόν, Western text.

question of choice. If either reading is original and right, we must suppose that this reading has been deliberately changed into the other. But what was the motive? The sense of *for I referred you to him* seems absolutely flawless. To the other, *for he sent him back to us*, it might be objected, by a punctilious critic, (*a*) that the words, if pressed strictly, ignore the essential matter, and should be rather " for so he has informed us "; and (*b*) that, in the style of St Luke, the procurator would not use the plural (though Latin) for himself only, and that, if " us " means "me and you," the procurator and the accusers, it is a form not very suitable to a situation in which these parties are not co-operators but rather adversaries. Pilate is not made to say "*We* have examined him," but "*I* have examined him in *your* presence[1]"; and so also he should say rather " Herod sent him back to *me*." And from a literary point of view, these objections, though small, may be sound. But are they such as would lead to a bold alteration of the text, and does it elsewhere appear that the texts of the Gospels, during the process of fixing, were subjected to revision of this kind, to corrections purely literary? The variations in them are generally either minute, and such as might arise from inadvertence, or on the other hand substantial, and explicable by some motive of religious interest. This variation is of neither class, and seems very difficult to account for, if we suppose that either reading is original and right.

[1] Luke xxiii 14.

What we should seek is rather the common original, which, by alternative corrections, might give rise to both. And there is a form which, in some respects, certainly satisfies this condition :—*for he sent him back to you*, ἀνέπεμψε γὰρ αὐτὸν πρὸς ὑμᾶς. This is at first sight not intelligible. It looks wrong ; and each of the traditional readings is an obvious way of simplifying it.

If then it really has a good meaning, it is preferable, in point of authority, to either of the traditional readings, which disprove one another.

Could then Pilate properly say to the accusers this :—" Nor did Herod find any ground for your accusations ; for he returned the prisoner to *you* " ? I think that not only is this possible, but it is the correct form, that which really expresses the legal relation of the parties. If Herod were invoked as a judge, then no doubt the procurator should say that, when Herod acquits, he returns or refers the prisoner to the first judge, Pilate :—" he sent him back to *me*." But, as we have seen above[1], Herod is not a judge, nor is invoked as such, nor acts as such. The procurator, the only judge, invites the tetrarch to say *whether or not he supports and concurs in the accusation of the priests*, whether, from his knowledge of Galilee, he considers the prisoner open to a charge of sedition. If Herod had answered in the affirmative, he, or rather some one on his behalf, would have appeared in the procurator's court as an *accuser*. It is proper and correct therefore to say,

[1] pp. 352 ff.

that, by answering in the negative, and refusing to join in the accusation, he remitted or returned the prisoner to the first *accusers*, whom he left to make out their accusation, without his help, if they could.

And further it is to be noted, that in this case the accusers, the members of the Sanhedrin, have a position different from that of ordinary prosecutors. They are not private persons, nor prosecutors merely. They are themselves magistrates of high dignity and competence, who have legally arrested and tried the prisoner, and could have punished him severely at their own discretion. It is only because they desire to put him to death, a sentence beyond their power, that they invoke the procurator and prefer a charge of treason. By so doing, they doubtless surrender custody to the extent of that purpose, but perhaps not, even technically, for all purposes. It is not clear that the procurator could, even then, assume absolute control and prohibit any further proceedings. He himself speaks rather as if, upon the dismissal of the capital charge, the question of other punishment would be matter for arrangement between him and them. He seems to propose, if they agree, to "give him a lesson and let him go." Substantially then, whether technically or not, the prisoner was still the prisoner of the Sanhedrin; and for this reason also it is proper for Pilate to say, that Herod, by dismissing the accusation, returned him, not "to me," but "to you."

It should be considered then, whether the reading ἀνέπεμψε γὰρ αὐτὸν πρὸς ὑμᾶς, *for he returned him to you*, while it accounts for the double tradition and is favoured by the joint evidence, is not also more consistent than either with that true sense of the legal situation, which distinguishes the third Gospel in this part.

LUKE XIII 32. "*This fox*[1]."

"Go ye and tell *this* fox"—πορευθέντες εἴπατε τῇ ἀλώπεκι ταύτῃ—runs the text; but why that pronoun is used, if, as we should suppose at first sight, and as is generally assumed, the words are merely a description of Herod and a reflexion upon his character, is not clear. We should expect "that fox" (ἐκείνῃ), as the Authorized Version gives it.

Possibly "this" may have suited the context of the anecdote in another document, and may be retained inadvertently; but that is not to be supposed, if any explanation is to be found in the context of Luke.

The question is perhaps connected with another, why he has chosen this place for inserting the invocation of the City:—"O Jerusalem, Jerusalem, thou that killest the prophets . . ." The invocation agrees almost verbally with *Matthew*[2], and is drawn evidently from the same source, where it must have been recorded, as a saying, without note of place and occasion. But whereas in the first Gospel it is spoken in the temple as the peroration of a discourse against the tyranny and crimes of the hierarchy,

[1] See above, p. 349.   [2] xxiii 37—39.

here it is made part (if we press the connexion strictly) of a reply given in Galilee to a warning against the tetrarch. It is true that, allowing for the method and style of St Luke, and his manner of working his materials together, we need not so press the connexion, and even should not. But there is only the more reason for asking, how the composer was led to make a juncture which is barely possible, and not, as in *Matthew*, natural. In *Luke* the invocation at first sight seems to hang on to the context solely by the words "thou that killest the prophets"; in all the rest the supporting anecdote seems to be forgotten.

May it be suggested that, in the view of the composer, there was another and a more intimate link between the anecdote and the invocation—a correspondence of simile or metaphor between the comparison of Christ and His converts to a *hen and her brood* and the designation of the alleged persecutor as a *fox*? The conception seems not unnatural.

And if this were so, there would be no longer any difficulty in accounting for the phrase "*this* fox." By "*this* fox" would be meant "the enemy here," in Galilee, as contrasted with other "foxes" or persecutors, the enemies in Jerusalem. Enemies *here* may be assured, that only *there* can designs against a prophet be accomplished.

That this is the intention we cannot safely assert, but the supposition is preferable to that of error or oversight in a matter so simple as the use of a pronoun.

It is perhaps an advantage in this interpretation, that the term *fox*, when conceived as part of a simile, a symbol for "persecutor," has not the personal note, which it has, if taken for a designation of the tetrarch, an equivalent for the name of Herod. With this latter sense, the words "Go ye and tell that fox" have a singular colour and are somewhat startling. But in "Go ye and tell *this* fox," understood as now proposed, nothing is asserted as from the speaker. The description signifies "the person here inimical to me and mine." It is relative to the warning of the Pharisees, and is no more applicable to the tetrarch than to any one in Galilee, who might be so conceived or so represented.

AUGUST, 1910.

I add here a few words on certain objections or difficulties, which have been suggested by critics of this essay.

One objection relates to the passage in the *Acts of the Apostles* alluding to the Passion[1], which I have discussed, but perhaps too summarily, at p. 373.

And being let go, they (Peter and John) went to their own company, and reported all that the chief priests and elders had said unto them. And when they heard that, they lifted up their voice to God with one accord, and said, Lord, thou art God, which hast made heaven, and earth, and the sea, and all that in them is: who by the mouth of thy servant David hast said, "Why did the heathen rage, and the people imagine vain things? The kings of the earth stood up, and the rulers were gathered together

[1] *Acts* iv 23–8.

against the Lord, and against his Christ." For of a truth against thy holy child Jesus, whom thou hast anointed, both Herod and Pontius Pilate, with the Gentiles, and the people of Israel, were gathered together, for to do whatsoever thy hand and thy counsel determined before to be done. . . .

Since the author of the third Gospel here names Herod among the enemies of the Saviour and as one of those who contributed to his death, we are bound (it is suggested) to interpret the act of "clothing him in fine apparel" as a hostile mockery, not as a friendly compliment.

To this I would say, that, if the allusion in the *Acts* were to be construed as history, and if the language of it were to be pressed to the full sense, then, without regard to the particular question of Herod's investiture, the allusion could not possibly be reconciled with the story of the Passion as related in the Gospel. Both as to Herod and as to Pilate, the allusion, so construed, would be unjustifiable. The allusion, taken strictly, would mean or suggest, that the tetrarch and the procurator were active against the Saviour, and wilfully promoted his condemnation. But, according to the Gospel, neither did so. Both on the contrary were favourable to the defendant, and publicly proclaimed him innocent of the charge upon which he was put to death. Such a discrepancy and contradiction, going to the root of the matter, would not be removed, or materially affected, by supposing that the tetrarch accompanied his favourable pronouncement by an insult which, however inconsistent, indecent, and

offensive, cannot have had any effect upon the trial
and issue.   Upon the question which we are considering, the allusion in the *Acts* has therefore, as
I conceive, no bearing.

But—to go for a moment beyond the question
—must we or should we hold that the allusion is
actually irreconcilable with the narrative in the
Gospel ? I think not. The allusion is not to be
construed as history ; and considering the context
in which it occurs, we cannot fairly extract from it
any precise account of the parts played by the actors
in the tragedy. The allusion is part of a prayer and
thanksgiving, passionate and eloquent, poetical and
rhetorical throughout, and nowhere more so than
in the allusive sentence. If we apply a strict and
historical interpretation to what is said of Pilate
and of Herod, how are we to deal in like manner
with the reference to their alleged associates, the
" nations " and " peoples of Israel " ? Who precisely
are these, and what part precisely does the allusion
assign to them ? The composer of the passage—
which does not purport to be, and perhaps is not,
an original work by the author of the *Acts*—is seek-
ing an analogy between the circumstances of the
Passion and the language of the Psalm. He is
frankly content with a general analogy, a loose and
poetical resemblance. The actors or agents who,
under Providence, were brought together to accomplish the destined event, answer sufficiently (so the
liturgist thinks) to the terms of the prophetic poem.
As he satisfies the " heathen " and the " people " of

the Psalmist by the fact that the actors in the story included both Gentiles and Jews, so he sees "the kings of the earth" in the procurator of Judaea and the tetrarch of Galilee. For such a purpose as this, it scarcely matters what precisely was the line of action pursued by the several performers. It is enough that they contributed in any degree, positively or negatively, to the issue. The concession of Pilate to the Sanhedrin is enough, upon this view, to include him among those "gathered together against the Messiah," notwithstanding his reluctance and persistent efforts on the other side. And similarly, by a stretch of interpretation not bolder, Herod's light and negligent treatment of the case is thought to justify the importation of his name, as a "king of the earth," notwithstanding his testimony to the prisoner's innocence. The whole conception of the composer is loose and inexact, but not more so in the reference to Herod than in the reference to Pilate and in other points of the analogy. The value, and even the propriety, of the method may be open to question; but this question does not turn particularly upon the allusion to the tetrarch, which, upon the statements of the Gospel, is neither more nor less justifiable than the rest.

It has been objected further, that, according to the interpretation of the Herodean episode suggested in this essay, the coincidences of fact and language, between this episode and the mockery by the soldiers as described in the other Gospels—an investiture and a jest in both places, and in both places the terms *to jest* and *to clothe*—must be supposed fortuitous ; and that such an accident is not credible.

Undoubtedly this objection has weight. The coincidences, if fortuitous, are improbable. But since improbable coincidences do occur, the objection is not decisive. It is for the reader to judge whether it outweighs the considerations on the other side : whether—as I should put it—on the ground of these coincidences, we ought to put upon the Herodean episode, in order to fill up the resemblance to the act of the soldiers, an interpretation which does not satisfy either the words or the sense, but attributes to the author an incoherent conception of the story and a language perversely inappropriate. If the mockery by the soldiers had not been related, no one, I believe, would have thought of the construction now put upon the interview with Herod as related by St Luke : it is not a natural or reasonable construction. If this be so, is the existence of the other episode, and the contact of the two in certain details of expression, sufficient reason for forcing the Herodean episode into a frame which it does not fit? As at present advised, I do not think so.

I take this opportunity to repair an omission, by remarking that, when I describe the author of the third Gospel and the *Acts* as "Luke" or "St Luke," I do not mean to express an opinion (to which I am not entitled) on the much-debated question of his identity. I follow tradition, as seems proper, upon a point which is not material to the present purpose.

INDEX

of 347; desires to see Christ 349 f., 359; Pilate sends Christ to H. 351 f.; motive of this reference 352 ff.; does not act as judge 354 ff.; story of the mockery of Christ by H. considered 356 ff., 362; disowns capital charge 357 f.; II. and the Sanhedrin 358, 360, 371; *strateumata* of 365 f.; "contemns" Christ 366 ff.; robing of Christ by 368 ff.; interest in miracles 371 f., 379; reference to in Acts 373, 386 ff.; H. in Gospel of Peter 374 f.; described as "this fox" 384 ff.

Herodians, the 344 f.

Herodias 342, 348

Herodorus 30

Herodotus and Homer 179 f.; dependent for some of his materials on the evidence of public monuments 309 ff., 319 ff.; influenced by popular poetry 310; quotations from poets in 310 f.; H.'s account of the battle of Plataea 312 f.; the Lady of Cos in 313 ff.; whence H. derived her story 314 ff.; story of Spartan herald in 319 ff.; the story of Cyrsilus in H. 323 ff.; H. gives the name of Cyrsilus as "Lycides" 326 f.; does not use patronymics 334

Hesiod 52

Hesychius 79

Hipparchus 171, 174

Holiness (ὁσία), Hymn to in *Bacchants* 12, 59, 127, 149, 157

Homer 52; the first 164; traditional beginning of "Homer" as definite book 167; adopted and arranged as the material

of education at Athens 168 ff., 195 f., 199, 237; recited at the Panathenaea 172, 179; Athenian "poetry of Homer" identical with the Cyclus 173, 177; *Iliad* and *Odyssey* parts of Cyclus 174; material for Cyclus 176; Herodotus and 179 f.; inconsistencies in the *Iliad* 181 ff.; various versions of the *Iliad* 184 ff.; why a harmony was attempted 189; rise of text-criticism on 190 f.; Alexandrian theory of 191; harmonist in *Odyssey* 191; effect of harmonistic theory on questions of origin, date, etc. of 192 ff.; illustration of harmonistic process 198 ff., 243; "wall" or "no wall," in *Iliad* 198 ff., 209; *Iliad*, Bk X (the *Doloneia*) 215 ff.; the reconciliation-scene (Idomeneus and Meriones) in *Iliad*, Bk XIII 232 ff. p. 238; "we" and "our" plurals proper in 233

Horace refers to a scene in Euripides' *Bacchants* 145–6

Iacchus at Eleusis 51

Idomeneus: the mutiny of 197 ff.; and Meriones 203 f., 210 f., 228; the *Aristeia* of 202 ff., 214 f., 241 ff.; *Aristeia* of not made for its present place in the *Iliad* 209, 214

Lampon, Herodotus' story of 319

Loisy, M., quoted 336 ff., 352, 364 f., 368, 373

Lycides, see Cyrsilus

Lycurgus and the "poetry of Homer" 169 ff.; and the story of Cyrsilus 324 ff.

CAMBRIDGE: PRINTED BY JOHN CLAY, M.A. AT THE UNIVERSITY PRESS.